PRICING FOR HIGHER PROFIT

PRICING
FOR
HIGHER
PROFIT

Criteria

Methods

Applications

SPENCER A. TUCKER, P. E.

Partner, Martin & Tucker
Management Consultants
Little Neck, New York

McGRAW-HILL   BOOK   COMPANY

New York   San Francisco   Toronto   London   Sydney

For Jeanette

Preface

Pricing is a contest between the individual seller and the individual buyer. The market is the referee; the competitors are the jeering section. But unlike sports contests, there are very few ground rules. The buyer is not concerned with the seller's costs nor with his need to make a profit. And the market is a potpourri of prices which allows a profit to some sellers and denies profit to others. "Market" or "going" prices represent a mixture of prices contributed by the community of competitors in the seller's markets and altered constantly by the vagaries of market demand.

No businessman can price successfully and in depth without a knowledge of his costs, competitive prices, market demand, and ideally, a basis for predicting competitors' behavior and especially their reaction to price change. Out of the interplay of these variables in any immediate pricing situation, there is always one best decision and optimum price available to the seller with the right tools.

The tools, methods, techniques, and applications are given in these pages. Such is the purpose of this book.

Who Should Price?

It is surprising that even in some of the best managed companies, pricing is done by whim, guess, hunch, instinct, emotion, and prayer— with some practices resembling early tribal rituals. Yet with an appreciation on management's part that pricing is the critical profit function, cost-estimating and pricing can achieve the echelon of importance it deserves. All too often, pricing is relegated to a clerk who performs the pricing function mechanically, or to a salesman who is more interested in generating revenue for commission purposes than he is in profit. And ironically, the time and cost of getting sound cost and pricing data are probably less than the typically indefensible, arbitrary gyrations, ceremonies, and magic pricing formulas prevalent in industry.

Pricing and responsibility for pricing are top management jobs. Pricing is the sole profit generator, the function that provides the profit opportunity which is enhanced or diluted in the company's internal operations. Why delegate the pricing function (perhaps by default) to a lower than top management level, unless management wishes to assign to that level the responsibility for attaining the company's target return on employed capital? Pricing generates profit or loss from the mix and volume of product. Obviously, pricing must produce the right kind of revenue which will cover all costs before there can be a profit. Any other activity in the company becomes academic in profit-planning until this primary task has first been accomplished.

The Book

This is a book on pricing methods which shows management how to obtain the most profit out of every pricing situation consistent with the use of production facilities and employment of capital. The book does not cover the legal implications of pricing because methods rather than policy is the subject stressed. Nor is there an attempt to go deeply into economic theories. The book covers pricing from the individual company's point of view as a vital part of its profit-planning. It accepts the market as an existing fact of life and emphasizes making the most out of the market rather than trying the change it.

The author recognizes that existing market prices are the result of a mixture of prices contributed by the community of competitors serving the market, and that the forces of demand and competition exert a more powerful impact on prices than any one company's pricing method. Economic theories of prices, markets, competitive behavior, and the like, indicate the existence, and to an extent, the direction and location of the nonprice factors bearing on the pricing task. However, these theories do not provide measurements of intensity and so simply remain theories for the economists to debate. As such, the derivation of these theories is beyond the scope of this book. However, some of these laws of economic behavior are immediately applicable and can be used effectively to improve the profits from pricing. Therefore, wherever applicable to specific and practical problems discussed in this book, they are presented, demonstrated, and used.

Pricing "Methods"

The book presents, illustrates, and applies profitable and rational pricing _methods_. The word method is frequently thought of as a procedure leading to a definite result. Thus one talks about welding methods, baking methods, etc. It should be understood that in our use of the term *pricing method,* there is no implied guarantee of results. If there were such guarantee, then, in the broadest sense possible, there would be only one pricing method, it would produce the best results, and everybody would use it. No one would be interested in pricing methods of any lower rank and it would be a waste of time to present them.

While the internal tangible factors about a seller's company are methodized into a pricing format, the external, intangible, unpredictable factors of the marketplace cannot be methodized as finite measurable elements. Only clairvoyance, extrasensory perception, radar, and a highly polished crystal ball could begin to accomplish that objective. Pricing methods spelled out in this book suggest different approaches that can be used for different businesses, once the external factors have been estimated by the pricer. The methods presented can be thought of as a systematic attack on price, pricing, and pricing decisions within the volatile framework of rapidly changing external conditions.

Content

Section 1 discusses pricing's role in profit-planning and some of the important external forces bearing on the pricing task. The author feels that an awareness of these factors broadens the pricer's perspective and makes him conscious of the depth of the problem as he prices each situation. Thus, after a price acceptable to the seller is reached, the pricer hopefully will consider the strategic factors before posting that price in the marketplace.

Section 2 presents the traditional pricing methods which are in general use today, their arbitrariness and deficiencies. Unfortunately, these methods dominate the pricing scene and are responsible for much of the chronic price attrition prevalent in many industries. Because of the almost universal use of these methods, the author believes that it would be difficult to promote the more rational pricing methods unless first the pitfalls of using the traditional methods are thoroughly analyzed and proven.

Traditional cost and pricing methods are confused by both accounting and economic dogma, each competing with the other and both vying for management acceptance. This leaves management in the unenviable position of being a technical arbitrator, of trying to unscramble an answer out of the muddle of impractical theory and technical gobbledegook. Worse yet, the practice of erecting prices traditionally based on arbitrary costs denies the existence of market demand and competition. This could cause the company to lose business on the one hand, and make it impossible to measure the profit contributions (if any) of the business they do get from such pricing, on the other.

All other things being equal, if a market price for an article was based on an individual seller's cost, then there would be as many market prices for that article as there are sellers. Obviously, only the seller with the lowest cost would get the order and he would continue to get this business until he exhausted his capacity. The fact is that a market price is not directly identified with one cost, one selling price, or óne seller. The "going" price is instead a mixture of demand and the price-offering community of all the sellers in that market. That is why no one price can provide the same amount of tangible benefit to all sellers who are capable of producing the article. The measurement of economic value to the seller of meeting a market price depends on what he uses for cost. If he uses traditional cost, he might wind up taking business he shouldn't and vice versa. If he disregards market price and builds his own price from his traditional cost, he denies the existence of competition and gets work only when his traditional cost produces a price at or below the market. Getting business on this basis can contribute to profit or not, but traditional data will never say which. But if the seller uses tangible, identifiable cost, only then does he have an objective measure of what meeting a market price will contribute to his profit, to his return for the use of facilities, to the return on his capital employed.

Section 3 provides the reader with rational cost-volume-profit analytic data and how these bear on the pricing task. Management's performance is pretty much gauged upon results achieved from things it can control. Costs fall into that category; pricing only partly. Tangible rather than traditional cost is the action tool from which the objective results of pricing can be measured. A sound knowledge of tangible cost is essential for successful pricing and provides the base from which the prospective results of a price under consideration is measured. The question is, which cost? Unfortunately, cost means different things to different companies. With cost traditionally arrived at, asking how a price is set is tantamount to asking how its cost was developed. This section demonstrates which costs are controlling in the pricing situation and shows how to use such costs in pricing decisions. More importantly, the impact of volume, product mix, and other internal variables is brought into the pricing task to show the reader how the rational approach will permit finding the best answer, to replace the usual frustrations and gnawing doubts when traditional methods are used.

In the multiproduct business enterprise of today, maximizing output and/or sales revenue does not necessarily guarantee maximum profits. Profits depend on the proper selection and balancing of the variables of prices, product mix, volume, costs, facility usage, and employment of capital. Sound pricing decisions can only be made when the seller knows the various sources of profit available from his company's profit segments, such as: product lines, customers, markets, territories, machines, salesmen, divisions, channels of distribution, etc. Proper pricing methods depend on knowing the relative contributions which each segment makes to the overall profit, and then striking the proper balance. Pricing therefore, is a profit-planning problem in which management analyzes the various alternatives and compares them in order to select the one which promises to be the most advantageous.

Section 4 gives the reader rational, specific methods for pricing products and orders. The reader is shown how a proper price decision is determined from the following data: gross profit contribution of the order; profit contribution per unit of facility time; and/or separate markups on the major elements of cost to yield a price which gives a desired return on the capital invested in those major cost elements. Once the profit contribution figure is firmly implanted as the only tangible measurement of economic value of a product or order, the contribution characteristics of the various profit segments of the seller are determined and used to target selling prices.

In the contribution-pricing method, the effect of product mix is demonstrated to lead the pricer to a profit-maximizing mixture of revenue. Then, using the basic contribution figure, product and product-line profitability are determined and used in guiding future prices. Various formulas are presented to suit the convenience of the pricer and his particular business. All are based on first knowing the seller's out-of-pocket costs and the measurable contribution against a known price, or for targeting a desired contribution level. Then, actual product cost estimates are presented and priced in certain model situations. The established market price list comes in for analysis to show that such a list cannot be a reflection of all of the sellers' costs. Rather, each seller must measure what contribution (and at which range of quantities) would be available to him if he meets any of these published prices. Then, a method for controlling and evaluating period contribution is presented.

In the facility-pricing method, the gross contribution of an order or product is compared with the time required on production facilities (or any other scarce factor) to evaluate the economical use of said facilities. A large amount of gross profit contribution provided by an order may not be desirable if the order uses a large amount of time of critical facilities. As a firm reaches a high level of capacity, this profit contribution per unit of facility time becomes a vital factor in pricing. The reader is shown how to price for maximum contribution per facility hour on orders competing for the same use of facility time, on list price decisions, and for quantity differentials. Then this measurement is applied to the appraisal of product-line profitability and for the pricing of the company's various profit segments. Instead of the classical approach to profit planning which starts with a forecasted but unqualified amount of revenue, a method for planning a specific product mix using target contribution levels and facility hours required, is presented. Then, a method of controlling this booking of contribution together with a build-up of facility hours is demonstrated.

In the chapter on pricing for desired return on product investment, a product or order is dissected into different cost elements according to the various levels of capital invested in it and separately marked up to provide the target return on capital. After measuring the gross contribution and return for each hour of facility time, this method evaluates any variance which exists between a market price under consideration and the target selling price which reflects the seller's desired return on the capital he has invested in an order. This method is crucial where no competitive benchmark prices exist for a product, which deprives the seller of a contribution measurement. It is especially valuable where the seller is an innovator. Several methods and formulas are presented to cover most of the general industry product characteristics. Then, a method of controlling the booking of contribution, facility hours committed versus the capital return target prices and pricing variances, is illustrated.

In the "criteria" chapter, suggestions are given for selecting the pricing method to use in special situations. Each case is demonstrated and documented to allow the reader to identify with his particular problem. Even though a pricer may use one or more of the rational pricing methods presented earlier, he is cautioned (with illustrative material) that slavish adherence to any one method during one phase of the business cycle, may be profit-draining as his specific operation changes.

The concluding chapter in this section deals with using the managerial control of pricing. First and foremost, methods are presented for evaluating the results of pricing separate and apart from the result of all other company operations. The bottom-line profit on the traditional form of profit-and-loss statement is actually a mixture of the results of pricing jumbled together with the results of operating performance, inventory change and the amount of fixed expenses capitalized in inventory as under- or over-absorbed. Such a profit result is inadequate for appraising the quality of the pricing function. Next, a series of management information reports is presented to enable management to "see" clearly their sources of profits from which they can guide their future pricing.

Section 5 deals with the installation, testing, and control of a complete pricing program in one specific company. The industry chosen to demonstrate the steps required in this example, represents probably the most difficult one for application of the pricing art and science, as it has almost every variable one could imagine: highly changeable intermix of products, investments, costs, volume, contribution rates, order sizes and types, common facilities, highly diversified markets, and unpredictable customer demand. Basic to the development of such an installation is the availability of a sound cost-estimating system. The modern machine-hour rate system is used in this instance. The machine-hour rate system is not developed in this Section or in this book, but the steps are shown to demonstrate the necessity for proper cost data.

Section 6 recognizes that the basic data required for sound pricing are useful for other internal managerial decisions. These basic data are used to show management how to select the most economical facility to run when there are several choices; how to approach make-or-buy decisions; how to justify capital expenditures for new equipment; sales compensations plans for generating the most profitable product mix; and worker, supervisory, and management financial wage incentive plans. The cornerstone of all these decisions is the contribution figure and how it is enhanced or diluted (with due consideration for the change in invested capital) by the aforementioned activities.

Summary

Our purpose in this book is to expose the pitfalls of traditional cost and pricing methods and then show the rich potentialities available in the rational approaches. Our treatment of pricing and the pricing methods used to increase profit and return on capital, are presented from the profit-planning viewpoint. The methods, procedures and applications are given in practical, how-to-do-it form and come from hundreds of client engagements over the past 27 years, as well as from surveys of pricing practices in other eminently successful companies.

If any of the data presented herein bears any resemblance to any company, that resemblance is unintentional and purely coincidental.

ACKNOWLEDGMENTS

Writing a book of this type requires the author to maintain perspective. From the wealth of data and experience he has accumulated over the past 27 years, this book could easily have been twice the size. During the outlining stages he sought and received generous advice from clients, from others in professional life, and from graduates of the Cost-Estimating and Pricing Institute which the author's firm conducts. For their valuable time and talented efforts, the author wishes to acknowledge the counsel of the following people:

W. E. Allaire, Profit-Planning Department, Warner Packaging, Bridgeport, Conn.; Warner W. Behley, Division Accountant, R. J. Reynolds Tobacco Co., Winston-Salem, N.C.; Thomas E. Brinkman, Vice President, Cincinnati Lithographing Co., Cincinnati, Ohio; Paul J. Casabonne, Plant Manager, Ethyl Corp., La Grange, Ga.; A. I. Cassidy, Corporate Accounting Manager, Anaconda Aluminum Co., Louisville, Ky.; Cameron Clark, Jr., President, Warner Packaging, Bridgeport, Conn.; J. E. Culhane, Accounting Manager, Weyerhaeuser Company, Chicago, Ill.; R. J. Doucette, Director of Management Services, Warner Packaging, Bridgeport, Conn.; G. J. Eberz, Manager of Sales Administration, Continental Can Co., New York; N. T. Fadero, Manager Systems & Procedures, Riegel Paper Corp., Charlotte, N.C.; Edward Green, President, Pandick-Newcomb Press, Inc., New York; Joseph F. Gross, Controller, Sample-Durick Co., Chicopee, Mass.; H. C. Haroun, Vice President–Operations, Pak-Well Paper Products Co., Portland, Oregon; A. D. Hoeppner, Product Director, Bemis Bro. Bag Co., Minneapolis, Minn.; S. J. Kitagawa, Cost Accountant, Rolph-Clark-Stone Ltd., Toronto, Canada; Zoltan S. Kolley, Director of Management Services, Rolph-Clark-Stone Ltd., Toronto Canada; Richard Kux, President, Kux Manufacturing Co., Detroit, Michigan; E. F. McCann, Continental Can Co., Chicago, Ill.; Clifton C. Meads, Vice President, Millhiser Plastics Co., Richmond, Va.; Mitchell Newman, Federal Carton Corp., North Bergen, N.J.; Gustav L. Nordstrom, Executive Director, Folding Paper Box Association of America, Chicago, Ill.; Derrick Pollard, Commerical Analyst, West Virginia Pulp and Paper, Newark, Del.; Sidney Rennert, Manager of Cost Accounting, Stein, Hall & Co., New York; Marshall M. Rose, Director of Administration & Finance, Transo Envelope Co., Chicago, Ill.; Don R. Russell, General Manager, Raymond Bag Co., Middletown, Ohio; Clayton E. Shrewsbury, Manager Engineering Accounting, R. J. Reynolds Tobacco Co., Winston-Salem, N.C.; Campbell Stuart, Control Manager, Canadian Industries Ltd., Montreal, Canada; Ernest Trotter, Publisher, Printing Magazine/National Lithographer, Oradell, N.J.; Dell H. Warnick, Supervisor Estimating Department, Stecher-Traung Lithograph Corp., Rochester, N.Y.; C. K. Watters, Vice President and General Sales Manager, Raymond Bag Co., Middletown, Ohio; Dwight Wheeler, Controller, Riegel Paper Corp., Charlotte, N.C.; Lawrence O. Wheeler; Franz von Ziegesar, Vice President, Bowne & Co., New York.

Lastly, but by no means least, thanks are due Mrs. Elizabeth Prendergast, the author's secretary, who laboriously typed the manuscript and to Miss Marie Zielinski who had the difficult task of proofreading the final manuscript.

Spencer A. Tucker

Contents

xv

Section 5 MECHANICS OF PRICING PROGRAM INSTALLATION

Section 6   USING BASIC PRICE DATA FOR OTHER OPERATING DECISIONS

List of Exhibits

Section 1

THE PRICING COMPLEX

CHAPTER 1 *The Role of Pricing in Industry*

Prices are a basic and critical factor in determining profits and, ultimately, the success or failure of a business enterprise.

There are many ways for money to flow out of a firm in the form of costs. But there is only one way to bring money in. That way is by the mechanics of pricing. Pricing is not only the sole revenue generator in a company, it is also the only profit contributor—assuming, of course, that the items sold cost a company less than the prices at which they are sold.

If prices are too low in comparison with costs, volume may be great but profitless. If prices are higher than competitors', volume and profit are reduced and invested capital and facilities are rendered idle. Between these two poles, the optimum profit to the company comes from sets of prices which make contributions to profits and are acceptable in the marketplace.

What Pricing Does

Pricing determines significantly the bottom-line figure on the operating statement. Pricing determines what products will and will not be sold, in what volumes, and with what profit. In more detailed terms, pricing specifies which equipment will be operated, what inventory commitments are to be made, what cash flow can be expected, where sales efforts should be applied, which markets should be approached and penetrated, and, ultimately, what return can be expected on the firm's invested capital. Therefore, pricing should not be given short shrift as an annoying but somehow necessary detail and relegated to an office clerk or estimator, unless management is quite prepared to assign to that individual full responsibility for the effective employment of the company's capital and resources.

The most modern, streamlined company—with the most productive workers, highest-speed equipment, highest quality of product, highest level of sales, and preeminent product acceptance in its markets—will lose money if the revenue produced from prices does not cover costs. While no one will disagree with this clearcut truism, the point needs strengthening since the medieval cost-price practices in many otherwise well-managed companies produce prices inadvertently pegged below costs. Even if prices are set with reference to costs, frequently the economic and strategic factors of market demand, competition, and product mix are ignored, thereby producing a lower return on the firm's invested capital than could otherwise be attained.

Pricing, and pricing alone, more than any other single decision-making activity, is responsible for most of the profit differences among similar firms.

How the order or product is priced will in itself determine the product mix that will be produced. The pricing action will make the product more or less attractive to the buyer; the major factor which determines the buyer's response. To the extent that costs of the mix produce both profit contributions and favorable responses from buyers, the volume sold will be profitable. The sales revenue, then, is a mixture of the various prices of the different products or orders, and the resultant period profit is a mixture of their profit contributions.

Balancing of Variables

Profits depend on a proper selection and balancing of prices against the variables of costs, volume, and product mix. Typically, orders and products differ widely in cost, volume, price, profit, and the use of facilities and capital. Orders also differ in terms of the specific product made, the markets sold to, the customer classes involved, the sales territories covered, and the channels of distribution used. Thus, profit is not a single-valued function of time or quantity, but is rather composed of a number of pooled segments from which a net profit ultimately develops. These sources or segments of profit are important from the viewpoint of evaluating strengths or weaknesses.

In pricing, though, management must know the relative contribution which each segment makes to the profit structure in order to strike a proper balance among prices, product mix, volume, and cost. Pricing, therefore, is a profit-planning problem in which management analyzes the various economic and strategic alternatives and compares them with each other to select the one which appears to be the most advantageous in each pricing situation.

The pricing method cannot be formularized because many factors cannot be measured objectively. Pricing is influenced greatly by, and must be related to, market conditions, competition, financial liquidity of the firm, inventory pressures, available productive capacity, investments in product line, etc.

Profits which result from the operation of a business as a whole cannot be greater than the net sum of the profits (or losses) contained in all its individual parts. These profit segments are sources for period profits and relate to individual orders at various prices, various costs, and various profit contributions. In multiproduct firms, orders have profit characteristics which go beyond the mere identification of order sizes or revenues. Orders go to different markets, geographic areas, and customers and customer classes; they are produced on different facilities and are parts of various product lines. Once these data have been sorted and analyzed by any desired segment, management has an objective guide to its sources of profits and can emphasize, eliminate, strengthen, and direct as required to enable the pricing program to attain the profit objective.

Pricing Art and Science

Pricing is at once a science and an art. It involves more than setting, meeting, raising, or lowering prices. Pricing goals involve more than keeping facilities active, workers busy, material consumption high, or revenue generated at peak levels. Maximization in any one or all of these areas is no guarantee of profit. Then, again, neither is slavishly following the pricing vagaries of market demand nor agreeing simply to follow competitive prices. Internally generated information about profit sources can be quite scientific, as later chapters will demonstrate. But, on the other hand, the pricer must be strategically artful in the way he handles this information and meshes it into the external, unpredictable, uncertain events of the marketplace.

Pricing is not a job like production scheduling or invoicing, to be decided and disposed of mechanically. Neither is pricing to be handled capriciously, arrived at by guesswork, or done in sheer desperation.

Scientific, artful pricing can provide the firm with the maximum profits obtainable during any specific state of economic weather. Otherwise, the company can be victimized by the vagaries of the market, its profit structure steered by customers and competition, and resultant profits produced by accident instead of by plan.

Objective cost data are essential in deciding whether to meet or withdraw from competitive prices. Only by showing the spread between costs and a price under consideration and then by balancing that margin against the use of facilities, the capital return goals, etc., is the seller able to decide how much value the order will contribute to his company and, therefore, whether he should accept or reject the price. These are the scientific, internal effects of the price proposal. However, the artful, strategic factors which must be considered simultaneously are reaction from competitors, effect of the price level in the marketplace, effect on other phases of the seller's business, creating or relieving bottlenecks, displacement of more profitable work later if the order is large and competes for the use of the same facilities, etc.

Pricing requires a combination of calculation and judgment. A price must be validated by immediate market conditions and modified by management, up, down, or out, as the need would indicate.

Management's Attitude toward Pricing

Managements tend to look for short cuts. Expenditure of time and involvement in "paperwork" are regarded as inefficient and something to be held to a minimum. The average executive is attracted by formulas and guideposts because these hold out the promise of expedient solutions to problems. This attraction is understandable in view of the maze of matters which compete daily for the executive's attention. However, some managers almost completely reject the notion that some of these guideposts may be arbitrary, indefensible, and therefore possibly misleading. "After all," they claim, "didn't we make money last year using these formulas?"

A formula gives the manager both needed security and needed time-savings but no threatening analysis into which he would have to delve. He has a decision to make; he applies a formula, gets the answer, and then moves on to the next task. The trouble is that the traditional, arbitrary, shallow pricing guidepost may be twisted which, in turn, leads to poor decisions and wrong actions.

Some executives make extravagant claims to being "practical." Much of this attitude is the result of being exposed to the threats of the "numbers game" and failing to understand its workings. Being practical, then, sometimes becomes a rejection of systems, procedures, and most formal, calculated data presentations. In some cases, also, an executive who has been "burned" by complex, illogical systems becomes "twice shy." This is especially true if he had used a "standard" pricing system which was administered by the accounting division without any reference to product mix, market demand, and competition. In one pricing conference at which the author was present, the president was handed data concerning a certain pricing decision. He commented, "Let's forget about all these numbers and really price this thing. What do you think gentlemen? Can we get x amount for this deal?" The "go–no-go" decision was reached purely by the votes of the head shakers and the head nodders.

Our experience indicates that many client executives do not ordinarily concern themselves with pricing details, there even being many instances in which executives were not intimately aware of how their products were priced. Even among officers who were familiar with overall company pricing policy, there were those who were not able to show how the policy was applied in any specific pricing decision. In other cases, we have witnessed an indifferent attitude toward the pricing of products. Even though subordinates were familiar with the basis of pricing, management did not have a formal review policy by which it could evaluate the results of both successful and rejected pricing proposals.

Pricing a product, an order, a contract, is one of the most critical decisions management is called upon to make. Pricing decisions, which integrate the firm's costs with market strategy, business conditions, intensity of competition, customer demand, production alternatives, product variables, channels of distribution, and financial characteristics, will determine the success or failure of a business. This coordination is management's job.

Price Determinants

Major determinants of price are the seller's costs, competitive prices, and market demand. Prices cannot always be based successfully on individual costs, but objective, traceable cost information must be available to measure how much an order will contribute to profits when meeting a "going" price. The seller's costs are specific and identified only with him. Prices, on the other hand, represent the community of competition in the seller's markets. For the seller arbitrarily to mark up his cost to arrive at a selling price is tantamount to denying the existence of this competition and market demand.* Costs should not be the sole determinant of prices, but they can be used to determine whether to withdraw from a price proposal or to continue to explore the alternatives.

Regardless of any other consideration, the price determines the spread between the seller's cost and the outside market and acts as a measure of value to the seller. The crucial point is *what kind of cost* the seller must use to make this evaluation and how he develops it. This question is one of the most contentious in the entire costs-for-pricing area around which much mystery, magic formula, and just plain nonsense still persist.

When cost-plus methods of pricing are used, and the "cost" portion of the formula is arbitrarily determined, the resultant price represents a compounding of errors: the indefensible cost allocation acts as a base upon which an illusionary price structure is erected that makes no allowance for competition and demand. A profit structure results from sales

* See Sec. 2: The Traditional Approach to Pricing.

bookings by accident when the seller happens to have prices lower than his competitors. These types of repetitive accidents must produce enough profit and must happen frequently enough to keep the seller in business. Obviously, if competitors using similar cost-plus formulas have substantially lower costs than the seller, the latter's days in business are numbered.

Pricing decisions involve more than setting prices for products offered to customers. More often than not, a pricing decision must be made whether or not to meet a competitor's price. Thus, in many industries, price-*setting* has given way to measuring just what the taking of competitively priced business is likely to contribute to the seller's profit structure. If information on the various profit segments is available, the seller has the opportunity of profit-*ranking* his products, orders, customers, and markets and balancing this information against the profitable time allocation of his facilities and employment of capital.

Obviously, an inefficient high-cost manufacturer cannot successfully price higher than his efficient competitor simply because he wishes to earn the same rate of return. The chances are good that if any manufacturer sought to earn the same return on all his products, orders, or product lines, he would price some output out of his markets.

Pricing Policy and Plan

The ultimate goal of a pricing policy is to formulate a program so that over the range of economic conditions the owners will obtain a satisfactory return on their invested capital in keeping with expected results. A proper and effective pricing policy is the result of coordination by management on costs, volume, prices, profit, competition, and market demand.

Many management people are now living through their first experiences in a tough, competitive environment and are finding it harder than ever to cope with competition to meet their profit objectives. How well they succeed will depend largely on how well they know and direct their profit structure, how well they can uncover strengths and weaknesses in the various profit segments of their operations, how well they get and use market and competitive information, and how well they make decisions on these data to implement an organized profit plan. The implication here is that executives must be responsive to a planning-oriented profit discipline.

Planning in this framework must be tied into a target return on the capital employed in each of the company's segments of profit generation. Moreover, such objective planning must be dovetailed with market-competition variables to optimize the product mix.

In most cases, factors governing prices are complex as well as dynamic. These factors cannot be waived aside by treating pricing as a hodge-podge of subjective decisions. A pricing policy and a set of objectives are vital for profit planning. These should be interwoven with prices which are to be used as part of the company's strategy in obtaining the profit objective. Then a knowledge of markets and competition will help marshal a series of pricing tactics to be used.

Pricing policy must be related to a base upon which results are expected to occur. Some firms use as an objective a target rate of return on total invested capital. Others express this goal as a return on sales. Because of the external variables of competition and market demand, a major portion of which deals with the uncertain future and the unpredictable actions of others, management is expected to have some latitude in manipulating its internal factors with these nonpricing externals to achieve its goal.

Usually there is enough room for seasoned judgment in pricing so that management is not expected to use a rigid price policy against the market forces. Rather, any price policy or method of attack should serve as a guide to pricing decisions after the appraisal of all factors and forces at work.

Of importance is a well-formulated statement of objectives, clearcut enough so key executives can communicate by means of a common language. From a statement of goals the company can then structure a formal policy. Typical statements of pricing policy include prices that maximize profits for the entire product line, prices that are flexibly geared to the market and to competitive reactions, prices that discourage new competitors from entering the market, prices that make a given return on capital per product line, prices that generate a minimum profit contribution per machine-hour, prices that increase the longevity and growth of the company, prices for new products to be developed after a thorough market research program, etc.

Information Flow

One of the essentials for intelligent pricing is a constant flow of reliable information from all activity areas within the company. This information should be in the form of a common language so that the different levels can establish effective communication with respect to costs, products, equipment, investment segments, markets, and competition. Price decisions must be coordinated with production, marketing, new-product and new-equipment investments, and other related decisions.

A sound program of management information should be used to coordinate these decisions so that management can be guided to act on the sum total of overall company effects instead of in the transient areas that are informally brought to its attention.

Later chapters will demonstrate how these data are developed and used.

The Rational Approach

The rational approach to pricing adopts no specific rules because once rules are set up, they tend to remain in effect when they no longer apply. A rigid pricing method is usually based on a company's own costs and thus makes no allowance for the external factors we have discussed. The rational approach adjusts to differing or changing circumstances, irrespective of the particular pricing method employed, without ever losing sight of the interplay of all the variables discussed in this chapter.

Summary

What this chapter attempts to do is to explain the various factors and forces which enter into the pricing decision, to indicate what information and systems will be required for a sound pricing program, and to criticize existing methods, attitudes, and certain information gaps. Basically, though, the author hopes that this chapter will place the pricing function in clearer perspective so that its value in the organizational spectrum will have a higher rank than heretofore.

In the following sections, complete systems of pricing will be presented and analyzed together with methods of developing and implementing the information. It is suggested that the cost-plus pricing methods given in Section 2 be read carefully as preparation for the information in the following sections.

CHAPTER 2 *External Factors in Pricing*

Sales are the result of many forces in addition to price. These forces are called external factors. Among them are market demand, competitive behavior, and alternative cost-price-quantity schedules, which are forecast to test the expected results of future demand and competition. Although basic economic theory is beyond the scope of this book, the fundamental mechanics are presented as minimum practical orientation to pricing management.

Elasticity of Demand

One of the most influential factors affecting the pricing decision is the *elasticity of demand* for the company's various products in its various markets. Elasticity of demand is a basic device for measuring the sensitivity of sales volume to a change in one of several internal operating factors. For example, how much will volume increase with a drop in prices of 2, 5, or 12 per cent for Product A in City Y? If the advertising budget is increased by 50 per cent, how much will sales rise? The response to these changes as measured in sales volume provides the company with a barometer of market characteristics which it can use in planning pricing and profit from operations.

It is important to realize that in forecasting profits from pricing, the price-quantity schedule is not the controlling factor, but rather the relation between sales and measurable demand. A firm cannot set prices in a vacuum; information must be available by which price elasticity and competitive reactions can be predicted within reasonable limits. This fact calls for some kind of empirical analysis.

Typically, sales forecasting is concerned with short-run decisions for existing products. Long-range forecasts are infrequently made, except for the new-product forecast which deals with the question of making a large initial investment. Demand projections for existing products can be done in a routine procedure by tabulating data from existing markets and past behavior of volume, sales, and costs. Since most of the demand factors are expected to change only slightly during the short-run period, the analysis can be performed simply by concentrating on the most vital factors. Among these are survey of customers' intentions; survey of the sales and marketing divisions; survey of industry-connected people, such as jobbers or distributors; survey of trade association data; survey of industry trend data; etc.

Measure of Elasticity

Elasticity of demand refers to how volume-sensitive a product is to change in price. If the percentage change in quantity sold is greater than the percentage change in price, the demand for that product is considered *elastic*. If it is less, it is *inelastic*. For example, if a 4 per cent decrease in price results in an 8 per cent increase in quantity sold, then the demand for that product is said to be elastic, with an *elasticity factor* of $8/4$ or 2. If a 10 per cent decrease in price causes a 5 per cent increase in quantity sold, the elasticity factor is $5/10$ or $1/2$. In formal economic practice, an elasticity factor of less than 1 represents inelastic demand.

Price-volume sensitivity or elasticity of demand is a valuable, strategic tool of pricing. Astute managers are aware of the demand elasticities of their various products and take advantage of this factor in their pricing policies. Demand information requires a constant policing of markets and ultimate consumers. Tricky markets are customers who use the sellers' products as their raw material. In many cases, the sellers' outputs are only a portion of the customers' products and involve a mixture of demand factors; for example, paper mills which sell to converters and printers; paperboard mills which sell to folding carton plants which in turn sell to manufacturers of frozen food, cosmetics, pharmaceuticals, toys, records; steel mills which sell to distributors who sell to job machine shops.

Price-volume sensitivity may be found in many familiar items. Television sets are a good example. If a certain popular line of TV sets dropped in price from $199.50 to $149.50 during a period of stable economic conditions in the industry, the quantity sold would probably rise noticeably. To conform to the economist's theory of demand elasticity, the increase in quantity would have to be at least 25 per cent to qualify the TV set as having an elastic demand.

An example of a product with an inelastic demand is table salt. If the present market price for table salt is 8 cents a box, raising the price to 9 cents or lowering it to 7 cents would not materially affect the quantity sold. As we shall see in later chapters, the seasoned executive will be able to cash in on the sensitivity of volume to price even though the elasticity factor is less than 1.

The following tabulation demonstrates arithmetically the classic approach to measuring elasticity of demand. The product costs $6 each with an unadjusted annual volume of 100,000 units and a selling price of $10. Total profit is $400,000:

1. Elastic demand (elasticity factor = 3)
   (a) Price decrease:

Price	Volume	Profit/Unit	Total Profit
$9	130,000	$3	$390,000

   (b) Price increase:

$11	70,000	$5	$350,000

2. Inelastic demand (elasticity factor = .5)
   (a) Price decrease:

$9	105,000	$3	$315,000

   (b) Price increase:

$11	95,000	$5	$475,000

If the price-volume sensitivity of products would behave predictably and consistently, lending itself to the type of arithmetic measurement shown above, it would provide a definite factor in a pricing formula. However, the marketplace (in the broadest sense) is filled with people: people who buy, people who sell, people who compete, people who react to price change, to styles and taste, to their own personal needs. People determine the changes in volume by their reactions to changes in prices, economic theory notwithstanding. That's why in some cases a price increase of 5 per cent can cut volume 30 per cent, a 5 per cent price decrease for the same product may raise volume only 8 per cent and a price decrease of 10 per cent may only raise volume to 14 per cent. Unfortunately, the elasticity factor is not linear in any amount nor in any direction.

Even if it were possible to predict the results of price reductions at various price levels, consideration must be given to the fact that increases in volume may develop only after intensive selling and advertising campaigns, especially if additional volume is being sought in new markets. In the case of a price increase, there may be a considerable loss of volume immediately, which may or may not be followed by a gradual recovery later as customers get accustomed to the higher prices. These are customer-based responses. But how about competitors?

Competitors do not remain passive in the face of price changes. Their responses will directly affect the volume response to price changes, compounding further the task of quantifying the elasticity factor. When the demand for a product is elastic, it is possible for an entire industry segment to price itself out of its markets or increase its total market potential. The task for the individual company is to find out the best combination of price and volume that yields the greatest profit. Knowledge of its markets, responses from customers, and reactions from competitors can be used as effective pricing tools.

Such practical information can be tabulated if properly developed:

Selling price	Marginal profit*	Estimated sales volume of units†	Total marginal profit contribution‡
$5	$1	250,000	$250,000
6	2	230,000	460,000
7	3	200,000	600,000
8	4	160,000	640,000
9	5	110,000	550,000

* Marginal profit = selling price − out-of-pocket cost of $4 per unit.
† Volume for which there is existing capacity.
‡ Contribution margin pay for fixed expenses and then profit.

Obviously, the company selling this product would want to peg its price level somewhere between $7 and $8.

Demand and the Specific Profit Structure

As will be discussed later, the profit-making characteristics of the firm are determined largely by its profit structure, which refers to the proportion of fixed costs present in total cost—the relationship between a company's fixed and variable costs.

Generally, where the demand for a product is elastic, higher profits can be made with lower prices, lower unit profit margins, and higher volume. Where the demand is inelastic, higher profits can be made with higher prices, larger unit profit margins, and lower volume. A company with a higher proportion of fixed costs would benefit from the former situation, i.e., higher volume at lower unit profit margins. This basic point is demonstrated in Exhibit 2-1.

The exhibit shows two different companies and their profit structures, both selling the same product at a unit selling price of $10. Both earn the same profit at 100,000 annual unit volume. The bottom of the exhibit shows how each company would react to changing selling prices under two elasticity factors. Obviously, Company B can not only produce

Exhibit 2-1. Effect of Demand Elasticity

Item	Company A: Low proportion of fixed cost	Company B: High proportion of fixed cost
Annual fixed cost...............	$ 200,000	$ 700,000
Annual variable cost:...........	700,000	200,000
Total cost...................	$ 900,000	$ 900,000
Profit.......................	100,000	100,000
Annual sales revenue.......	$1,000,000	$1,000,000
Unit volume...................	100,000 pieces	100,000 pieces
"Normal" unit SP..............	$10	$10
Unit "profit"..................	$ 1	$ 1
Unit contribution*.............	$ 3	$ 8
Annual contribution*..........	$ 300,000	$ 800,000
Drop price 15% to.............	$ 8.50	$ 8.50
1. Elasticity factor of 1:		
New volume.................	115,000	115,000
New sales revenue...........	$ 977,500	$ 977,500
Annual total cost.............	$1,005,000	$ 930,000
Profit or (loss).............	$ (27,500)	$ 47,500
Unit contribution...........	$ 1.50	$ 6.50
Annual contribution..........	$ 172,500	$ 747,500
2. Elasticity factor of 2:		
New volume.................	130,000	130,000
New sales revenue...........	$1,105,000	$1,105,000
Annual total cost.............	$1,110,000	$ 960,000
Profit or (loss).............	$ (5,000)	$ 145,000
Unit contribution...........	$ 1.50	$ 6.50
Annual contribution..........	$ 195,000	$ 845,000

* Contribution = revenue − variable costs.

profits in spite of the drop in selling prices, it can also produce greater profits as the elasticity factor rises. Company A, with a lower level of fixed expenses, shows a loss under both conditions.

One point should be made clear: a major factor for the changes in profits of both companies is the respective levels of variable expenses per unit which affect the amount of marginal income contributed (sales less variable costs). In the case of Company A, the drop in prices eliminates half of this contribution. In Company B, the reduction is only 19 per cent. Thus, it is the *rate* of increased marginal contribution with greater volume that is controlling. With reduced prices, Company A has a marginal contribution of $1.50 per unit; Company B, $6.50 per unit, or over four times as fast.

This is one reason, when considering both the elasticity of demand and the different fixed-cost proportions as well as the different changes in marginal contribution rates, that a price which is as high as the "market can bear" is *not necessarily* the most profitable price.

Pricing Strategy

Since every business is confronted by certain rates of demand for its products and since the quantity changes will affect the firm's cost-volume-price relationship, management must have at least a general knowledge of the elasticity of demand for its products in its various markets. Otherwise, management should consider engaging in some controlled experiments to be able to evaluate the elasticity factors.

After these data are available, the profit-planning division can prepare cost-profit schedules showing alternate projections of profit-structure data at different prices and volume levels. In other words, before the pricing program is set, it is necessary for management to select factors of demand, competition, and cost that are relevant to each pricing problem. At the same time, formal research effort must be made to get quantitative estimates for each of these elements.

Surprising results are produced from even the first attempts at price-demand experimentation. One major meat-packing firm discovered that a relatively inelastic demand existed within a given price range for a group of its products. As soon as it discovered this fact, it raised prices somewhat without any noticeable drop-off in volume and enjoyed an appreciable increase in profits.

But regardless of the specific elasticity of demand existing in an industry, if the company is operating in a highly competitive market, the seller's firm is constantly faced with an elastic demand schedule. If the seller's prices are reduced, the competitor's customers will be attracted and vice versa if prices are increased. This condition limits the pricing independence of the individual company, and thereby costs are not too controlling. As was said in the previous chapter, costs under these circumstances are more important for determining which items to make, which to drop, and which are more profitable, than for basing prices.

Market Segmentation

Another nonprice tool which can be used to advantage is the segmentation of the company's market to expose different layers of customer demand. Existing or potential customers will buy a range of similar products at varying prices and in different volumes. Higher-priced items will yield lower sales at greater profit margins; lower-priced items will produce greater sales volume but with lower unit profits. If customers are separated into classes, the seller can take advantage of the differences in the demand elasticities.

Frequently, it is necessary to differentiate the product to justify the different prices offered to the various layers of customer demand. This differentiation may result in offering the basic product in both standard and deluxe models or offering the product under advertised brand names and under unadvertised private labels. Often this technique is used to occupy some capacity of facilities which are also used to produce the company's regular line.

However, when market segmentation is used as one of management's tools, care must be exercised to avoid actions which may make it difficult to maintain the company's prices in its more profitable market segments. Thus a company should not sell the lower-priced items to a class of customers which competes with the company's regular customers.

Market Force

Management frequently asks, "What does a product cost?" The accountant may give an answer that includes all direct variable costs plus other period costs developed per unit at a volume rate which is expected to recover these expenses. This "standard" cost may not be tolerable in price competition. In many cases, the volume rate selected upon which to unitize the period costs may produce a cost that is too "big" when compared with present market or competitive prices. The test of the cost is not the addition of a markup for pricing but rather the comparison with the market which will show the return to the company if it meets the competitive price.

The concept of formula pricing, e.g., Price = cost + profit, is totally unrealistic because it ignores the nonprice factors. Instead, the basis for successful pricing is Profits = market price — your cost. Regardless of the costing concept employed in the company, costs must be compared to the external bench mark of the competitive market price. From this simple comparison, management can be directed to lower or to increase its target return on invested capital; to shift sales emphasis on its various products to its various customers, end markets, etc.; to add or drop a product or customers, etc.

CHAPTER 3

The Role of Cost in Pricing

The three points of the pricing triad are costs, competition, and market demand. Dealing effectively with competition requires another triangular relationship: product improvement and innovation, sales promotion, and pricing. Prices, to be successful as one of management's attack weapons, must be backed up with the type of information which enables sound decisions.

Costs Essential

It is vital that management know intimately the ingredients and behavior of product costs in order to price products most advantageously within the turbulent environment of competition, vagaries of demand, and product mix. Then a company can accelerate cost recovery, evaluate proposals to change selling prices, segment the market to gain advantage of the different layers of customer demand, select most profitable business when capacity is limited, determine the price at which to refuse an order, distinguish between volume which adds to the peaks and that which creates bottlenecks, and determine which work to abandon when more attractive opportunities are available.

Even though costs generally do not determine prices, costs for pricing purposes are essential both for measuring the profit contribution of the selling transaction and as data for interproduct comparisons and rankings. Costs for pricing require both estimates of future cost magnitude and behavior and a study of the profit structure of the firm.

Knowing what the costs are becomes essential when prices for products have to be determined. Naturally, a company that has a good costing system will tend to give costs a greater emphasis in its pricing policies than a company that is not so fully acquainted with the costs of its products.

Cost-Price Relationships

Normally, the capacity of the United States to produce exceeds the demand for such production. In this buyers' market, the customer and not the seller determines the price. Regardless of sellers' prices, the buyer in the long run will determine what the price will be and how much will be accepted at any price. Therefore, only after a price acceptable to the buyer is reached does the question of cost enter the picture. Then the question for the seller is: Can the product be made and sold at a cost which will leave a profit satisfactory to the seller? This measure of the profit contribution of the sale transaction is the starting point in formulating a pricing attack.

If the demand for products is low, prices are lower than if demand is high. It's as simple as that. Therefore, the price that a buyer is willing to pay for a product will not be necessarily related to what the product costs the manufacturer. The price will instead depend on what the buyer will have to pay for it elsewhere. Costs only indicate the minimum sales price at which costs will be recovered; they do not show the profit margin that the market is ready to accept. That's why selling prices rarely have a rigid relationship to cost. What buyers pay for a product need not bear a direct relation to what it costs any seller to make.

From the customer's point of view, a successful price is one which makes him buy. From the seller's viewpoint, a successful price is one which produces a profit. While the buyer is not interested in the seller's cost, the seller must know his own costs and have some idea of competitors' prices. Reconciling (balancing) these two elements for the seller leads to a policy of successful pricing.

Cost plays an important but limited part in pricing. It indicates whether the product can be made and sold profitably at any price. But it does not indicate the amount of markup or markdown on cost which will be accepted by buyers.

Where selling prices are established in a market and an individual company has practically no latitude for independent pricing, proper costs allow measurement of profit contribution which leads to a decision to sell at the prevailing price or to withdraw. Most important, proper costs serve to guide management in the design of the most profitable product mix and in determining how much cost can be incurred without sacrificing profit.

However, when a company is a price leader in its industry and can pursue a policy of independent pricing, pricing can be tied to a target profit markup on cost expressed as an objective return on its total capital employed. Often this technique is employed for pricing a brand new product, whether the company is a price leader or not.

On the other hand, when a company is neither a price leader nor follower but rather operates with others in a highly competitive market, it can maximize its profits by a judicious balance of cost, volume, prices, and product mix phased in with the external influences of the marketplace.

Results of Inadequate Costs

A company that does not know the cost of making, selling, and distributing its own products is like an unguided missile. It may take off, but nobody knows where it will land. So it is with cost systems. A company manufactures products, but if it cannot predict in advance what the products' sales will contribute to its profits, it is in the dark and must wait until the operating results are published. This is management "after the facts" and is surely too late for guiding pricing; the lack of profits is a fact, and a rigid pricing precedent may have been set in the company's markets.

Yet numerous companies operate on the basis of poor cost information—which, of course, may be at one and the same time a source of delight to their competitors as well as a major headache to them because of the necessity of now having to meet lower prices. That doesn't mean that companies which use poor costing methods have poor production methods. It does mean that regardless of methods or the degree of plant streamlining, product costs are not an effective guide to pricing.

Poor costs for pricing purposes have led some managements to push the wrong product or product line, drop the wrong product, extend excessive service to the wrong customer or market, and make a host of other profit-draining mistakes. Frequently, a desired profit may amount to only a few pennies per product. It follows, therefore, that a loss of merely these same pennies can mean failure to operate profitably. Errors in pennies can be the result of inaccuracy and sloppy record keeping, but they can also be caused ultimately by an improper segregation of costs of widely differing behavior patterns. Usually, the latter type of error accounts for most poor operating results.

Management decisions are divided into two basic groups: short-term and long-term. Probably the large majority of day-to-day management decisions are of short-run nature; pricing decisions represent most of these. Costs, similarly, have a short-term as well as a long-term nature, but unfortunately these different behaviors of costs are not too often taken into consideration either in classic cost accounting or in the process of pricing. Thus, pricing practices in many instances fail to relate the short-term decision to the short-term cost.

Basic Information Required

Before a pricing plan can be installed, it is first necessary to assemble the basic cost facts and marshal the physical data of the company. Questions like these must be answered: What products are to be manufactured? In what proportions or mix? In which markets? At what prices? Will new products be introduced? Will new equipment be needed? What will be the rate of operation. How many shifts are planned? What will be our plant capacity? How reliable are our production standards? What is the expected level of fixed expenses? Which equipment will be discontinued? What will our operating costs be? What rate of return is desired on total invested capital?

The answers to all these questions can be translated into cost facts and embodied in the form of an expense budget which is included in the profit plan. Of course, the pivotal planning function centers around the sales forecast and the projection of the specifics of future product sales. But the core of the pricing task centers around the development of sound costs which are estimated to be required to support the sales projection.

Not all costs are incurred necessarily in one total in the budget. Some, such as material, are incurred with the volume of output, per piece if you will. Other costs, such as machine depreciation, are incurred annually. Some costs are more identified with the productive effort than others. Direct labor is usually considered a manufacturing cost, whereas executive salaries are classified as a nonmanufacturing cost.

The vital point to bear in mind is that changes in price will change volume output; while some manufacturing costs will vary directly with this change, other manufacturing costs will vary somewhat disproportionately to the output change. On the other hand, it is possible for some nonmanufacturing costs to vary or remain fixed with the change in volume output. With the exception of sales commission, it is rare for a nonmanufacturing cost to vary directly with changes in output.

Completed costs, whether budgeted by production center or products, should be assembled and summarized separately so as to disclose the various elements of material, labor, factory overhead, administrative overhead, and the like.

To be valuable for pricing purposes, any cost system has to be flexible enough to provide the information required at different times as a response to changing conditions. A cost system represents only an assembly of facts presented in an orderly manner for the purpose of obtaining some predetermined answer. Consequently, a cost system must be uniform and consistent for the individual company. If the methods used in organizing the data are changed, the results will also differ. For this reason, the cost of a product may never be a single, precisely calculated figure; it is a figure obtained to fulfill a specific function in a company, whether for pricing, profitability determinations, or control. That is why it is of the utmost importance to decide in advance, before organizing any cost system, what will be the purpose of the system and which objectives the company will try to reach with it.

Future Costs Essential

What kinds of costs are required in pricing? Surely raw accounting costs will not do because they are historical and do not indicate what future costs are likely to be. Costs for pricing deal with the future. Current or past information may not provide a proper basis for pricing measurement nor for profit projections unless we are willing to assume that what has happened in the past will happen in the future—with respect to product mix, volume levels, price levels, customer actions, competitive responses, and all other interrelated variables of operations.

Product costs used for determining pricing actions must be based on expected purchase costs of raw materials, labor wage scales, and other expenses to be incurred. Products and manufacturing may be divided basically into those which are made to order and those which are made in anticipation of future orders. The first group can be characterized as custom or job shop operations; the second as mass produced in predetermined lot sizes or catalog type. The job shop effort has to wait until orders are placed. The second type of manufacturing proceeds on a planned rate of output without regard to specific orders. For either type of manufacturing category the need for predictable future costs is essential.

Besides knowledge of production costs, information about development, promotion, marketing, and distribution costs is needed. Development costs may be related to a product, to a product line, or to a period in which there is expected a general development program. Promotional costs include advertising and selling costs, whether applicable to a product line, a territory, or a market.

Historical and "standard" costs provide only a *guide* to current or future costs. When costs of material, labor, facilities, and services change, costs previously recorded have to be restated in dollars having the same purchasing power as the dollars in which the selling prices are being quoted. One of the deficiencies in the use of costs for pricing is the inclusion of the depreciation expense based on the original or acquisition cost of the capital asset in use. This deficiency calls for a "price level" adjustment on the acquisition cost so that it will reflect current dollars. Current dollars in an inflationary economy have a lower purchasing power than original dollars. Thus the depreciation expense would have to be inflated to make provision for the future replacement of assets in current dollars.

Information on product cost must be regularly presented to management for consideration of selling prices and the constant question of deciding what to do about meeting, beating, or withdrawing from competitive prices. The planned cost, rather than the past costs, is the deciding factor, so that management can know in advance the relative profit contributions of the various products that it is planning for present and future markets.

Costs Start the Pricing Process

A cost system worth its salt must reflect accurately and currently all changes in the company so that management may price effectively in its markets, channel its sales efforts into the most profitable areas, enhance profitable facilities, discard unvirile facilities, and plan for expansion. Management must know its costs while the events are current, not after the fact when the events have become ancient history. A proper cost system must be able to predict in advance, within close limits, the ultimate costs of making the product.

For pricing, costs are only the starting point. Since competition and customer demand must be considered, selling prices rarely have a rigid relationship to cost. Pricing is more an overall total-product planning task in which management analyzes the possible courses, balances one with the other, and then selects the one which promises to be the best. In selling, management must direct the sales effort into the most profitable channels for the most profitable facilities. No matter from what areas profits ultimately develop, *the basic function of cost is to help management find its sources of profit.*

For a company to operate profitably, expenses must be properly identified, classified, reported, and allocated to the various products. In the "competition sets the price" attitude, a manufacturer should enter into the transaction with a full knowledge of his cost "floor" even though he sells at someone else's price level. Traditional cost systems do not produce this kind of information, and often companies find themselves selling below their actual out-of-pocket costs.

While, in general, selling prices of certain products are not established on the basis of production costs, the total aggregate selling prices of a company's products over a period of time must exceed the total cost of making those products. Within a specified period there are many fluctuations in cost and selling price because of the nature of the particular product, the time of the year, the customers' demands. A proper set of cost data skillfully used will allow the manufacturer to exploit such factors to his own advantage and thus obtain a greater gap between the total period costs and sales income. Of course, costs stated on the estimating sheet must be close to expected future costs; otherwise the manufacturer could be misled into making a wrong decision.

Cost-estimating

Cost-estimating for pricing purposes may be defined as the process of calculating the expected cost of articles to be produced when past experience does not provide the historical cost of identical items produced under identical conditions.

All pricing problems have both long- and short-range components. While fixed costs must be allocated to provide a complete recovery of expenses at the end of a given period, the short-range impact also must be given consideration. Both long- and short-range volume differentials in cost must be available to permit accurate pricing decisions.

Product costs based upon normal volume and mix of facilities are not sufficient for short-range pricing. The term "short-range" refers to any period in which there are costs that do not change with volume. This period is characterized by the stability of fixed costs and the fact that the industrial manager usually cannot adapt his productive capacity to take advantage of sudden increases in the demand for his product, nor can he substantially change his production costs overnight.

Academic approaches to product costing state that every price should cover the "full" cost of the product. Yet, the amount of overhead apportioned to a product is never precisely measurable, and there are always degrees of interpolation existing between even the closest allocation bases. Customers are not interested in the seller's allocation basis or the amount of projected activity expected, nor in that of his competitors. Allocations are done for the information of the seller and should not be done for the benefit of the customer.

Because of this "unitizing" of period costs, the actual amount carried by each unit or product cannot really be known until after the number of units have been produced—at the end of the period. That's why the getting or losing of a particular order may in itself affect the cost of filling it—as well as affecting the cost of all the other units produced.

Classification of Costs

Costs may be classified into fixed and variable, manufacturing and nonmanufacturing, direct and indirect, controllable and noncontrollable, and many other categories. In costs for pricing purposes, management must know which costs vary with volume and which do not. Thus, when management is considering additional volume which will not involve additional facilities to produce, fixed costs may not be included in such a proposal, and the contribution made to profits from this volume increment would be the difference between the incremental variable costs and the revenue. In other cases, if the volume increment being proposed requires additional equipment, both fixed as well as variable costs have to be considered.

In other instances, it may be helpful to know the direct charges incurred by the product apart from the general and administrative costs, which are not related directly to the product. The use of these cost classifications will be discussed in detail in a later chapter.

After costs have been identified and categorized, they must be reported in a form suitable for convenient evaluation and application. Costs take different forms, change at different rates, and occur at different places in the company's geography. Reporting methods must take these characteristics into consideration. One would not report the cost of machine depreciation in the way purchase of a lubricant is reported.

Other Uses for Cost Data

A proper cost system also helps determine which machines or production centers in a plant are the most profitable. This consideration is important since it enables management to reflect this profitability in its sales emphasis. Inaccurate, illogical cost information can result in sales emphasis channeled in the wrong direction, applied to the poorest products or markets. In some cost systems, the level of materials costs becomes the sole guide to prices, even though a product may be produced on expensive facilities. Sales of this type make the manufacturer a jobber of someone else's raw materials instead of a merchandiser of his production facilities, thus diluting the profit return on capital equipment.

In a multiproduct company, proper costs also help determine which products will be manufactured, in what quantities, in what volume, on which facilities, and for what markets. Costs show the relationship of profitability of facilities or products to the marketing costs required to promote and sell the products.

Costs are also essential for the planning of expansions, whether in terms of equipment, markets, product lines, sales territories, or the like. In planning for the longer term, management must know in advance the expected results of a future course of action. Proper costs and cost separation are essential for applying the break-even technique to company operations and to the analysis of cost-volume-profit relationships.

For the shorter term, proper costs separated into their fixed and variable elements will give the out-of-pocket as well as the break-even point of specific orders, facilities, market areas, and the like. This procedure enables management to attract work to use unfilled capacity or to fill out a product line. However, the acceptance of this type of work requires discretion to avoid causing bottlenecks in the plant or occupying facilities at a time when more profitable work is available in the immediate future.

Management's Attitude toward Cost Information

Executives tend to underrate or overemphasize the importance of costs in pricing. Some dismiss costs by an attitude of "competition sets the price." Others overplay the importance of costs by rigidly adhering to the notion that costs determine prices. Costs, competition, and demand all must be considered in the pricing decision. In some cases, costs may have little direct effect on prices. In other situations, prices may tend to establish costs. Even when costs have little immediate influence on pricing, they are essential for evaluating such internal proposals as which products to push, which to drop, which to innovate, etc.

Successful competitive pricing is not simply a process of assigning an economic value to the item being priced. Nor is it just a matter of following competitive prices of the same or similar items. Even if either or both of these procedures succeeded in generating sales, the revenue could be profitless at best or loss producing at worst.

Obviously, cost is a primary factor in pricing decisions. No matter how a price is arrived at in the management inner sanctum, that price should be compared with its cost before posting in the marketplace. While this procedure may appear to be obvious and basic to profit control, a surprisingly large number of managements believe that any mistake made by neglecting this comparison can be compensated for later by increases in volume.

THE TRADITIONAL APPROACH TO PRICING

CHAPTER 4 *Cost-estimating Methods*

The cost of a product is not necessarily an exact, specific sum. Its amount depends on concurrent manufacture of other products and on the activity of the facilities involved in its production. Cost determination is based on many variables, not the least of which is allocation of overhead to the product. Usually, when an executive inquires about the cost of a specific product, he is given figures developed by the orthodox accounting approach. While this figure may be useful for internal managerial decisions, it tends to be inadequate for pricing purposes.

Cost-estimating Formulas

The key to the cost-estimating puzzle is the way period or time expenses are allocated, unitized, and charged to the individual product. The direct product costs, such as direct labor and direct materials, pose no special allocation problem. These costs are generated with the manufacture of the product and do not exist if the product is not made. These direct costs are part of a group called variable costs. The period portion of variable costs is not variable directly with the product but rather changes in total with overall company output. These period variable costs are not traceable to a specific product; an example is sales clerical salaries. There are also the fixed period costs which remain constant over the short term, generally considered to be a one-year operating period. These costs are not identifiable in any manner with the product; an example is real estate taxes. These expenses occur at the same amount irrespective of volume and exist regardless of the booking of any order or group of orders.

Over the years, myriad formulas have cropped up, each claiming to be the best way of allocating period expenses to the product or order so that each carries "its proper share," "pulls its own weight," is "fairly charged." Cost-estimating became hampered by unnecessary complications and illogical theories. Short cuts, formulas, magic numbers, factors, and percentages confused the cost-finding process and generated tons of paper work. Often these methods arose out of a need for quick quotations; many managements never recognized product costing as a science. Once the idea of the magic number became implanted, it was hard to pry loose, especially if management was able to point to a profit figure on a recent operating statement.

Unfortunately, the use of the magic number does not *find* costs, it *forces* them. Period costs get spread with a bulldozer, filling in holes and leveling peaks. Management is victimized by the current short-cut formula in use and alternately rides the peaks of profit and the valleys of loss as the formula approaches or departs from actual costs.

Traditional Cost-estimating Methods

The following is a list of current methods being used to estimate product costs. Two products are shown for each example for comparative purposes. In all cases, the two products are the same and are made by the same company. Product 1 is produced on slow, old, inexpensive facilities; Product 2 is manufactured on fast, modern, expensive equipment. An understanding of these methods will assist the reader in the analysis of current pricing methods given in the following section:

METHOD A: *Total Overhead Costs Applied on the Basis of Direct Labor Cost*

Item	Product 1	Product 2
Direct material...........................	$ 9.00	$ 9.00
Direct labor..............................	8.00	3.00
Overhead = 150% of direct labor...........	12.00	4.50
Total cost.............................	$29.00	$16.50

Comment: This method assumes a direct relationship between overhead costs and direct labor costs. It is perfectly possible for low-labor items to require massive overhead expense support, and vice versa. This method will undercost expensive work, such as Product 2, and overcost work requiring a higher amount of direct labor, which may be true of work produced on slow, old equipment, as in Product 1. The effect is to keep the expensive facilities very busy, especially those on which the unit direct labor cost is low. In some instances, this method has led to overtime, multiple-shift operations and even to a duplication of facilities. When profits do not provide the expected objective, the tendency is to secure volume by "desperation pricing" in order to avoid excess idle capacity. Frequently, this desperation pricing results in selling below out-of-pocket costs. This method victimizes the user to the extent of his direct labor content in any product; product mix becomes customer dominated and not seller controlled; the company generates a great amount of unprofitable volume; and usually any profit is made by accident and not by plan.

METHOD B: *Total Overhead Costs Applied on the Basis of Direct Labor plus Direct Material Costs*

Item	Product 1	Product 2
Direct material + direct labor..........................	$17.00	$12.00
Overhead = 33⅓% of direct material + direct labor.......	5.67	4.00
Total cost...	$22.67	$16.00

Comment: This method assumes a direct relationship between overhead costs and the sum of direct materials and direct labor costs. There may not be any sensible relationship between overhead expense and the amount of raw materials used in the product. Raw material content can be very high and the cost of facilities used to manufacture the product can be very low, so that the product becomes overloaded with overhead expense because of its inherently high material-cost content. Naturally, the reverse is also true. In other cases, the labor and materials can both be low or high. This method is a compounding of illogical relationships, the overhead being assigned by two elements of direct cost, both of which may vary considerably without having any real appreciable effect on the overhead actually incurred. Orders having the lowest combination of materials and labor wind up with the least overhead charge. This practice limits volume on expensive facilities where most of the company's investments exist if the material cost is a large portion of product cost. The method also victimizes the user as in the foregoing Method A, but to an even greater extent because of the interplay of cost with a changing product mix. For example, if Product 1's material and labor cost of $17 had a different mixture, say, $16 for material and $1 for labor instead of what is shown above, then the one-third for overhead could be far too much. If the proportions were changed in the other direction, the one-third could be too little. If Product 2 had a different breakdown, say $2 for material and $10 for labor, the distorting effect of the one-third overhead charge would be even more serious because of the nature of Product 2's facility cost.

METHOD C: *Total Overhead Costs Applied on the Basis of Direct Material Costs*

Item	Product 1	Product 2
Direct material............................	$ 9	$ 9
Direct labor...............................	8	3
Overhead = 100% of direct material.........	9	9
Total cost..............................	$26	$21

Comment: This method, similar to Method A in the sense that only one cost factor is used as the allocation base, makes product cost the accident of the material content. In this case, even though both products are made on facilities which differ considerably in capital cost, the method assumes that the incurred overhead is the same. Products made at high speed on expensive equipment will not be charged with much overhead if the material cost in the product happens to be low. In the reverse case, products which make little use of capital facilities and incur little overhead cost will be charged with a great amount of overhead cost if the material in the product happens to be high. This method is very simple to compute and use, but its valid application is limited to bulk materials industries such as forgings, cement, sugar, paint, bread, and the like. In these cases, this method is applied on a weight instead of a dollar basis. For example, if a brass foundry produces 800,000 pounds of castings per month of uniform style and weight and the overhead expenses for the month are $80,000, the *overhead per pound* is 10 cents. Thus, the overhead cost estimate for a casting weighing 5 pounds would be 50 cents. If however, the foundry's products are *not* uniform and it produces a variety of castings which vary in weight, shape, and style, requiring all manner of coremaking, this method becomes inequitable. Under this circumstance, the simple but heavy casting will be overcost, and the complex but light casting will be undercost.

METHOD D: *Total Overhead Costs Applied on Unit of Product Basis*

Item	Product 1	Product 2
Direct material.............	$ 9	$ 9
Direct labor................	8	3
Unit overhead..............	5	5
Total cost................	$22	$17

Comment: In this method, the expected output is divided into the total budgeted overhead to get the cost per unit. Here we are assuming overhead costs of $100,000 per year and output at 20,000 units per year, or $5 per unit. This method is a more direct method of charging overhead cost—but only in severely limited cases. It can be used only where one product is made or where products are few, closely related, and have some common denominator such as weight or volume. Examples of industries where the use of this method may be considered safe, but still not logical, are the shoe industry and the mattress industry, where the size is standard and the grades held fairly close. In the above case, the illogical effect shows up by assigning as much overhead to one product as to the other in spite of the wide gaps between their use of facilities and actual incurrence of overhead costs.

Observation: It is interesting to note that in the foregoing four cost methods, Product 2 shows a lower total cost. This fact is not to imply that Product 2's cost should be lower or higher than Product 1. Although the overhead assigned to Product 2 probably should be higher, there is no reason to expect that its total costs will be, even though both have the same cost of material. The products may be totally different or, and this is of major moment, the comparison may be drawn to show the probable costs of making the *same* product both presently and also under a proposed new method involving a substantial capital outlay. In this event, management would want to see a lower total cost (in the Product 2 column) before authorizing the change. The implication is that the adoption of newer methods while raising *annual* overhead (to the extent of the additional depreciation of new facilities) should be offset by a lower unit direct labor cost.

METHOD E: *Overhead Applied on the Basis of Conversion Costs*

Item	Product 1	Product 2
Direct material...	$ 9.00	$ 9.00
Conversion costs:		
Direct labor.......................................	8.00	3.00
Direct manufacturing overhead.......................	2.00	7.00
Period overhead = 125% of conversion cost..............	12.50	12.50
Total cost.......................................	$31.50	$31.50

Comment: This method assumes that overhead costs vary directly in accordance with direct conversion costs and is similar to Method A, in which only the direct labor was used as the basis of allocation, except that some direct overhead is charged directly to products and the balance to be allocated is only the period or fixed component of overhead. This refinement does not change the logic, only the numbers. Consider the above case where the sums of direct labor and direct overhead are both $10. Does this mean that the depreciation expense for the equipment (a period fixed cost) is the same for both products? Does it mean that the space occupied, and thereby the real estate taxes (another period fixed cost), for each piece of equipment used for the two products will be the same? Certainly there could be substantial differences which might lead to vastly different total product costs. This method is an attempt to divorce material as one of the bases of allocating overhead and is a step in the right direction. This method also recognizes that those overhead costs which are directly identified with a piece of equipment (and thence with the product) should be charged directly without the necessity for an arbitrary allocation. This is creditable and another step in the proper direction. Other rationales for this method include one which recognizes the process of conversion as the service being sold and thereby attempts to apportion fixed overhead in accordance with the respective capital investments in each product. Again, the desire to assign value to a product based on investment levels is sound, but only if the various layers of capital and their respective degrees of risk are considered. But this method amounts to a blanket average and is not specific enough.

METHOD F: *Manufacturing Overhead Applied by the Machine-hour Rate Method**

Item	Product 1	Product 2
Direct material...	$ 9.00	$ 9.00
Conversion costs:		
Direct labor..	8.00	3.00
Manufacturing overhead............................	4.00	10.00
Total manufacturing cost..........................	$21.00	$22.00
Nonmanufacturing cost = 10% of manufacturing cost......	2.10	2.20
Total cost..	$23.10	$24.20

* Spencer A. Tucker, *Cost-estimating and Pricing with Machine-hour Rates,* Prentice-Hall, Inc., Englewood Cliffs, N.J., 1962.

Comment: A machine-hour rate is the cost of operating one production center for one hour in the processing of orders or products. Some machine-hour rate plans include only manufacturing costs; others include nonmanufacturing costs as well. The machine-hour rate, then, is a *rate of conversion cost.* For example, assume that Product 1 has to pass through just one piece of equipment in its process. If this machine carries a machine-hour rate of $2 (manufacturing cost only) and Product 1 uses that machine for 2 hours, the conversion cost is then 2 hours at $2 per hour or $4. If Product 2 also requires processing through one machine for 15 minutes and its machine-hour rate is $40, obviously its conversion cost is $0.25 \times \$40 = \$10$. The machine-hour rate method is the most equitable way of allocating overhead since the apportioned overhead cost reaches the product cost by way of the facilities used. In this way overhead is charged by the way it is incurred and where it is incurred, instead of where the impact of overhead incurrence is obscured. This method, however, includes only manufacturing cost in the conversion cost rate, leaves the nonmanufacturing cost to be allocated by percentages, and may or may not be equitable depending on the specific company and its product characteristics. For example, in some industries one product may require much more or much less nonmanufacturing support than a fixed percentage on manufacturing cost would yield. The following two methods show the logical refinements of the machine-hour rate method.

METHOD G: *Total Overhead Costs Applied by the Machine-hour Rate Method*

Item	Product 1	Product 2
Direct material............	$ 9	$ 9
Conversion costs:		
Direct labor.............	8	3
Total overhead...........	5	18
Total cost............	$22	$30

Comments: The method used here is similar to Method F with this exception: the conversion rate is all-inclusive of manufacturing and non-manufacturing costs; nonmanufacturing costs are not applied by a percentage of another total. In Method F, total overhead costs were shown to be $6.10 ($4.00 + $2.10) for Product 1 and $12.20 ($10.00 + $2.20) for Product 2. When the machine-hour rate is all-inclusive, the total overhead costs are $5 and $18 respectively, indicating a possibly greater cause-and-effect relationship between each product and the amount of nonmanufacturing overhead charged. Even though this method shows a greater degree of refinement, we have to go one step further before it can be used for pricing.

Recommended Cost-estimating Method

A method which is presented in detail in Section 5 is discussed briefly here to provide a comparison:

METHOD H: *Fixed and Variable Overhead Costs Applied by the Machine-hour Rate Method*

Item	Product 1	Product 2
Direct material............................	$ 9.00	$ 9.00
Direct conversion costs:		
Direct labor............................	8.00	3.00
Direct overhead (facility).............	3.40	9.80
Direct overhead (order)..................	0.40	2.10
Period variable costs....................	1.60	1.80
Period fixed costs.......................	1.10	1.90
Total cost..........................	$23.50	$27.60

Comment: In this method, overhead is applied to products through the medium of the cost of facility usage, as in the previous two methods, but with the exceptions that (1) the machine-hour rate is an all-inclusive overhead rate and (2) the costs which behave differently are treated differently. This method is known as the two-part machine-hour rate system[*] wherein a machine-hour rate is expressed in the direct cost per hour and the "full" cost per hour. Thus, a machine-hour rate for a given production center could be $36.75 "full" cost, of which $22.45 is the direct-cost component. Since the fixed costs are reflected in "full" costs by an assumed rate of expected activity, the "full" costs, even though they may represent the result of cause-and-effect relationships, are nonetheless arbitrary because of the unknown element of future activity. If the market-place is not ready to accept such a "full" cost (since it represents only the projections of one manufacturer without reference to competitive price levels), management is faced with a reduction in its price if it wishes to get the order. In this event, it is essential that management knows its floor on cost—its out-of-pocket cost level. This method of cost-estimating provides simultaneously both out-of-pocket and "full" costs. A word of explanation is in order regarding the two types of direct overhead charges shown. The direct overhead (facility) refers to those charges which are incurred directly by a machine, such as electricity for operating, machine supplies which vary directly with volume, and the like. Direct overhead (order) represents those overhead charges which are incurred by the order, such as freight out, salesman's commissions, and any other direct order charge which requires no statistical allocation.

[*] See Sec. 5.

Summary of the Eight Cost Methods

Obviously, great differences exist among the eight methods illustrated:

Total costs estimated	Product 1	Product 2
Method A.....................	$29.00	$16.50
Method B.....................	$22.67	$16.00
Method C.....................	$26.00	$21.00
Method D.....................	$22.00	$17.00
Method E.....................	$31.50	$31.50
Method F.....................	$23.10	$24.20
Method G.....................	$22.00	$30.00
Method H (recommended).........	$23.50	$27.60

Which cost is correct? Regardless of whether management intends to use estimated costs for pricing or for other internal decisions, the cost method must produce a reliable answer. It should be clear from this comparison that much damage can be done to the firm's profit objective as well as to the market price levels if illogical cost methods are used as the basis for price. Yet it has been the author's experience that all these methods are used by groups of competing companies serving the same markets. Often, then, a company gets the order which it thinks is profitable solely on the basis of the cost method used. One can look at this situation as involving competition based on cost-estimating methods rather than on the basis of quality, performance, and modern processing methods.

Summary

When a manufacturer offers a product for sale he is really offering to make his services, facilities, and technical knowledge available to his customers. Ideally, the customer should pay for a portion of each of these items so that the manufacturer gets back all the costs he has incurred. The industrialist suffers the risks of operating his business by investing capital in machinery, buildings, inventory, labor force, and other factors of production. Against these risks, the manufacturer balances his profits and the selling prices that should bring in the expected revenues. When estimated costs are wrong, regardless of the pricing method used, anticipated profit contributions shrink and/or orders are lost.

The seller must apportion the various categories of cost to products or to facilities which produce his output. Direct costs which vary with volume are identifiable with, and traceable to, output and call for no special allocation to products. The allocation of fixed or time costs to products requires the use of one of a great number of allocation bases, each of which has some degree of logic but is nonetheless arbitrary. The contention that a given allocation method is the "right one" is indefensible because of the lack of direct, traceable relation between the cost and the product. This attempt to unitize time costs can victimize the manufacturer and distort the basis on which prices are decided. In a multiproduct business, the use of magic numbers for cost-estimating distorts information needed for analyzing the product mix and facility usage.

Later chapters will suggest rational approaches to cost-estimating for pricing purposes and will apply them in specific situations where there are the volatile interplays of costs, volume, prices, profit, product mix, facility usages, market forces, and competitive behavior. The pricing technique will show how these operational variables can be quite different from company to company and from one situation and time to another situation and time.

CHAPTER 5

Cost-plus Pricing Methods

Unless a company follows a market-dictated policy of pricing its products without any reference to its own costs, it is bound to have some kind of pricing policy. Surveys of business practices in setting prices have shown the most prevalent attitude to be pricing which bears some "equitable" relation to costs. As in the allocation of period costs to products (discussed in the previous chapter), here, too, the notion persists that the fairest kind of pricing involves a common markup shared over all product costs. Businessmen believe that this policy is most defensible in justifying to others. But in many cases, the formula approach is regarded as only a first approximation of price.

Definition

Cost-plus pricing is the practice of adding to an estimated product cost an amount of money to arrive at a selling price. This added money is considered the profit expectation if the sale is made on the basis of adding this anticipated profit to total or "full" costs. However, not all cost-plus methods use "full" costs as the markup base; some methods use only a portion of the total product costs, in which case the margin of markup (generally larger) serves to cover the balance of nonestimated costs plus the expected profit.

Whatever the segment of cost marked up, i.e., total or partial cost, the nature of the cost is subject to some variation from company to company. In some instances, actual or present costs are used; in other cases, expected or future costs are used; and in some cases, standard costs are used. Standard cost is an estimate of what costs would be at some normal rate of output, such as 80 per cent of capacity, at a standard or optimum level of productivity.

41

The Profit Markup

The derivation of the markup may also vary from method to method. Some markups are calculated to provide a certain return on sales; others give a desired rate of return on invested capital. In some methods, different elements of the product's cost are marked up at different rates to reflect the differences in invested capital in those elements.

Not all methods for arriving at a markup are as rational as the above. In the author's experience, a majority of managers set (or attempt to set) prices on the basis of a fair profit. This profit percentage, more often than not, is a fixed rate on cost regardless of the ingredients of product-cost structure, i.e., heavy in raw material content and light in the use of facilities and vice versa. Naturally, this "fair" profit percentage differs from industry to industry as well as from company to company within an industry. Where there is no price policy, the amount of markup tends to be set arbitrarily. The defense rationale is that companies want no more than a fair profit, even though no one knows how much this figure should be.

The percentage or the amount added for the profit markup differs considerably among industries, among companies in the same industries, and even among the different product lines within a firm. If an average had to be given, its level would hover around 10 per cent—a most convenient, round number. The differences in the profit percentage are sometimes due to the characteristic industry differences, e.g., heavy capital equipment industry versus a hand-assembly industry which uses the output of other manufacturers. Other variances from the average are caused by different degrees of competitive intensity in an industry, market, and/or particular geographic area where freight is an important cost factor. Other differences come from the nature of the cost base and the extent to which some profit has already been included by padding overhead cost. In most cases, though, the differences in the markup percentages are more the result of habit patterns and local concepts of "fair and just" profit.

Starting Point

Regardless of the cost-plus method used, the starting point is the cost estimate. Cost-plus methods are variously successful and unsuccessful based on the method of estimating product cost (see Chapter 4) combined with the external effects of market demand and competitive prices.

Some cost-plus methods start with a defensible cost-estimated base and then dilute the effects by a rigid approach to establishing prices. Others have an underlying poor cost estimate but then apply a reasoned approach to competitive and market conditions. Obviously, neither practice succeeds for too long. The most reliable approach combines the best elements of each.

Cost-plus pricing takes a number of forms. The following topics in this chapter discuss the more popular ones. The concluding chapter in this section summarizes the deficiencies of the various methods given and presents the rationales for current usage.

"Full"-cost Pricing

"Full"-cost pricing is probably the most popular of the cost-plus pricing methods because to businessmen it seems the fair and safe way to price. It also is easiest to explain and justify to customers and others. But the method was developed by accountants for use by businessmen, and so the chief concern underlying "full"-cost pricing is that all products must bear their "full" share of costs. The assumption is that if all these assigned costs are covered by the selling prices, a full recovery of all costs will be achieved.

The term "full" costs is intended to convey an impression of total costs. However, when practitioners of this method refer to "full" costs they mean fully allocated costs, but the reader should bear in mind that it is possible to obtain "full" costs without allocation methods. The author will refer to these as total costs and will treat both of them in this chapter.

Fully allocated costs are those costs assigned to products using common or joint facilities of the firm, which are distributed on the basis of expected future activity. Facilities refer to production machinery, administrative services, selling, distribution, marketing, promotion, and/or warehousing services. Typical products and industries falling into this category are multiproduct firms which produce many different fabricated parts on common equipment, such as job machine shops, commercial printers, paperboard package converting firms, iron and brass foundries, etc. These companies may be considered job shops or converters because they produce only to customer specifications and not in anticipation of orders. Companies which do produce in anticipation of orders are usually mass production firms producing a standard or catalog line of products at a predetermined rate of output.

There are also companies which produce a variety of products on separate, nonjoint production facilities but which use common administrative, selling, and distribution facilities for the benefit of the entire product mix. The cost of sharing these services is also generally allocated to the products or orders on an expected volume basis.

Total costs represent costs which are all identifiable with and directly traceable to the product. This type of cost is typical of companies producing a limited and rather homogeneous line of similarly priced products in which no allocation (or a bare minimum) of any type of cost is used.

Whether "full" or total costs are used, the concept and application are very much the same. The exception is that "full" costs contain the arbitrary element of expected future activity.

Most firms start with an estimate of the known, tangible elements of their costs which appear obvious. These costs are usually the direct material and direct labor costs. From this point on it's anybody's ball game, as shown by the eight cost-estimating methods analyzed in Chapter 4. Let's take a few examples to see how these methods work.

Markup on Total Costs for Return on Sales

The following is the annual operating data of a company:

Direct labor...	$100,000
Direct material......................................	200,000
Factory overhead....................................	150,000
Selling, general, and administrative (S, G, and A) overhead.	50,000
Total Cost..	$500,000
Pretax profit.......................................	50,000
Sales..	$550,000

In terms of individual product cost, unit direct labor and unit direct material present no great estimating problem. The only problem is how to get a portion of the annual factory overhead and annual selling, general, and administrative overhead costs tacked onto the labor and material figure. Out of the many choices available, we shall test these four typical formulas:

FORMULA A: Assign factory overhead as 150 per cent of direct labor and to the sum of labor, material, and factory overhead, add one-ninth for the balance of the overhead.

FORMULA B: Assign all overhead as 200 per cent of direct labor.

FORMULA C: Assign all overhead as 100 per cent or direct material cost.

FORMULA D: Assign factory overhead as 75 per cent of direct material cost and assign the balance of overhead as 50 per cent of direct labor cost.

It can be clearly seen that any of these methods applied to the labor and/or material costs will recover the total overhead on an *annual* basis, since this is where the ratios or formulas were derived. However, when applied on a unit product basis, the final total costs can be appallingly different. When a standard percentage profit markup, such as 10 per cent, is used, the results are just as different. "Full"-cost prices for three different products in the company's product line are developed in Exhibit 5-1 using the above four formulas.

EXHIBIT 5-1. FOUR FORMULAS USED FOR "FULL"-COST PRICING

Formula	Product 1	Product 2	Product 3
Direct labor	$ 2.00	$ 6.00	$24.00
Direct material	18.00	10.00	4.00
Formula A:			
Factory overhead	3.00	9.00	36.00
S, G, and A overhead	2.55	2.77	7.11
Total cost	25.55	27.77	71.11
10% markup	2.56	2.78	7.11
Selling price	$28.11	$30.55	$78.22
Formula B:			
Total overhead	4.00	12.00	48.00
Total cost	24.00	28.00	76.00
10% markup	2.40	2.80	7.60
Selling price	$26.40	$30.80	$83.60
Formula C:			
Total overhead	18.00	10.00	4.00
Total cost	38.00	26.00	32.00
10% markup	3.80	2.60	3.20
Selling price	$41.80	$28.60	$35.20
Formula D:			
Factory overhead	13.50	7.50	3.00
S, G, and A overhead	1.00	3.00	12.00
Total cost	34.50	26.50	43.00
10% markup	3.45	2.65	4.30
Selling price	$37.95	$29.15	$47.30

Even if competitors use this type of pricing, the order is placed with the lowest bidder. That means that if this company uses Formula B for Product 1, Formula C for Product 2, and Formula C for Product 3, it stands the best chance of selling those products. No one of these formulas produces a consistently low price for all three products, not that there is anything virtuous about a low price. If the company should choose Formula B across the board, it will be lowest for Product 1 but highest for Products 2 and 3. If it chooses Formula C consistently, it will be highest for Product 1 but lowest for Products 2 and 3.

What should the price be? is better phrased: What cost is right? What cost is best? What cost should be used?

Is the $83.60 price for Product 3 near what it should be, or is $35.20 more nearly right? From the way the system is set up, who knows? One might be tempted to elect the higher figure because of the large amount of direct labor. What this system does not show is that the relatively high direct labor could be the result of assembly by hand or on old, slow, inexpensive facilities. In that event, the chargeable overhead would be low, making the $35.20 more representative. Moreover, is the $41.80 price for Product 1 near what it should be, or is $26.40 a better one? Here one might be tempted to select the lower price because of the small amount of direct labor. But perhaps Product 1 is made on modern, expensive, high-speed facilities, thereby requiring a small amount of unit direct labor. Because of this higher investment in these facilities, the higher price might not even be high enough.

Generally, these methods tend to undercost products made on expensive facilities and overcost those having higher levels of labor and materials, which have no relationship to the amount of overhead incurred. *When price is a direct markup on cost, expensive facilities are usually kept very active and inexpensive facilities remain relatively idle.* These activities are sometimes the result of the company's getting enough volume when it *accidentally* happens to be the lowest bidder in the marketplace. Any profit which may develop at the end of an operating period is mistakenly credited to the company's ownership and highly active use of expensive equipment. Ironically, this error sometimes prompts management to purchase even more new capital equipment. When profits begin to wane, management searches for more volume to keep its equipment busy. This kind of approach drives a company to the practice of desperation pricing with the consequent disastrous results for itself and for the spoiling of the market.

The only time a product's unit cost and price will have the same proportions as that shown in the annual operating data is when the product's unit direct labor and direct material costs are in a 1:2 ratio. That still does not necessarily mean that the cost of that product is near what it should be. Product A in the following is made on expensive equipment and Product B is not:

Item	Product A	Product B
Direct labor..............	$10	$ 2
Direct material...........	20	4
Factory overhead.........	15	3
S, G, and A..............	5	1
Total.................	$50	$10
Markup 10%..............	5	1
Selling price.............	$55	$11

When the magnitudes of the direct labor and/or the direct materials cost act as a lever for apportioning overhead expenses, the specifics of actual overhead cost incurrence is ignored. Thus, even though the cost proportions of the above products are identical with the annual operating data, it is within the realm of reason to say that Product A is undercosted and underpriced and perhaps should sell for $85 and that Product B is overcosted and overpriced and perhaps should sell for $8.

Some companies attempt to compensate for obvious differences in a product's use of overhead by varying their pencentage markup. Using

EXHIBIT 5-2. "FULL"-COST PRICING WITH VARIABLE MARKUP

Formula	Product 1 (markup 5%)	Product 2 (markup 15%)	Product 3 (markup 10%)
Formula A:			
Total cost....................	$25.55	$27.77	$71.11
Markup.....................	1.28	4.17	7.11
Selling price................	$26.83	$31.94	$78.22
Formula B:			
Total cost....................	$24.00	$28.00	$76.00
Markup.....................	1.20	4.20	7.60
Selling price................	$25.20	$32.20	$83.60
Formula C:			
Total cost....................	$38.00	$26.00	$32.00
Markup.....................	1.90	3.90	3.20
Selling price................	$39.90	$29.90	$35.20
Formula D:			
Total cost....................	$34.50	$26.50	$43.00
Markup.....................	1.73	3.98	4.30
Selling price................	$36.23	$30.48	$47.30

the data of Exhibit 5-1, assume that Product 2 is considered the most expensive with Product 3 and Product 1 following in order; markups assigned may be 15, 10, and 5 per cent, repectively. Using the same four formulas results in the pricing shown in Exhibit 5-2.

This method does not contribute to the determination of the pricing floor nor does it assure market acceptance any more than the uniform markup does. Here the expensive work could be further overpriced, especially if used with Formula B. Ironically, the larger markup used to reward for the use of expensive facilities could restrict volume for this product, which, in turn, could actually boost its unit overhead cost. When total costs are used as a guide and not as a bible for pricing, some price trimming is done for the sake of booking an acceptable level

of orders. The questions are: How far down to trim? Of what use
are formula prices which are bound to be changed anyway?

Undoubtedly, at the beginning of the period, management has some
idea of how much of each of the three products is expected to be sold.
This is called the company's *product mix.* Of course, management could
be in the business of making and selling fifty different products, in which
case the problem becomes far more complex than it is now. Based on
the cost-price method used it will sell more of some products and less
of others than originally projected in its planned product mix. Therefore,
pricing is the major determinant of product mix, and the final operating
results reflect the actual mixture of unit costs and unit profits as contributed by the sales volume of the respective products.

Is the information shown on the cost-price estimates any guide to how
competitive prices can and should be met? Suppose Method B is the
one used in the company and the "going" price for Product 3 is $29
or $35 or $54. Should the company agree to meet any of these three
prices? On what basis can it agree and be certain that it will not incur
a cash loss, an out-of-pocket loss? The one additional piece of cost information lacking in this kind of pricing approach is the amount of variable
or direct overhead cost, which in some instances can be as much as
or greater than either the direct labor or the direct material figure. The
absolute floor on prices is the total *direct* cost of the product, not known
under this method.

Summary of Method

COST DEFECTS:

1. No cause-and-effect relationship between cost to be distributed and
basis of apportionment
2. Overhead costs allocated are dominated by gross amounts of unrelated costs
3. No distinction made for different facility costs and usages
4. No consideration for different investments in various cost elements
5. Products made on expensive machines are undercosted
6. Inexpensive work is overcosted
7. Costs highly distorted if wide range of facilities and products are
present
8. Cost variances difficult to trace

PRICING DEFECTS:

1. No knowledge of price floor, cannot meet competition intelligently
2. Competitive prices and customer demand ignored
3. Orders priced above total cost would be accepted

4. Market spoiled by underpricing expensive products
5. Product mix customer dominated instead of company controlled
6. Tendency to reject orders which do not at least cover total costs

Markup on "Full" Costs for Return on Sales

Probably the most prevalent method in cost-plus pricing is based on fully allocated costs. Whereas the total-cost pricing method uses a convenient but illogical basis for apportioning overhead expenses to the product, the "full"-cost method of pricing is an attempt to establish fair and equitable overhead cost distribution based on cause-and-effect relationships and future activity. Then a markup on these costs is used to arrive at a selling price. Rather than attempt to assign overhead costs directly to the product, this method assigns such costs to the production event which generates the cost, i.e., the facility, and then converts the facility-overhead cost to product overhead costs by considering the time the product uses the facility. (See Methods F, G, and H of Chapter 4.)

The end result is a cost rate (machine-hour rate)* for each production center or machine. Thus, if a quantity of product is processed through three machines to completion, the *conversion cost* (which includes direct labor and either manufacturing overhead or all overhead) would be developed as follows:

	Product X		
Production center	Hours required to process	Machine-hour rate (MHR)	Conversion cost
Print.............	4.5	$22	$ 99
Cut.............	6	18	108
Glue.............	2.3	30	69
Total direct labor and overhead.	...	...	$276

Then added to this conversion cost would be the cost of raw material and a markup to arrive at selling price.

Generally, the steps in developing a machine-hour rate are:

1. Establish production centers by type of machine, by department, by product line, etc.

* Spencer A. Tucker, *Cost-estimating and Pricing with Machine-hour Rates,* Prentice-Hall, Inc., Englewood Cliffs, N.J., 1962.

2. Distribute to each production center all annual manufacturing costs (with or without nonmanufacturing costs) on a cause-and-effect basis, i.e., electricity on the basis of horsepower-hours; machine repairs on the basis of expected hours and machine value; real estate taxes on the basis of machine space occupied; fringe benefits on the basis of direct labor cost, etc.

3. Divide these annual conversion costs by the forecasted (expected) number of hours each production center or machine is expected to operate in the coming year to get a rate of conversion cost per hour—the machine-hour rate.

The steps in arriving at the selling price of a product are:

1. List the production center processing steps required for manufacturing the product, indicating the corresponding machine-hour rate.

2. From a schedule of production standards (work measurement basis) apply the number of processing hours required by the product at each production center.

3. Extend required processing hours by the respective machine-hour rates to get conversion cost at each center. Total all conversion costs.

4. Add to total conversion costs the cost of the raw material, special tools, etc., involved in the quantity of product and add any nonmanufacturing overhead cost not included in the machine-hour rates.

5. Add special order charges not included in the machine-hour rates, i.e., commission, freight out, royalties, etc., to get total costs.

6. Mark up total costs by a percentage to get selling price.

Exhibit 5-3 shows the construction of the total overhead portion of a machine-hour rate for two printing presses, one expensive, the other worth very little. The hourly direct labor cost is a direct cost and is therefore added to the overhead portion of the rate, rather than allocated.

If the various bases used to allocate the different costs are found to be correct, if the expected annual hours become the actual hours at the end of the year, and if products are sold at a price no lower than the "full" costs estimated, the use of the two rates shown will recover all the budgeted expenses. Obviously, the mix of the hours projected is a reflection of the expected product mix. That is, the proportions of the various products sold will determine the respective annual hourly usages of the two presses. It is this mixture of facility usage which causes more difficulty than the inequities in the allocation bases. In some instances, a company will not even make the distinction among its facilities but will instead develop an overall average machine-hour rate by dividing

EXHIBIT 5-3. BASIC MACHINE-HOUR RATE DEVELOPMENT

Overhead Expense Element	Total for Two Presses	Allocated to Production Center	
		A	B
		4-color 61-in. Offset	1-color Flatbed Letterpress
Building expense.........................	$ 6,000	$ 5,000	$1,000
Machinery expense......................	44,000	40,000	4,000
Indirect labor Expense..................	10,000	8,000	2,000
General expense........................	8,000	6,000	2,000
Total overhead.......................	$68,000	$59,000	$9,000
Annual expected hours.................	2,000	1,000	1,000
Machine-hour rate (overhead only)........	$34.00	$59.00	$ 9.00
Hourly direct labor cost.................	....	14.00	4.00
Total machine-hour rate................	....	$73.00	$13.00

the total annual overhead cost by the total annual hours of all its facilities. This process would give the $34 per hour figure as shown on Exhibit 5-3.

Obviously, the average rate does not recognize the widely differing hours used by other facilities. Thus, the total of 2,000 hours for both Production Centers A and B could be composed of the hours shown on the exhibit, or 500 hours of A and 1,500 hours of B, vice versa, or any combination which would total 2,000 hours.

When individual production center hourly distinctions have been made, the recovery of cost depends on the accuracy of these activity projections, as follows:

Annual hours	MHR	
	A	B
1,000 of A...........	$ 73.00	
1,000 of B...........	...	$13.00
500 of A............	$132.00	
1,500 of B...........	...	$10.00
1,500 of A...........	$ 53.33	
500 of B............	...	$22.00

(Notice that the overall overhead rate would still show a $34 per hour figure irrespective of the variation in the two components of hours.)

An incorrect projection of annual hours could have a disastrous effect on operating results if prices are built directly on top of these fully allocated costs. If activity is overstated on expensive facilities, the conversion rate (machine-hour rate) will not be high enough to recover all the costs. As we stated earlier, this could lead to a high rate of actual activity which might deceive management into the purchase of additional facilities. Conversely, if activity is understated on expensive facilities, the conversion rate could be high enough to price the company out of its markets, thereby depriving it of recovering the typically high ownership and operating costs associated with expensive equipment.

The above does not mean that correct hourly projections are the panacea for successful "full"-cost pricing. While the techniques of developing these projections are outside the scope of this book, it may be helpful to discuss the subject briefly. Some companies use historical data or modified historical hours. This method is the same as saying that they expect to make the same products as last year, in the same proportions, and with the same use of machine time. On the other hand, they may adjust the entire bundle by a percentage to account for what they believe the future period will produce. Others just budget production for a coming period without any reference to past activity. Some companies use maximum capacity hours as the activity figure irrespective of the percentage of capacity they expect to operate at. Some use a long-range sales expectancy as an activity base. In other instances, a sales forecast is made for the next twelve months by product line, and then the products are analyzed for facility usages to be required.

Of course, the use of any of these bases is not a guarantee of the right magic number. They are simply arithmetic exercises performed to satisfy certain people for certain reasons. The last word on any number produced is the customer and competition.

Exhibit 5-4 compares the construction of a selling price, using the total cost method with total overhead applied as a percentage of direct labor, with the machine-hour rate–"full"-cost method. Examples show two classes of work, one produced on inexpensive facilities, the other on more expensive equipment. Notice that a uniform 10 per cent markup is used for both classes of work. It should be pointed out that in some companies the level of the markup percentage changes to account for work in different product lines and for goods sold to different markets.

There is no doubt that the machine-hour rate method distributes overhead more fairly than the technique of applying overhead as a percentage of another unrelated cost, such as direct labor. The latter method overcosts (and therefore overprices) inexpensive work and undercosts

EXHIBIT 5-4. COMPARISON BETWEEN TRADITIONAL AND MHR ESTIMATING METHODS: FOLDING-CARTON ESTIMATES

Operation	Facility-hours Required for Order	Overhead as Per Cent of Direct Labor Method		MHR Method	
		Hourly Direct Labor Cost	Direct Labor Job Cost	MHR	Conversion Cost
1. Inexpensive job A:					
Print 1 color...........	9	$5.50	$49.50	$15.00	$135.00
Cut and crease.........	10	5.25	52.50	13.00	130.00
Straight-line glue.......	5	8.50	42.50	21.00	105.00
Total direct labor cost.....			$144.50		
OH = 200% of direct labor...			289.00		
Total conversion cost.......			433.50		370.00
Direct material cost........			213.00		213.00
Total cost........			$646.50	"Full" cost....	$583.00
Markup 10%........			64.65		58.30
Selling price........			$711.15	....	$641.30
2. Expensive job B:					
4-color offset........	15	$15.00	$225.00	$64.00	$960.00
Bobst cut........	25	7.50	187.50	32.50	812.50
Right-angle glue........	40	9.50	380.00	28.20	1,128.00
Total direct labor cost.....			$792.50		
OH = 200% of direct labor...			1,585.00		
Total conversion cost.......			2,377.50		2,900.50
Direct material cost........			840.50		840.50
Total cost........			$3,218.00	"Full" cost....	$3,741.00
Markup 10%........			321.80		374.10
Selling price........			$3,539.80	....	$4,115.10

(and underprices) expensive work because the arbitrary application of overhead cost as 200 per cent of direct labor does not discriminate for the use and cost of the specific facilities costs entering into the production of each order.

Again, this method doesn't make "full" costs effective for pricing. Suppose, for example, that the market price for Job A is $560 or $410. How does the seller know if he would be safe in meeting that price—even though he realizes the arbitrary nature of the "full" cost? Obviously, what is missing from either method is the knowledge of his cost floor, a level which he could not afford to price below without taking money directly out of his pocket.

Summary of Method

COST DEFECTS:

1. Exaggerates accuracy of allocated costs
2. Assumes ultimate logic in cause-and-effect relationships leading to the selection of allocation factors
3. Arbitrarily unitizes fixed period costs and converted to direct costs on the basis of unknown future volume and activity
4. Alternately undercosts and overcosts products as product mix and actual activity departs from original plan
5. Produces product cost in inverse relationship to economic conditions
6. Makes cost variances difficult to trace

PRICING DEFECTS

1. Provides no knowledge of price floor; cannot meet competition intelligently
2. Ignores competitive prices and customer demand
3. Would accept orders priced above "full" cost
4. Would tend to reject orders priced below "full" costs
5. Overprices products in periods of poorer economic conditions
6. Underprices products in periods of better economic conditions
7. Spoils market in periods of better economic conditions

Unrealistic Pricing

When pricing is left in the hands of traditional accountants, the recommended actions sometimes can be most unbusinesslike. For example, let's consider the case of a company that makes only one product and how it would price it under "full"-cost pricing. The company's total annual costs are comprised of a direct manufacturing cost of $2 each and fixed manufacturing and nonmanufacturing costs of $200,000 per year. The company expects to produce and sell 100,000 units during the coming year. Using the "full"-cost method, the selling price per unit would be calculated as follows:

Direct manufacturing cost per unit..............	$2.00
Fixed cost per unit ($200,000 ÷ 100,000)........	2.00
Total cost...................................	$4.00
10% markup..................................	0.40
Selling price...............................	$4.40

It is possible for a competitor to project his expected production of units at a higher or lower level, and it is likewise conceivable that a competitor's annual fixed costs could also be different. These could exist even if a competitor's direct costs were the same. The result is an inter-mixture of conjectured forecasts and different cost bases. Thus, what a unit fixed cost is for one manufacturer may be nowhere close to what it is for others making the identical product.

Nevertheless, let us assume that the $4.40 selling price is below competitive levels, which makes sales rise rapidly. Thus, the accountant is given a forecasted 40 per cent increase in sales volume for the next year. Using the same cost-pricing formula, he develops this price:

Direct manufacturing cost per unit..............	$2.00
Fixed cost per unit ($200,000 ÷ 140,000)........	1.43
Total cost...................................	$3.43
10% markup..................................	0.34
Selling price...............................	$3.77

When the accountant gives this new price to management, he is telling them in effect *to reduce prices despite the rapid rise in sales.*

The next year new competitors start to produce this same product. (The same would hold true for a slowdown in the general business picture.) In either event, sales for this company drop, and the company forecasts an annual volume of only 60,000 units. The accountant would then price the product as follows;

Direct manufacturing cost per unit..............	$2.00
Fixed cost per unit ($200,000 ÷ 60,000)..........	3.33
Total cost...................................	$5.33
10% markup..................................	0.53
Selling price...............................	$5.86

When the accountant gives this new price to management, he is telling them to raise prices or lose money. The notion of increasing prices in the face of additional competitive invasion or in poor economic times is ludicrous. Yet the "full"-cost method tells management *to decrease prices when it is taking business away from competitors and to increase prices when it is losing business to competitors.*

Of course, this example is oversimplified because only one product is involved. However, in the multiproduct business of today, the problem is vastly more complex because of product mix, facility mix, varying facility costs, and volume of product variations. Basically, this method requires any price to completely recover all costs regardless of the volume, regardless of business conditions, and regardless of competitive prices. This forces some costs, which are not identified with products, to be unitized to the product as a function of some selected volume or activity level. In effect, "full"-cost pricing forces fixed costs, which are incurred by time period, to become direct product costs.

This "full"-cost method is referred to by accountants as absorption-costing, wherein there is a compulsion to have every unit of product carry a portion of the fixed costs regardless of how the output quantity varies. Thus, regardless of the annual quantity output, the "full" cost of each unit will be made to vary inversely with volume to absorb the company's annual expenses. The trouble with absorption costs for pricing purposes is the ignoring of competitive prices and the company's need to survive, as the following example will illustrate:

A company has an annual fixed cost of $30,000, all associated with one facility. In pricing the same product in good times and bad, absorption data would show:

Item	Good times (3,000 hours)	Poor times (1,000 hours)
Direct costs..................................	$12.00	$12.00
Fixed costs ($30,000 ÷ activity hours)...........	10.00	30.00
"Full" cost..................................	$22.00	$42.00
Selling price.................................	$24.20	$46.20

If these data were used in pricing, the businessman would be put in the extremely *unbusinesslike position of decreasing prices in good times and raising prices in poor times.* Yet the traditional approach requires that if volume is one-third as much, then allocated fixed unit costs have to be increased three times as much to compensate. This concept would be fine if products could be sold on that basis, but it is like putting a gun to a customer's head and demanding that he become the seller's partner and buy at a higher price because of the seller's decreased activity.

Let's say that in the period of poorer economic weather, the "going" selling price is not $46.20, but only $23. The traditionalist would be prompted immediately to turn it down. This action would deprive the seller of the margin of $11 to contribute to annual fixed costs at a time when he needed it the most. Of course, it is assumed that the seller's cost records are separated to show variable costs separately from period costs. When fixed and variable costs are jumbled together, the company has little chance of determining its floor on prices in order to measure just what cash margin would be contributed towards a recovery of its fixed period costs.

The reverse happens with absorption cost-pricing in boom times. Here the unitizing of period costs makes the customer a willing partner in the higher activity of his supplier because he winds up with bargain prices.

Return-on-capital Pricing

Return-on-capital pricing is really another form of cost-plus pricing, but instead of the profit markup being targeted to a return on cost or sales, the markup is related in some way to a desired rate-of-return on capital. However, since the specific amount of capital invested and the desired return are both personal company matters and not necessarily the same as competitors', the price calculated can be considered only a target and not a guarantee of customer acceptability. Thus, in terms of competition and the market, this method has pricing limitations.

However, regardless of the no-guarantee-of-results aspect of this form of pricing, the expression of profit as a return on capital seems to be more rational than the slavish adherence to an unknown fair markup on cost.

Return-on-capital price formulas are designed to provide the same return on each order or product; they may differentiate among products and product lines and may be applied to total costs or to different segments of costs.

Comparison of Methods

The return-on-capital method can be expressed for the total company's operation as well as for some of its profit segments, such as units, products, product lines. In pricing, the markup used on cost may be a simple markup which has been equated to total capital invested in the product, or distinctions may be made for the different kinds of investment in the product. In this latter case, more than one markup is used.

The following methods are the ones in general use:

A. *Markup on annual cost for return on capital:* Generally, this formula is obtained from the operating results and balance-sheet data of a previous period:

$$
\begin{aligned}
\text{Total capital employed} &\ldots\ldots \$1{,}000{,}000 \\
\text{Total annual cost} &\ldots\ldots\ldots \$1{,}250{,}000 \\
\text{Desired rate of return} &\ldots\ldots\ldots 15\%
\end{aligned}
$$

The formula is

$$
\begin{aligned}
\text{Per cent markup on cost} &= \frac{\text{total capital employed}}{\text{total annual cost of return}} \times \text{desired rate} \\
&= \frac{\$1{,}000{,}000}{\$1{,}250{,}000} \times 0.15 \\
&= 12\%
\end{aligned}
$$

Thus, when costs *annually* are marked up 12 per cent, the return on total capital employed (TCE) will be 15 per cent. That is, a 12 per cent markup on the $1,250,000 annual cost produces a profit of $150,000, which is a 15 per cent return on the $1 million total capital employed.

Applying this method to two different products:

Item	Product A	Product B
Total cost...............	$11.00	$11.00
Markup 12%.............	1.32	1.32
Selling price.............	$12.32	$12.32

If the company makes only these two products and the expected volume of the mix in the profit plan is attained, the return target is achieved. However, since the markup approach ignores competition and demand, Product A may be priced below market levels and Product B above, which will undoubtedly result in a shift in the planned mix and a consequent decrease in the profit target. To repeat, a target selling price pegged to a desired return on capital doesn't guarantee that it is acceptable in the marketplace. The projection of a target price is just one company's expression of its particular employment of capital and with what return it agrees to be satisfied.

The basic fallacies underlying this method are:

1. It assumes that the relationship between capital, revenue, and profit developed from annual data will obtain on an individual order basis. In fact, when the markup percentages are carried to the order pricing point, severe distortions in price may be generated, resulting in the usual high activity in items priced below the market and vice versa.

2. It makes no distinction for the various kinds of capital risk present in any product or order; product mix is assumed to be constant.

3. It treats variable capital the same as fixed capital in aiming for a target return.

B. *Markup on annual cost for separate returns on variable and fixed capital:* In most manufacturing enterprises, fixed capital remains substantially the same for varying levels of volume. Fixed capital as stated on the balance sheet decreases by the passage of time due to the economic depletion of the asset as caused by additional annual depreciation. Variable capital, on the other hand, represented by cash, receivables, and the various levels of inventory, usually changes as the sales volume changes. This characteristic can generally be expressed as a ratio between sales dollars and supporting variable capital dollars. Thus, a comparison of the annual profit-and-loss statement with the balance sheet may show $1 million of sales revenue to $250,000 of variable capital, in which case variable capital is said to be 25 per cent of sales.

A formula approach to pricing which gives effect to the changes in total capital employed with changes in revenue can be obtained from the following arrangement of the data:

$$
\begin{array}{ll}
\text{Total annual cost.} & \text{\$770,000} \\
\text{Volume of sales in units.} & \text{100,000} \\
\text{Desired rate of return on TCE.} & 20\% \\
\text{Ratio of variable capital to sales.} & 28\% \\
\text{Fixed capital.} & \text{\$200,000}
\end{array}
$$

A selling price per unit which will provide a 20 per cent return on both elements of capital regardless of the changes in total capital employed with changes in revenue is obtained from the following formula:

Unit selling price

$$
= \frac{(\text{annual cost} + \% \text{ return} \times \text{fixed capital})/\text{volume of units}}{1 - (\% \text{ return} \times \text{ratio of variable capital to sales})}
$$

When the previous data have been substituted in this formula, the following unit selling price is produced:

$$
\text{Price} = \frac{(\$770,000 + .20 \times \$200,000)/100,000}{1 - (.20 \times .28)}
$$

$$
= \frac{\$8.10}{.944}
$$

$$
= \$8.58
$$

Thus, for a unit cost of $7.70 ($770,000/100,000), a unit selling price of $8.58 will provide a 20 per cent return on both the variable and fixed capital portions of the total capital employed, under the condition that the annual unit sales volume be 100,000. Because the change in total capital employed is not proportionate to the change in sales revenue, the selling price which will produce the same return is not the same for all sales volumes. For example, suppose it is desired to find out what the price must be for an annual volume of 150,000 units:

$$\text{Price} = \frac{(\$1,155,000 + .20 \times \$200,000)/150,000}{1 - (.20 \times .28)}$$
$$= \frac{\$7.97}{.944}$$
$$= \$8.44$$

The basic fallacies of this method are:

1. Annual units are assumed to be homogeneous, i.e., that each product unit is identical, and there is no product mix.

2. Annual units are assumed to cost exactly the same and to have the same ingredients of invested capital, i.e., heavy in equipment usage and light in materials, or vice versa.

3. Annual units are assumed to have the same characteristic needs for variable capital per sales dollar; therefore, the proportion in each is identical.

Summary

Because a company has developed a formularized selling price with the finest system in the universe does not mean that it will sell its products. Markup on a seller's cost or a margin added to cost to generate a desired return on capital are both hopes. This hope is converted into reality if the formula price accidentally corresponds to the market price then prevailing. However, if a company makes a unique product not available elsewhere, it has an excellent chance of developing a pricing policy based directly on its own costs or targeted directly to the company's investment and the sought-for return. In a competitive market, prices based on a seller's costs are useful only as guides and should not be used as the basis for "go or no-go" pricing decisions.

CHAPTER 6 *Summary and Rationale for Cost-plus Pricing Methods*

As we have seen, cost-plus pricing methods take a number of forms. All these methods proceed by formula and make no concessions to external influences. Underlying all the methods is the assumption that prices based on an individual seller's costs will be acceptable and attractive to buyers. Even though some managements say that they use formula prices as an approximation, they admit that their prices must be manipulated in the marketplace because of buyer resistance, cost advantages or disadvantages over competitors, desire to expand market share in a given product line, segmenting the market to reach different layers of demand, etc.

Because of such price adjustments, economists are discounting the importance of formula pricing in favor of a reasoned or flexible approach to pricing. If formula prices are computed only to be abandoned in the face of market forces, why use them?

Product-order pricing is probably the most difficult as well as the most critical decision-making area in which to develop general principles or formulas. Pricing is at once an art as well as a science, combining internal cost and capital data, external market information, and the judgment of management regarding effects, both economic and strategic. Pricing is influenced by a host of factors, some objective as relating to internal information, the uncertain externals regarding market factors, and behavior and types of competition. It is not difficult to understand, therefore, why management people are unable to describe their pricing policy in definite terms. Not that a rigid pricing formula is desirable; quite the reverse. Instead, pricing should be a continuous process of scrutiny, test of alternatives, and balanced decisions that mesh the variables of internal and external factors.

Cost-Price Distortion

Managements who use formula-based costs and formula-type pricing are engaging in exercises which do not strengthen either their knowledge or profit. In the first instance, "full" or total costs are computed using various methods which are all equally defensible but not objective or traceable to the specific product being manufactured and sold. Therefore, each different method produces a different cost result. Then, regardless of the specific markup applied, management gets the notion of a unit profit developing if he sells his product at the formula price. This notion is highly illusionary in view of the arbitrary allocation of common or joint costs associated with a multiproduct company. The markup on a seller's costs denies the existence of competition and market forces. It fails to take into account the buyer's needs and willingness to pay and what prices competitors are offering.

For a business to grow and prosper, its management must not blindly follow competitors' prices, nor slavishly follow rigid cost methods or inflexible pricing formulas. There is no single cost figure for any one product upon which management can erect its selling price. Even if one were found, management could have no assurance that the markup to the selling price figure would be acceptable. First must come the realization that cost is only one factor to consider. Second must be the understanding that it is not the average cost figure which is important, but rather the composition of costs and the behavior of each type that are vital. Thus, management should be able to distinguish between variable and fixed costs, between traceable and blanket or common costs, between avoidable and unavoidable costs. The cost to be used for pricing decisions is one which is objective, free from arbitrary allocation or apportionment, tangibly, traceably, and identifiably related to the product, and discontinuable if the product is not manufactured. In this sense, such costs can be called marginal or incremental costs. In contrast to these costs are the blanket, period, or fixed costs which proceed unchanged with or without the product and which have been incurred to provide capacity. The scrambling together of all costs regardless of their individual behaviors produces misleading costs and illusionary prices.

Summary of Cost-Price Relationship

The relationship between costs and prices is varied:

1. Accounting cost may sometimes be used in pricing, or it may be used after an adjustment reflecting future conditions. In some cases, accounting cost is never a short-term determinant of price.

2. Total unit cost may be considered to be the minimum below which prices may not go in the *long* run. In this sense only, normal total unit cost may be indicative of the normal selling price.

3. Out-of-pocket unit costs fixes the minimum price over the short run.

4. In prices fixed by policy, unit out-of-pocket costs determine the amount contributed by product unit to common costs and profit.

5. Even when prices cannot be based directly on cost, it is a basis for measuring profitablility and for order acceptance or rejection. Costs, separated into fixed and variable elements, can be directly assigned to individual product, product lines, customers, sales territories, orders, etc. In this way, the cost-revenue-contribution relationships by these aggregates may be used to direct the selling and production efforts of the company.

6. Pricing decisions deal with the future; therefore, expected costs are more important than historical costs or current costs unless the latter are adjusted to provide for future changes.

7. In multiproduct manufacture, it is essential to show that each product line and product is recovering its own direct (out-of-pocket) costs and contributing something toward meeting the general (period, fixed) expenses of the business common to all products.

Who Gets the Order?

Application of a uniform markup to all of a seller's products discounts completely that various products may have to face different kinds of pressures from different markets. Competition and demand can be different for each of his products and may each face different demand elasticities. The same holds true for attempting to obtain the same return on capital for each of the seller's products. This practice can frequently cut off profit at the top of the line by pricing the prestige item below what buyers would be willing to pay, and it could reduce sales volume at the bottom of the line by overpricing items that are exposed to intense competition. Both can lead to profitless operations.

But who gets the order? What action should be taken?

1. If competitors' "full" product costs are the same as the seller's, the order is generally placed with the company having the smallest markup. (At what profit?)

2. If competitors' "full" product costs are different from the seller's (either below or above), the order usually goes to the firm whose combination of cost and markup results in the lowest price. (At what profit?)

3. If competitors' costs are not known to the seller, the seller will only get orders under those unpredictable and accidental situations in which he unknowingly has the lowest price. (At what profit?)

4. If competitors use modern cost-estimating and pricing methods against the cost-plus pricing method of the seller, the seller will price himself out of his markets in poor economic times and will underprice in boom times. (Low-volume inadequate recovery of costs versus high-volume profit-draining operations)

5. If competitors' prices are below the seller's "full" costs, the seller rejects work, perhaps at a time when he needs it the most.

6. The almost infinite interplay among the variables of costing and pricing methods between the seller and his competitors and the fact that business conditions compound the problem even further, the pricing problem cannot be solved in any other way than by guesswork.

7. Under these conditions, if the seller is a multiproduct company with a constantly changing product mix made on common facilities, all that will help is prayer.

Rationales for Cost-plus Pricing

Many managements say they use cost-plus pricing. They say that they add a "fair" markup to average unit costs to provide a "reasonable" return on their invested capital—even though neither they nor anyone else seems to know how much this markup should be. This "plus" in cost-plus pricing is rarely a plus because it is affected by the specific nature of the cost computation as well as by the behavior of competition and market forces.

When questioned, managements give various reasons for using cost-plus pricing:

1. Instinct tells them that their method produces the "right" price.

2. Some claim loyalty to their trade association as they believe that any price below "full" cost would be price-cutting and anything higher than their standard markup would be price-gouging.

3. Some say that they have been making a profit using the cost-plus method and see no reason to change.

4. Some believe that prices above their standard markup would invite competitive invasion; others think that if they raised their prices other competitors would not follow suit and they would be out in left field.

5. Some believe that buyers are aware of costs and would be suspicious of prices above or below their regular prices.

6. Others think that a large turnover of products is the pathway to profits and would be difficult to achieve with higher prices.

7. Some believe it is morally wrong to earn too much profit.

8. Some managements think that if they priced below "full" cost to take advantage of an immediate opportunity, their competitors would follow suit to spoil the market.

9. Others believe that decreasing prices will not affect demand and volume.

10. Some believe it is improper to sell below "full" costs.

11. Others believe that once prices are lowered they are difficult to raise.

12. Some object to the fact that their price cuts will not be passed on by their customers.

13. Others believe that prices are implanted in the minds of their buyers and that buyers dislike price changes.

14. Some think that the market stability of prices should not be changed.

15. Others believe that it is the logical way to maximize profits in the long run.

16. Some managements realize that while it is not the most profitable way of pricing, it is the safest way.

17. Some say that cost-plus pricing is really not strictly adhered to, that most managements only say they adhere to it to impress investigators by their "respectable" approach.

18. Others say that since short-run profit maximization is really not the company's goal, cost-plus pricing is not illogical after all.

19. Some managements prefer to maximize volume rather than to raise prices because in this way they project their image of a just price and a fair margin.

20. Other businessmen believe that a cost-plus price sets a floor on their prices, refusing to commit their facilities to work which would yield substandard profits.

21. Cost-plus pricing keeps the company from losing money by getting orders. (But not from losing money by *not* getting orders. It sets a ceiling on profits but sets no floors!)

22. Some public corporations use cost-plus pricing as a device to smooth out profit peaks which would otherwise be available by more modern pricing methods. This attitude is prevalent among corporations who receive critical attention from union officials, and whose position in an inflation economy makes their prices pivotal.

23. A large portion of industry uses formula pricing as a desperation measure in the face of no other acceptable substitute.

Summary of Deficiences in Cost-plus Pricing

1. It completely ignores market demand and does not consider the buyer's needs, ability, and/or willingness to pay. Market demand is the major volume-generating factor with volume levels differing for each different set of prices. While the elasticity of demand is not an accurate

nor an absolutely reliable indicator of price-volume sensitivity, some consideration must be given to it in pricing, otherwise the adding up of anyone's cost plus a markup would yield an attractive price and a profitable volume. What buyers are willing to pay for an item has no relation necessarily to what it costs any specific seller to produce. The seller cannot aim a gun at a buyer's head and force him to buy at the seller's price. The buyer will turn elsewhere: perhaps to a competitor, perhaps to another industry for a substitute of similar function; or perhaps he will switch to a different product.

2. In effect, it denies the existence of competition. A price erected on a seller's "full" cost can compete with a competitor's price only if the competitor's combination of cost and markup produces the same price. If both use the same cost-plus method of pricing and each seller's costs and markups are computed differently, the order generally will go to the seller with the lowest price. Competitors' behavior must be a factor to be reckoned with in pricing.

3. It assumes absolute accuracy and logic in the allocation of common costs irrespective of the fact that various sets of allocation factors may be equally defended by a set of cause-and-effect rationales. Different allocation methods will produce significantly different costs, especially in multiproduct firms where common facilities are employed and product mix does not stand still. The figures used for "full" costs are usually less objective and tangible than their use in pricing warrants. When a product is priced below market prices because of increasing volume, the costing rates (machine-hour rates) become reduced and prices continue to drop until orders exceed manufacturing capacity. Annual profits decrease because the increase in volume does not produce enough revenue to offset the dropping of prices. Conversely, when a product is priced above market prices because of decreasing volume, the costing rates become increased to compensate for the loss in volume. The higher the prices, the lower the volume, and this vicious circle theoretically drives the costing rates and prices to even higher levels with the ultimate point being infinite cost, infinite price, and zero volume.

4. Whatever the extent of the markup, it ignores the need for different products to earn different rates of return on capital because of the typical varying proportions of materials and conversion costs. Similarly, it ignores the opportunity that each product has to earn different rates of return in terms of the marketplace. Thus, the extremes are between products which earn too little compared to their heavier capital investment and those which require little return but are overpriced.

5. Most importantly, cost-plus methods fail to distinguish between fixed and variable costs—between those costs which are directly traceable to and identifiable with a specific product and those costs which

provide the capacity and readiness to do business and are incurred with the passage of time. Thus, orders which do not cover "full" costs, but which can make a contribution to profits, are rejected. Orders which are priced above "full" costs, regardless of the effect of arbitrary allocation method used, are considered real profit-makers. Thus, management operates between low volume on unrealistically high prices and low-profit high-volume work, booking orders through the accident of being the lowest bidder—and earning profits by the uncontrollable combining of whatever accidental profit occurs frequently enough in its bookings.

Obviously, there are times when market and competitive price conditions may not permit the seller to recover his "full" product costs. Therefore, before the seller can agree to meet "going" prices, he must have a knowledge of his absolute price floor. Then he can begin to determine the minimum margin above this cost at which to enter the market if he so desires. The seller's price floor is his cash outlay or out-of-pocket costs.

In a multiproduct company, the "full" cost of a single product can be determined only by the arbitrary allocation of certain kinds of cost. The vital decision on price is that the selling price of a single product or order cover at least its out-of-pocket cost and then provide an amount above that level to *contribute* toward paying some of the common or joint costs associated with all the products made to the extent of what the market will permit. In making the price decision, management must accept or reject the proposed contribution, based on the use of the facilities and employed capital it would have to use for the order against the alternative use of the same resources for competing work on which a greater return may be earned.

To get this *single most vital piece of pricing and profit-planning information,* the seller must separate out-of-pocket costs from all his other costs in his company. Only in this way is the seller able to measure the contribution available from any price.

THE RATIONAL APPROACH TO PRICING

CHAPTER 7 *Pricing and the Profit Structure*

Profit is the difference between revenue and costs. The traditional profit-and-loss statement shows the computed profits that have been generated on a definite volume of business in a specific time period. This profit statement applies to no other period nor to any other volume or mix regardless of the period. Hidden within the figures on this statement are the mixtures of cost behaviors, price levels, operating performances, and product activity. This statement doesn't give the slightest clue as to the source or sources of profit. Hence, use of this kind of operating statement as a managing device is an abdication of the managerial task—acting after the facts—on a historical potpourri.

The Profit Structure

Not all costs change in proportion to revenue, and profits do not change in proportion to either costs or revenue. Not all costs change at the same rate and in the same way. Neither is each element of cost affected by the same cause in the same way. Some costs change directly with volume, such as direct labor and material. Some costs remain constant with volume, such as real estate taxes and machine depreciation (assuming no capital additions within the operating period). Some costs change in step fashion with volume, such as supervisory expense and some types of office clerical salaries.

This is why a given increase in revenue will not necessarily cause the same increase in profits. As a matter of fact, it is possible for an increased revenue to produce a loss where before the increase a profit existed. In the following tabulation, the original selling price for an annual volume of 100,000 units is $28 each; then management is persuaded that it could get a volume increase of 30 per cent by reducing the price per unit to $21:

Item	Original conditions	Volume increased 30%
Units sold....................	100,000	130,000
Variable cost per unit..........	$10	$10
Annual constant cost..........	$1,500,000	$1,500,000
Annual variable cost...........	1,000,000	1,300,000
Total cost.................	$2,500,000	$2,800,000
Selling price per unit...........	$28	$21
Annual revenue...............	2,800,000	2,730,000
Pretax profit or (loss)...........	$ 300,000	($ 70,000)

This result could occur when management did not know how the specific cost ingredients of its profit structure behaved in response to volume. Naturally, not all companies will respond to the same price and volume change in the same way. The way each would react is a function of its specific profit structure—its economic personality.

This type of response occurs in companies making a single product as well as in those making several products. In cases where multiproducts are made on common or joint facilities, decision making is based on guesswork, not fact, unless management has a clearcut picture of the behaviors of its costs. The specific nature of costs makes the prediction of profits at different volumes impossible by the use of classical profit-and-loss statement as a base. In the case of a company producing more than one item, usual in most manufacturing enterprises, a change in sales volume or revenue may or may not contain the same proportions of the various products. The presence of different amounts of various products made and sold is known as *product mix* or sales mixture. This product mix does not conveniently stand still. It changes in response to prices, to actions of the competitive community, and to demand. Unless management reflects in its pricing actions the likely effect of product mix changes and their consequent impact on the costs generated, the company could be sailing into dangerous waters.

Profit Analysis

Analyzing profit and examining the behavior of the cost, price, and product mix ingredients which cause it is vital to the management of any business at any time, to say nothing of its absolute necessity in planning the pricing action.

Changes in profits come in two basic ways: changes in revenue and changes in cost. Obviously, the revenue change comes from the combination of changes in prices and volume. If more than one product is being

1ade and sold, however, the revenue and cost changes are each affected
y the product mix, i.e., the volume of product related to its specific
·rice and cost. Obviously, not all products carry the same profit margins
or are they always sold in the same proportions. Therefore, the net
·hange in profits is the result of the interplay of all factors. In short,
·hanges in selling prices cause changes in product mix, which cause
·hanges in revenue and volume; these, in turn, cause changes in costs in a
·ever-ending cycle. Only a comprehensive analysis can show the effect of
·ll the forces.

·ffect of Volume

If all costs varied or were controllable with the physical volume of
·roduction, the total cost to make and sell would vary directly with
·olume and therefore the cost and profit of each product unit would
·emain the same. For example, if 200,000 units cost $2,000,000 to make
·nd sell, and if 300,000 units cost $3,000,000 to make and sell, it is ob-
·ious that each unit costs $10. But because of the presence of typical
·onstant or fixed expenses, which are incurred only with the passage
· time, it is impossible for such a direct proportion to exist. Fixed ex-
·enses do not vary with volume, and in the typical manufacturing enter-
·rise, these expenses usually remain constant throughout the operating
·ear from a volume level of zero output up to the level of operation
·r which they were intended.

Considering these fixed expenses as time or period costs leads to this
·mple comparative analysis for the same company:

Type of cost	200,000 units sold	300,000 units sold
·lume (variable, out-of-pocket, direct) costs..........................	$1,000,000	$1,500,000
·xed (constant, period, time) costs..............	1,000,000	1,000,000
·otal costs......................................	$2,000,000	$2,500,000
·nit "full" costs..............................	$10.00	$8.33

Volume in itself exerts a dual pressure on profits. It affects both the
·evenue and the unit costs. As the number of units sold drops, revenue
·lls and unit costs rise. If both factors are present and worsening, costs
·nd revenue soon meet and losses begin. The above analysis is simple
·nce the separation of volume and time costs has been accomplished.
·ut in a multiproduct company experiencing the usual changing product

mix, profit analysis is complicated if not impossible using conventiona
profit-and-loss statements.

Price-change Proposals

Evaluating proposals to change selling prices is a task faced frequentl
by management. Often management is confronted with questions of ob
taining additional volume from other markets if its normal prices ar
reduced. Unless proper data are available, management might agree t
such a reduction and achieve a poor result, or it might be misled int
turning down such a proposal and deprive itself of an increased prof
opportunity. The solution to the problem is available from an analys
of the company's profit structure. Let's say that a company is attemptin
to predict what additional profits will develop from a 40 per cent increas
in unit sales volume. The use of traditional profit-and-loss data for bot
the original sales level as well as for the 40 per cent increase woul
show (product mix and prices assumed constant):

Type of cost	Original sales level $1,000,000	Sales level increased to $1,400,000	Increase, %
Direct labor costs......................	$250,000	$ 350,000	40
Direct material costs...................	300,000	420,000	40
Factory overhead costs.................	200,000	280,000	40
Selling, general, and administrative costs.	150,000	210,000	40
Total costs........................	$900,000	$1,260,000	40
Pretax profit.........................	$100,000	$ 140,000	40
Profit return on sales, %...............	10	10	0

When management approaches profit and cost behavior in this manne
it is making the following incorrect assumptions:

1. That all costs change in the same way with a change in revenu
Above analysis shows that since revenue increased 40 per cent, ever
cost in the company also increased 40 per cent.

2. That all costs change in the same way with a change in volum
of units sold. The analysis also shows that since volume of units sol
increased 40 per cent, every cost in the company also increased 40 pe
cent.

3. That all revenue dollars carry the same "profit," i.e., that the sam
10 per cent profit is earned on all sales.

4. In particular, that the same 10 per cent profit is earned on an
sales increase above $1,000,000.

If the additional 40 per cent volume had to be priced 10 per cent lower in order for the company to book it, management might be prompted to turn it down. Its reasoning would be that since the same 10 per cent profit would be made on this incremental volume as well as on the original volume, the additional volume would be profitless after the 10 per cent price decrease. Decisions on this type of traditional data could deprive a company of legitimate sources of profit.

Incremental Profit

Exhibit 7-1 shows what a proper analysis would look like. In this tabulation, volume and time costs are separated. The fixed-cost portions of

EXHIBIT 7-1. COST-VOLUME-PROFIT ANALYSIS (PRODUCT MIX
AND PRICES ASSUMED CONSTANT)

Item	Original sales level $1,000,000	Sales level increased 40% $1,400,000	Incremental sales $400,000
Variable costs:			
Direct labor..................	$ 250,000	$ 350,000	$100,000
Direct materials..............	300,000	420,000	120,000
Factory overhead.............	125,000	175,000	50,000
S, G, and A..................	25,000	35,000	10,000
Total variable costs..........	$ 700,000	$ 980,000	$280,000
Fixed costs:			
Factory overhead.............	$ 75,000	$ 75,000	0
S, G, and A..................	125,000	125,000	0
Total fixed costs.............	$ 200,000	$ 200,000	0
Total costs.................	$ 900,000	$1,180,000	$280,000
Pretax profit..................	$ 100,000	$ 220,000	$120,000
Profit, %.....................	10	15.7	30

the Factory Overhead and Selling, General, and Administrative cost categories have been extracted and held constant over the volume increment. (Of course, this assumes that the company has the available capacity to produce this increment.) Only the variable costs are shown to move with volume changes. In other words, the variable costs are the only costs identified and traceable to the volume increase. The fixed costs incurred only by time period remain constant.

Thus, while profit is 10 per cent at the original sales level, it increases to 15.7 per cent because of the "spreading" of the fixed costs over a greater revenue. Because the only costs incurred specifically to produce the additional 40 per cent volume are the variable costs, the profits on just the incremental portion alone are 30 per cent. This contradicts the traditional notion that the same profit is earned on all revenue dollars, and shows management that, if necessary, a 10 per cent price decrease on this portion can be made without wiping out incremental profits.

Exhibit 7-2 shows how a proper analysis can show the effect of a 10 per cent price reduction on this 40 per cent volume increment. Here the various classifications have been condensed into variable and fixed segments. Since prices on just the 40 per cent volume increment have been reduced 40 per cent, the revenues for the combined sales as well as for the increment have been reduced to give effect to this price change.

EXHIBIT 7-2. COST-VOLUME-PROFIT ANALYSIS WITH PRICE REDUCTION
(PRODUCT MIX CONSTANT AND PRICES REDUCED 10 PER CENT
ON THE 40 PER CENT VOLUME INCREASE)

Item	Original sales level $1,000,000	Sales volume increased 40% $1,360,000	Incremental sales $360,000
Variable costs..................	$ 700,000	$ 980,000	$280,000
Fixed costs.....................	200,000	200,000	0
Total costs...................	$ 900,000	$1,180,000	$280,000
Pretax profit..................	$ 100,000	$ 180,000	$ 80,000
Profit, %.....................	10	13.2	22.2
Contribution..................	$ 300,000	$ 380,000	$ 80,000

Since the incremental volume of units remain the same, the variable costs are the same as those shown in the previous exhibit. And, of course, since the time costs are not readily discontinued or adjustable with revenue, the fixed costs remain the same. The data show that even if prices were reduced 10 per cent on just the incremental portion, profits for that portion would be 22.2 per cent, further discrediting the traditional approach to uniform profit-making.

A further calculation inserted on this exhibit because of its vital nature in pricing is the figures for the *contribution*. Contribution measurement is one of the pivotal factors and will be discussed at length throughout the remainder of this book. The dollar amount of contribution is obtained by subtracting the variable costs from the revenue. While the example shown develops contribution from annual data, the major use of this figure comes when management is developing unit prices. Rather than using profit, which is the result of intermixing volume and time costs, i.e., identifiable and nontraceable costs, the contribution figure is preferable to use as a measurement of economic value because it is the result of subtracting two tangible, nonarbitrary, identifiable amounts: The contribution amount is the sum left over from revenue after paying the out-of-pocket costs and is used to pay the fixed expenses with any overage being profit.

It should be realized that the profit responses of the 40 per cent increment shown in Exhibits 7-1 and 7-2 are specifically related only to the company under analysis and for no other company unless it has an identical profit structure. Exhibit 7-1 shows that a 40 per cent increase in sales revenue and unit volume produces a 120 per cent increase in profits (not a 0 per cent increase). Exhibit 7-2 shows that a 40 per cent increase in unit volume with a price decrease of 10 per cent on this increment (increase of 36 per cent in revenue) produces an 80 per cent increase in profit. If management had turned down the offer of a 10 per cent price decrease on the 40 per cent additional volume, it would have deprived itself of this additional $80,000 in profit.

This type of analysis is crucial in the pricing function, especially on a unit-by-unit basis in a multiproduct operation. Besides its use in pricing, profit analysis is vital for profit-planning and decision making in all areas of the enterprise, as later chapters will show. First and foremost must come the separation of costs into their respective behavior categories.

These examples have been presented to show management the importance of sound profit analysis in guiding its pricing decisions. Obviously, there are other pricing considerations, such as competitive reactions and market demand, which must be recognized.

CHAPTER 8   *Identifying the Variable Factor in Pricing*

For the determination of profit at any time, at any volume, at any price level, and for any condition of product mix, proper cost classification and analysis are required. As we have said, some costs vary closely with changes in volume, whereas others remain unchanged in total amount regardless of changes in sales activity or production volume. Costs which change with volume are usually called *variable* costs and those which don't over the short term are called *fixed* costs. When fixed and variable costs are scrambled together into a total unit cost, it is impossible to relate volume to costs; hence, pricing and other decisions are weakened. This problem can be resolved by obtaining costs that have been subdivided into their fixed and variable elements. Then the effect of volume becomes immediately apparent. When these segregated data are applied to segments of the profit structure, sources of profit as well as areas of strengths and weaknesses are revealed.

Direct Variable Costs

Some variable costs are called *direct* costs because they are incurred directly with production. Thus, as production is increased in a period, a proportionately higher amount of productive labor, materials, etc., has to be used and paid for. In pricing, though, we have to know the variable cost factor at the unit product level—the period figure being useful only for budgeting expenses. Here is where the problem becomes somewhat confusing. For example, in a one-product firm, that product has substantially the same amount of *unit* direct cost regardless of the total output of the firm. As the output in any period rises, the expenditure for direct costs increases in proportion, but that is not related to the *unit direct cost* of the product as that cost could remain the same per unit regardless of output. The reverse is true of a fixed cost which remains the same in the period regardless of production fluctuations. It is in this instance, if fixed costs are unitized, that the *unit fixed cost* of the product will

79

vary inversely with volume. Thus, at the unit of product level, a direct cost might appear to be a fixed cost and a fixed cost a direct cost.

In pricing, direct costs are also known as out-of-pocket costs, since it is these costs which are incremental to the decision to make and sell and which require outlay of immediate cash to support. One test of a unit direct cost is whether it is readily discontinuable or whether it will not exist if an order is not booked.

Direct costs may be said to include those costs which the product incurs unit by unit in any area of the company. These will include such obvious costs as productive labor and electrical energy charges at production centers, as well as charges directly incurred by the order, such as materials, sales commissions, royalties, freight out, etc. The major criterion of a direct cost is that it be traceably and tangibly generated by, and identified with, the specific product being made and sold.

While there are some direct costs which vary directly or almost automatically with volume, there are some variable costs which increase with volume but not in direct proportion.

Period Variable Costs

Pricing decisions must be based on a knowledge of the specific behavior of various costs used in the enterprise. The first task is to separate from total costs, and then study, costs which have a decreasing identifiability with the product. The highest ranking of product cost identifiability goes to the unit direct or out-of-pocket costs. But there are costs which, while not directly related to the product, do vary in some way with the volume of production.

In a broad sense and taken over the long term, fixed or constant costs, such as depreciation of equipment, can be considered variable as management adds investment from time to time. Administrative salaries, traditionally considered fixed, can also become variable as management tries to adjust its expenses to periods of business downturns.

Here, though, we are concerned with the type of cost which varies over the operating year and which, while not directly identified with specific products and therefore not varying unit by unit, does vary by changes in specific levels of operation or by activity in entire product lines. Such costs are those paid for factory supervisors, some classes of maintenance people, administrative clerical people, sales clerical staffing, and the like. It is interesting to note that, while period variable costs cannot be directly traced to product units, they often can be identified directly with entire product lines, especially since changes in total activity of product lines usually result in a greater number of transactions, clerical activity, specific maintenance problems, quality control efforts, etc. Therefore, in our future discussions and examples, we shall consider that within a defined product mix there is a reasonable relationship between period variable costs and direct costs in total but not necessarily unit by unit.

Period Fixed Costs

Fixed costs are known by many other names. Interchanging these names does not change the behavior characteristics as could happen with the various classifications of variable costs. Identifying different levels of fixed costs is done for purposes of management control, even though all are usually incurred in one fixed sum for the operating year.

Specific programmed costs: These costs, while fixed in amount for the year, refer to the costs assigned by management to specific projects to fulfill company objectives. Sometimes they are called *managed costs* because they are subject to management evaluation and change. Incurred depreciation costs as the result of acquiring new equipment or adding to factory space are good examples, but there are other specific programmed period costs which are used to generate additional revenue, such as the costs of opening a district sales office or warehouse, the reduction in costs that comes from installing special quality control devices in a product line, or a special advertising program to push a particular product line. These costs are known as separable rather than common because they may be charged (without arbitrary allocation) directly to the product line or activity which is the recipient of the cost increase or decrease.

General programmed costs: While these costs are also fixed for the operating year, they are incurred for the benefit of the entire enterprise and are common rather than separable, even though they may be discontinued by management action. Typical of these costs are general and administrative salaries, research and development, selling, marketing, and promotional costs.

Constant costs: These fixed costs are neither separable nor discontinuable. They are common and inescapable costs as long as the enterprise is to continue in business. Among these costs are depreciation, real estate taxes, interest on mortgages, rent, etc.

In pricing, all period fixed costs are referred to as fixed costs with the understanding that all elements of these costs incurred during the operating year have been included.

Cost-Volume-Profit Analysis

Practically every action or planned decision in a company will affect costs, prices, volume, and/or profits. The cost-volume-profit (cvp) analysis discloses the interplay of all these factors in a way which aids management to select the best courses of action from which to make the best price decision.

Mix of product, also known as the sales mixture, refers to the variety and quantities of products made and sold by one company during a specific period. Since it is usual for each of the products in the company's line to contribute differently to the company's profits, obviously any shift in one class of products over another will have a pronounced effect on the profit results obtained. One goal of cvp analysis is to give management accurate and objective data about the contributions made by each product so that the sales effort can then be directed accordingly.

In this respect, one of the most significant pieces of data produced by a cvp analysis is the marginal income ratio, often called the contribution ratio or profit-volume ratio (PV). This ratio is the percentage of the sales dollar available to cover fixed costs and profits after deducting variable costs. For example, in the following data:

Sales.................	$1,000
Variable costs..........	600
Fixed costs............	300
Profit................	$100

the contribution ratio or PV is the contribution money of $400 ($1,000 — $600) divided by the sales revenue. This equals $400/$1,000 or 40 per cent and the PV is said to be .40. This means that 40 cents out of every sales dollar goes towards paying fixed expenses and providing a profit. Thus the contribution of $400 pays the $300 fixed cost and leaves a profit of $100. It should be mentioned at this point that the $300 of fixed cost referred to is not allocated but pertains to a cost specifically related to the $1,000 sales activity.

When the PV is known, it is possible to determine the effect on profits that additional business will produce. If $500 of additional business is being considered, we are able to calculate the additional profit as being $500 × .40, or $200. Under these circumstances the $300 of fixed expenses has already been paid for by the $1,000 of sales, leaving a $100 profit. For instance, $1,200 in sales would produce $180 in profit. This simple example immediately reveals a facet of this company's profit structure, namely, that an increase of 20 per cent in sales produces an 80 per cent increase in profit. Again, this example does not mean that all businesses will respond to the same sales increase in the same way. How each company will respond is a function of its specific cvp characteristics—its profit structure. Obviously, this simple analysis could not have been made unless all costs had previously been separated into their variable and fixed elements.

How CVP Data Are Used

Cost-volume-profit analysis is vital for decision making in the areas of pricing, selective selling, volume compensation, which products to make, to buy, the effect of price on volume, effect of volume on costs, which product to add, to drop, how the product mix should be changed, etc.

For example, suppose a company makes a comparative analysis between two of its products:

Item	Product A	Product B
Selling price..................	$10.00	$15.00
"Full" cost....................	9.00	13.50
Profit........................	$ 1.00	$ 1.50
Return on sales, %............	10	10

It finds that both products earn (ostensibly) the same profit percentage of sales and are therefore thought to be equally profitable. However, realizing the arbitrary nature of the fixed-cost allocation contained in the "full" cost figure, the company prepares cost-volume-profit data and adds the following:

Item	Product A	Product B
Variable cost..................	$4.00	$10.00
Contribution..................	6.00	5.00
PV........................	.60	.33

When this type of analysis is made, management realizes that both products do not contribute the same degree of economic value to its firm as was thought because of the uniform profit percentage. Nor is management deceived by the higher price of Product B. Not only does the sale of each unit of Product A produce a higher tangible cash contribution, it also generates a much higher contribution rate (PV) on its price and thus helps cover the company's *period* (not allocated) fixed costs at a faster rate.

When cvp data are available, management can take steps to direct sales emphasis towards products of greater contribution. When variable and fixed costs are not separated, but appear scrambled together into one total ("full"), management has no objective basis for evaluating one product with another or for measuring the value of one selling price over another. The only alternative is to compare the respective selling prices, which the above example shows could be quite misleading.

Another reason the contribution figure is a much more useful figure than the profit is the arbitrary nature of the fixed expenses allocated to the various products, as discussed earlier. A variable or out-of-pocket cost is directly identified with the product, but the fixed cost is incurred with time. In order to unitize the fixed expense, it is necessary to force it arithmetically into becoming a direct cost by distributing it to the various product lines (or the production centers involved in their manufacture) on the basis of some future expectation of volume or activity of each. Since the unitized fixed cost is arbitrary it makes the "full" cost as well as the unit profit arbitrary also.

This same approach is used in making the pricing decision on a "going" market price. In many instances a market price for a product is sensible for one company to take and for another to reject if the price is below a company's out-of-pocket costs. The out-of-pocket price should be the floor on prices, below which no businessman would want to go. Selling a product at just the out-of-pocket cost level is an exercise in evenly trading dollar bills. Without cvp data, this might very well happen. Take the following example in which two similar companies are bidding for the same order:

Item	Company A	Company B
Selling price quoted.............	$11	$11
"Full" cost....................	10	10

But, let's assume that the "going" market price is $9.00. Obviously, with only "full"-cost information available, both companies would be inclined to turn down the order. However, with cvp data, the cost ingredients might look like this:

Item	Company A	Company B
Out-of-pocket cost.........................	$6.00	$8.50
Unitized fixed cost.........................	4.00	1.50
Contribution at a $9 selling price............	3.00	0.50

(Variations in out-of-pocket and fixed costs of the magnitudes shown for the same product occur because of differences in labor rates, productivities, material costs, specific fixed expenses, and volume projections.)

Obviously, Company A is in a much better position to accept the order at $9.00, whereas the contribution appears very marginal for Company B. One thing is sure: if the market price dropped below $8.50 and Company B accepted orders for that product, each increase in volume would generate specific cash losses (in addition to losing any contribution that product would make to the payment of Company B's annual period fixed expenses). Contrary to popular notion, volume will not compensate for price in all cases. In this instance, increasing volume can only make cash losses worse.

In directing the product mix of a company, emphasis should be placed on achieving the maximum amount of contribution money for the least amount of revenue (consistent with the use of capital and the availability of facilities). In many client engagements the question is frequently asked, "Why did we make less money this year on more sales?" Often, the answer rests with the fact that sales were being increased for the sake of generating revenue (volume) instead of contribution dollars. Naturally, in these cases, contribution information was missing because of the lack of cvp data—data in which volume and period costs are separated.

As an example of this, let's examine a simplified case in which one company earns more profit from less sales revenue on fewer items than another similar company over a period of one year. Each company produces the same product:

Item	Company X	Company Y
Unit selling price.....................	$15	$17
Volume of units sold.................	100,000	130,000
Total sales revenue.................	$1,500,000	$1,950,000
oop cost per unit....................	$12	$15
Contribution per unit...............	$ 3	$ 2
Total contribution...................	$ 300,000	$ 260,000
Less: annual fixed expenses..........	200,000	200,000
Pretax profits.......................	$ 100,000	$ 60,000

Company Y's out-of-pocket (oop) unit costs can be higher for various reasons: higher direct selling costs, poorer manufacturing productivity, higher cost of materials, higher waste, etc. But regardless of its higher selling price, greater number of units sold, and larger sales revenue, it makes a profit 40 per cent below Company X. Obviously, in this example, Company X used cvp data and Company Y operated on the hope that maximizing both price and volume was the pathway to higher profit. If it had separated its volume and period costs and measured contributions and had had a knowledge of the price-volume characteristics of its markets, it could have found the *combination* of price and volume which could have increased its profits.

CVP and the Changing Product Mix

In multiproduct companies, the effect of volume selling for its own sake is more critical. Exhibit 8-1 shows data for four different products made by the same company. The two mixes are presented to show the results produced by "gross dollar selling" versus a well-directed product mix. In the revised or Case B mix, more profit is earned on the same

EXHIBIT 8-1. HOW PRODUCT MIX AFFECTS PROFITS

Cost elements	Product 1	Product 2	Product 3	Product 4	Total
oop (variable)/thousand..............	$11.00	$5.00	$12.00	$ 8.50	
Selling prices/thousand..............	12.00	9.00	14.00	10.00	
Contribution/thousand..............	1.00	4.00	2.00	1.50	
Case A mix:					
Units sold, in millions..............	40	5	30	10	85
Revenue generated.................	$480,000	$45,000	$420,000	$100,000	$1,045,000
Contributions obtained.............	$ 40,000	$20,000	$ 60,000	$ 15,000	$ 135,000
Less: fixed expenses................	....	....	....	....	$ 200,000
Net loss........................	....	....	....	....	$(65,000)
Case B mix:					
Units sold, in millions..............	5	40	10	30	85
Revenue generated.................	$60,000	$360,000	$140,000	$300,000	$860,000
Contributions obtained.............	$ 5,000	$160,000	$ 20,000	$ 45,000	$230,000
Less: fixed expenses................	....	....	....	....	$200,000
Net profit.......................	....	....	....	....	$ 30,000

unit volume and less sales revenues. Often, when cvp data are not available, salesmen will generally push the products carrying higher prices, especially if their compensation is based on a percentage commission on booked sales dollars. The difference in results of $95,000 between the two cases is simply the result of placing emphasis on dollar contribution instead of on the revenue dollar. Besides which, the lower revenue could reduce the company's involvements in additional inventory, working space, and transaction costs. The selling prices shown are "going" market prices which the company has decided not to alter.

Pricing and Product Mix

Exhibit 8-2 shows another company's experience with changing prices and the effect on product mix. In Case 1 mix, the company followed a subjective policy of pricing at some uniform contribution level. This

EXHIBIT 8-2. PRICING AND PRODUCT MIX

Cost elements	Product A	Product B	Product C	Product D	Total
Unit oop cost....................	$ 9.00	$10.00	$11.00	$12.00	
Case 1 mix:					
Unit selling price................	$15.00	$16.00	$17.00	$18.00	
Unit contribution................	6.00	6.00	6.00	6.00	
Units sold, thousands............	50	60	40	30	180
Total revenue generated..........	$750,000	$960,000	$680,000	$540,000	$2,930,000
Total contribution generated......	$300,000	$360,000	$240,000	$180,000	$1,080,000
Less: fixed expenses..............	....	....	....	....	1,000,000
Net profit....................	....	....	....	....	$ 80,000
Case 2 mix:					
Unit selling price................	$14.00	$19.00	$18.00	$20.00	
Unit contribution................	5.00	9.00	7.00	8.00	
Unit sold, thousands.............	70	40	40	25	170
Total revenue generated..........	$980,000	$760,000	$720,000	$500,000	$2,960,000
Total contribution generated......	350,000	$360,000	$280,000	$200,000	$1,190,000
Less: fixed expenses.............	....	....	....	....	1,000,000
Net profit....................	....	....	....	....	$ 190,000

policy, in effect, ignored the presence of market forces and especially the elasticity of demand. When the pricing gave effect to these strategic factors, the mix of Case 2 resulted. In Product A, management estimated that the drop in price would be more than offset by an increase in volume which would more than restore the previous contribution in Case 1 mix. Product B was priced below competitive levels in Case 1 mix and adjusted for this condition in the Case 2 mix. Here the increase in price of $3 increased contribution by 50 per cent, which just offset the one-third drop in volume. In Product C, management found that its demand was inelastic, i.e., a small increase in price did not affect volume with a consequent increase in contribution. In Product D also, the $2 increase in price increased contribution enough to more than offset the drop in volume. Thus, the results of Case 2 mix produced more than twice the profit at less unit sales volume and at approximately the same sales revenue.

CHAPTER 9 *Fundamental Pricing Data*

In the multiproduct business enterprise of today, maximizing output and/or sales revenue does not necessarily guarantee maximum profits. These actions may in fact reduce profits as demonstrated in the previous chapter. Profits depend on the proper selection and balancing of the variables of prices, product mix, volume, and costs. Every business consists of a number of segments: divisions, product lines, territories, products, facilities, end markets, classes of customers, channels of distribution. Proper pricing methods depend on knowing the relative contributions which each segment makes to the overall profit and then striking the proper balance. Pricing, therefore, is a profit-planning problem in which management analyzes and compares the various alternatives in order to select the one which promises to be the most advantageous.

A rational approach to pricing adopts no specific rules because once rules are set up, they tend to remain in effect when they no longer apply. The rational approach adjusts to differing or changing circumstances, irrespective of the particular pricing method employed. But regardless of which pricing method is used, it must be recognized that the major determinants of prices are market demand, competition, and cost.

Pricing decisions involve more than setting prices for products offered to customers. More often than not, a pricing decision must be made whether or not to meet a competitive or market price. Thus, price-*setting* has given way to measuring the economic benefits (contributions) to the seller of meeting a competitive price.

Basic Requirements

For sound pricing, product costs must be stated in terms of their out-of-pocket costs. Whether or not a unitized fixed cost is shown, the product cost must be separated so that the out-of-pocket level stands out and can be used for contribution measurements. Pricing based on costs

89

which have not been so separated is usually accompanied by feelings of uncertainty. If a seller's price is rejected, has the cost been estimated as too high? Are the allocation methods correct? If the seller's price is readily accepted, was the price too low? If the price quoted was too high, should it be shaved? By how much? How low is safe?

In any estimate prepared for bid on which all costs are shown, there are both the known, tangible elements of cost and those which are arbitrary. The known elements are, of course, directly identified with the order; the arbitrary component is statistically allocated with any of several methods—all of which may be defended by rationalizing in one way or another. The sole tangible piece of cost information is the variable or out-of-pocket cost, the costs that are incurred specifically for the order and wouldn't be incurred without the order. Out-of-pocket costs consist of direct labor, direct materials, and direct overhead cost, whether at the manufacturing or nonmanufacturing level.

Price Floor

It follows then that the price floor of any order is its direct variable or out-of-pocket costs. Of course, if all orders throughout the operating year are sold at just the oop level, the company will incur a loss to the extent of its fixed expenses. That is, when all output is sold at oop cost, the annual contribution is zero. No businessman would want to continue this practice for very long, and surely he would not want to sell below his oop cost level.

Of course, there are several rationales for selling at the oop level or below. In periods of business downturn, a manufacturer may sell at just his oop cost level if it allows him to keep his doors open by which he can maintain a skeleton force of highly skilled labor. The critical shortage of such labor in normal business times and the high cost of training workers to the manufacturer's specific methods may justify such floor selling prices. In normal times, a seller may sell at his oop level or even below it if the work is part of an otherwise profitable package of orders to a customer. In this case, if the loss work is a small portion of what the customer buys in the year and does not seriously dilute the yearly contribution amount from the customer, then this pricing action is more strategic than economic and may be considered sound business. Of course, this action assumes that the seller does not have the option of dropping the loss work from the customer's entire purchasing package.

Regardless of these strategic reasons, taking an order priced below the out-of-pocket cost is like receiving $1,000 from a customer's order and then paying out $1,100 in direct labor, direct materials, and direct overhead costs to produce it. Therefore, in attempting to meet competitive prices, shouldn't a knowledge of oop costs be known in advance?

The following example will demonstrate the point. In this example, the identical product is being estimated by four hypothetical companies having identical facilities:

Unit costs	Company A	Company B	Company C	Company D
oop (known).............	$ 9.20	$ 7.80	$10.60	$ 8.80
Unitized fixed (arbitrary)..	3.10	6.40	3.60	5.20
"Full" (partially arbitrary)............	$12.30	$14.20	$14.20	$14.00

The first question to clear up is why the oop and fixed costs are so different for the same product made on similar facilities. Since the oop cost is a variable cost directly identified with the product, differences among the four companies can be explained by the fact that there are differences in hourly wages paid to workers, productivity, quality, material costs, delivery effectiveness, etc. Fixed-costs differences can result from differences in administrative salaries, depreciation practices, rent costs, etc. But these costs are not identifiable with a product or order since they are incurred by time and not by volume. Therefore, they are unitized to the product as a function of expected sales activity, which no one knows will come to fruition. The optimism or pessimism felt by the individual company about its future expectations reflects itself in this unitizing and generally constitutes the major reason for the unit fixed-cost differences. That is, the effect of higher annual fixed costs can be reversed at the unit cost level by the projection of an optimistically high activity projection.

In the above tabulation, if both Companies B and C based their selling prices on their "full" costs and were rejected because a competitive price of $12 existed, neither company could decide objectively whether it was safe to meet it, unless it first knew its oop costs. At the "going" selling price of $12, contributions would be $2.80, $4.20, $1.40, and $3.20. Obviously, the order brings more benefit to Company B than to Company C. However, if the "going" market price were $10, the contributions would be $0.80, $2.20, ($0.60), and $1.20; Company C could not take the order. Increasing volume for Company C in this instance cannot compensate for price; it can only make losses worse. However, the other companies can be receiving contributions in the amounts shown regardless of Company C's actions.

Contribution Pool

Just as the same product produced by different companies can yield different contribution rates (PVs), neither will each sales dollar per product in a multiproduct firm carry the same PV. Without a knowledge of its price floor, management may pursue a policy of selling for the sake of booking revenue dollars instead of for generating contribution money. Sometimes this practice takes the form of desperation pricing to keep facilities busy in the mistaken notion that the more the capacity booked, the more profits will be. Again, profits, if any, are made by accident and not by plan; the ironic result is to credit any profits to

EXHIBIT 9-1. THE CONTRIBUTION POOL

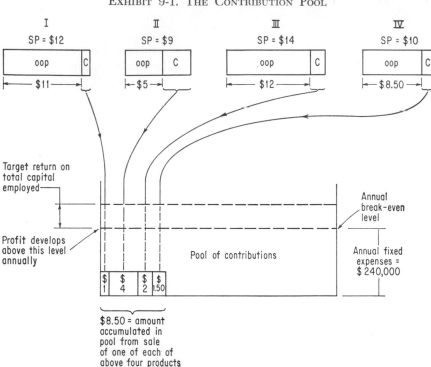

the high activity of facilities, which often prompts management to acquire additional facilities which it might attempt to keep just as busy. This, in turn, because of the pricing-for-volume yardstick, can provoke competitive retaliation, driving market prices down to where an entire industry cannot show an adequate return on invested capital.

As a company books orders at given prices, the combined contributions thus generated during the operating year must exceed the annual fixed expenses if an annual profit is to be earned. Exhibit 9-1 shows graphically how contributions from each of four products of a manufacturing company are pooled. By thus exposing the tangible economic value of each of the four product types, management is in a better position to know which products to push and which to discourage, which are the real contributors and which simply have a high price but do little more than swap dollar bills between the supplier and the seller.

The pool concept is a vital tool in pricing because, in any period, profits are the difference between the contributions pooled in the period and the fixed expenses *prorated* (not allocated) to the period under measurement. Thus, if annual fixed expenses are $240,000 and monthly contributions pool to $25,000, profit for that month is the $25,000 less the prorated fixed expenses of $20,000 ($240,000/12), or $5,000. Of course, when the pooled contributions equal the fixed expenses for any period, the company is at its break-even point for that measurement period.

With these data available, management can see that the sale of one of Product 2 contributes four times as much as the sale of one of Product 1, even though the latter sells for one-third more revenue. Obviously, a judicious direction of the product mix will cause the level of pooled contributions to build up at a faster rate. But it is one thing to want a favorable product mix and another to be able to get it. The activity which has to be directed towards this management goal is the sales effort. But as long as management continues to employ the classical method of basing sales compensation on sales revenue, it will have no assurance that the favorable mix will be generated. This type of plan only encourages the inflow of revenue dollars. In many client engagements where sales compensation plans were involved, a plan based on applying commission directly on contribution dollars has paid rich profit rewards to the company. A specific sales compensation plan of this type will be discussed in Chapter 20.

Exhibit 9-2 shows the relationship of oop costs, fixed costs, contribution, revenue, and profit.

Price and Contribution

When contribution data are available on specific selling prices, management can use this information in various ways:

1. To price individual products and/or orders
2. To target prices for desired PV to classes of customers, for end markets, etc.
3. To identify characteristically the most profitable products, customers, end markets, etc.
4. To disclose which products need attention
5. To select and improve the product mix
6. To determine the pricing floor
7. To evaluate proposals to increase profits by increasing prices and/or increasing volume

8. To clarify the understanding of costs by management people responsible for pricing

9. To get all departments to speak a common language in talking about profits

10. To provide an easier way to predict profits available in future proposals

11. To provide a better reward-for-performance basis of compensating the selling effort

EXHIBIT 9-2. CONTRIBUTION VERSUS VOLUME

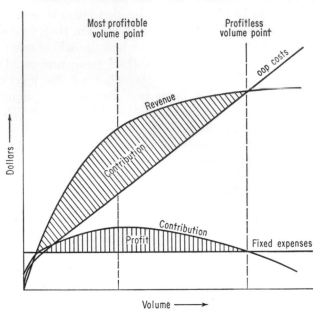

By having the contribution measurement, management has an absolute basis for evaluating the effect of price change on profits. Perhaps this simple example will help to dramatize the point: If a product is priced at $30 and has an oop cost of $29, its contribution is $1. If this product's price is increased just $1 to $31, the contribution is doubled ($2) and the booking at that slight price increase has the same effect on profit as if double the quantity of that product ($60) was sold at the $30 price.

Basic Price Data

The most basic and essential single piece of economic data for pricing is a knowledge of the oop cost of a product or order. Then the pricer can measure contributions from meeting competitive prices and/or he can establish selling prices of his own based on specific contribution targets.

Selling prices practically determine the volume of business that can be generated in all the company's products. Because of the influence of competitive and demand factors, pricing cannot be considered apart from volume. The pricing task might be to find the most profitable combination of volume and price for a product, or it might be to find how much an increment in volume of a certain product at a given price will add to volume. Hence, the pricer must estimate the profit that can be obtained from alternative price-volume combinations through the company's line of products.

In traditional "full"-cost data used for pricing, the getting of a specific order in itself affects the cost of filling it. Each time a new price-volume proposal is at hand, the accountants must go through the laborious task of recomputing the spread of fixed costs in order to present management with a "unit cost" figure. Not only is the approach invalid, but pricing decisions often have to be made promptly; otherwise an opportunity can be lost if the price is delayed by accounting gyrations and endless recalculations.

With the basic contribution pricing data, management can make immediate decisions on price and volume because the oop costs are incremental and have practically no effect on period fixed costs.

Price Leading or Following

Where there are established market prices for products, an individual company may not have the ability to take independent action with respect to the prices it would like to get. In this case, product costs are useless in *setting* prices because the company can only sell at the "going" price or withdraw. The company's oop costs are essential to show what contribution would be available if the "going" price were met. In this sense, oop costs are used to *analyze* a price structure, not to *establish* a price structure. Out-of-pocket costs and contribution measurements also allow the company to improve overall period profit by revising its mix in order to obtain the maximum amount of contribution dollars in a period, consistent with the least amount of revenue, employment of capital, and use of facilities. That is, the company is able to determine how much oop cost can be incurred without sacrificing profit. In following prices set by industry leaders, the company is more concerned with what products to make and what orders to take than with how to price them.

However, when a company is a price leader in its industry or offers products uniquely different from others, then it may be able to price independently and use its costs as a basis for selling prices. In terms of numbers of businessmen in the United States, most companies do not fall into this category.

The Competitor's Price

Management usually becomes informed of competitive price levels through its sales force. However, there are many inaccuracies, purposeful or otherwise, which arise between the buyer's representative and the seller's representative. In this human transaction questions of personality and business ethics crop up.

Questions which arise when a competitive price is reported to the selling management are: Which salesman reported the price? What kind of a man is he? Is he more interested in commission and would he book any type of revenue for the sake of that commission? Or is he a selective salesman who believes he is selling the best kind of work for his company? Is his report the only one or are there other corroborating reports? Is the purchasing agent on a "fishing expedition" attempting to get information to use against another one of his suppliers? Is the purchasing agent telling the truth in telling the seller's salesman what the going price is? Or is the purchaser trying to set one supplier against the other hoping to drive prices down in a retaliatory spiral? If the competitor's price is lower on an order, is it for this order only or is it part of a general price reduction?

Before Meeting a Competitive Price

Before the decision is made to meet a lower price (after measuring contribution, etc.), the seller should know the habits and practices of his customers and competitors. Are competitors quoting on the same product specifications? Does the buyer know if there are any differences? What kind of value does the buyer's representative place on the product? Is it the same as the seller's or his competitors? Which of the buyer's representatives is making the judgment of value? This decision can range from the president down to the shipping clerk. Does the buyer buy solely by price without reference to value? Is he afraid of paying more for the seller's product even though he knows that there is proportionately greater value in that product than represented by the higher price? Does the buyer buy what he wants even though it is not at the lowest price? Has the buyer been told to buy always at the lowest price?

Pricing in a competitive market is an exercise in tactics and strategy. Thus, price actions should be based on some kind of *intelligence system*. Not that undercover espionage is being recommended, but through a careful collecting of pertinent data involving financial statements, credit reports, trade association participation, behavior in the marketplace, information from former employees, and the like, a composite image of the competitor can be constructed. If the competitor is offering lower prices, ask these questions: Does he believe that volume is a panacea for profit? Have his prices dropped immediately after he bought a new expensive machine? Is he pricing desperately in an effort to generate enough volume to keep the new machine busy? Is his price low one day and high the next? Does he steer away from small orders? How well does he pay his bills? How are his collections? Is he making a profit? On all product lines? How long is he producing the product line which he is selling below your prices? Has he evaluated the market elasticity and is he trying to get it to pay off for him at a lower price level? Does he know the effect on his profit structure of lower prices and what a burden this will impose on his break-even point? Has he laid off some of his workers recently where other sellers have not? Is he pricing low because his backlog is low, and is he trying to cover fixed costs? Is this lower price an exception? Is he trying to "get his foot in the door" with an important customer? Has he followed suit when other competitors have raised prices? Is he just trying to gain technical experience on a new facility and is pricing to obtain the activity? Is he in for the "long pull" or is he an opportunist looking for fast profits? Is he actively interested in solidly promoting his good name and reputation? What do reports say about the quality of his output?

Usually, the oop costs, such as labor, material, and supplies, are more similar among competitors than the various elements of fixed costs. The oop costs reflect the product characteristics, whereas the fixed costs represent the individual's company's ideas of how the business should be managed and administered. Thus, by plotting estimates of a competitor's profit and sales for several periods, the seller finds it possible to arrive at an estimate of his average PV. The more segments of his business which can be involved in this analysis, the better. This analytic effort can not only guide the seller in his day-to-day pricing problems but can give him a new viewpoint in competitive relations by answering some of the aforementioned questions.

These and many more questions have to be answered in order to get some idea of the strengths and weaknesses of the opposition. But, of course, it will pay the seller to be introspective about himself and the image he gives to competitors and customers. A seller might believe his company to project a fine image in the minds of his regular customers, but it might be evaluated differently in the minds of prospective new customers with whom the seller had no previous contact.

Meeting a Competitive Price

Here are the possible consequences of meeting a lower price. For one thing, the lower price can set a dangerous precedent in the market which will take major surgery to remove. While the value of the product has not changed by virtue of the lower price, some competitors may be so irresponsible as not to care, and it takes just one lower price (from perhaps a poor businessman) to get other sellers thinking about it. The chain reaction in price reductions sets in like panic selling in the stock market. It does take guts sometimes not to meet a competitive price. Then, again, lowering prices even temporarily runs the risk of changing the products' values in the minds of the customer. Customers become accustomed to lower prices and the entire price level drops, stays there, and perhaps gets worse. Prices sometimes get so low that sellers withdraw one by one from booking orders so poorly priced. Then one competitor decides to return to higher levels and all follow suit until the next time when someone decides to cut prices and the vicious cycle starts all over again.

Sometimes lower prices allow greater market penetration, opening potential which was not available before. But, again, will the combination of contribution-volume produce more profit than before such market penetration was attempted? Or will the lower prices permit a deeper penetration into the layers of demand? In the latter case, new classes of customers may become interested in buying the product. The perfect example is the limited edition $25 book which skimmed the top prestige layer of the market. When that layer had been exhausted, the cost of the book was successively reduced and its form and price successively changed as each next lower layer of the market was exhausted until it was offered in a 75-cent soft cover edition to the deepest layer of demand in tremendous volume.

There is also the possibility that the lowering of prices may cause the product to be withdrawn from its present market, thereby causing changes to be made in the internal operations of the sellers. And perhaps in the period during which prices were spiraling downward, the sellers left themselves a legacy of the continuous obligation to provide some form of service after the sale.

Perhaps a major consequence of blindly meeting lowered prices is the effect this action will have on the quality of sales service which had been more than simply order taking. A company could be enjoying adequate sales activity on a product priced somewhat higher than competitive levels because of the reputation and reliability of the company and perhaps because of the loyalty of customers. Under pressure from salesmen to reduce price to generate more volume, the seller takes on the appearance of his competitors and part of the company's image is lost. Now he is in the same boat with all other competitors and has to fight to hold his previous share of the market. Salesmen become order takers, and the combination of lower price and volume severely deteriorates their profit position.

CHAPTER 10   *Basic Price Calculations*

Having invalidated the "full"-cost figure as useful in pricing decisions, we must turn our attention to the notion of unit profit before going further in price calculations.

Unit Profits

If a seller has only direct, out-of-pocket costs in conducting his business, the difference between that figure and the selling price will be considered a profit on every unit sold. However, when a seller incurs a period or time cost which is fixed in amount during the operating year (does not vary with the number of units sold), then no profit develops until that fixed cost has been paid for. Since the vast majority of businesses operate with some kind of fixed cost, it can be said that there is no such thing as an order or unit profit.

By the same token, it cannot be said that a price is a profitable one if it is in excess of "full" costs, nor can we say that a price pegged below the "full"-cost level is unprofitable. If a selling price is in excess of "full" cost in which the seller obtains less activity volume than he originally projected, thus minimizing the amount of unitized fixed cost, it is possible for that price to show an eventual loss. The reverse is also true. For example, let's take a simple case of a retailer of candy bars who buys them from his supplier at 8 cents and sells them for 10 cents each. His only fixed cost is his rent of $1,000 per year. If he desires to project an estimate of "full" cost on each, he would have to forecast an expected volume level. Let's assume he projects a volume of 100,000 bars per year:

Item	One bar	100,000 bars per year
Sales revenue	$0.10	$10,000
Out-of-pocket cost	0.08	8,000
Unitized fixed cost	0.01	1,000 (annual total)
Total cost	$0.09	$ 9,000
"Profit"	$0.01	$ 1,000

Seems reasonable, doesn't it? The only trouble is it won't work in pricing. The only single condition under which profit per bar will be 1 cent is if, in fact, 100,000 bars are actually sold during the year. If fewer bars are sold, the unit profit is less; if more bars are sold, the unit profit is more. If, during the year one bar happens to sell for 15 cents, far above the "full"-cost level, that 6 cents cannot be called profit unless at least 100,000 bars wind up being sold. The trouble is that no one knows in advance whether or not this will actually be the figure sold. Should only 25,000 bars be sold in that year, all except one being sold at 15 cents, the entire operation is still a loss and that 15-cent sale cannot be considered as contributing to profits.

In the reverse case, if actual activity turns out to be 200,000 bars sold for the year, "full" cost are 8½ cents each and any bars sold at anything above this level are actually profitable.

Every time the retailer sells a candy bar at 10 cents, he generates a *contribution* of 2 cents. This contribution figure is the only tangible piece of benefit he receives from making a sale. The point is that enough of these 2-cent contribution pieces must be generated to pay the annual rent of $1,000. Obviously, this would be $1,000/$0.02, or 50,000 bars. This figure is the man's break-even point: the level of sales volume which produced pooled contributions equal to the period fixed expenses. If 50,000 candy bars is the volume break-even point, then, when the 50,001st bar is sold, the full profit on that bar is 2 cents. If only 50,001 bars are sold in the year, the total true profit for the year's operations would be just 2 cents.

The unit profit notion implies that each time the man sells a candy bar, a profit of 1 cent is earned. Obviously, this cannot be correct since below the 50,000 annual volume level, losses are being incurred and above that level, a profit of 2 cents each is being earned.

From this simple example, we can define contribution in two ways:

1. *Below the break-even point:* Contribution monies are pooled first to pay the fixed expenses, and the PV indicates the speed of accomplishment.

2. *Above the break-even point:* Previously pooled contributions have fully paid for the fixed expenses, and contribution above the break-even point *is* profit and the rate of profit is the PV.

Obviously, the faster contribution money is generated, the sooner the break-even point will be reached and passed. But one thing should be made crystal clear at this point: assume that instead of a candy store operation, we are talking about a typical manufacturing company which operates in a competitive market in which market prices fall on either side of this manufacturer's "full" cost. How successful will he be if he pursues a policy of "full"-cost pricing until he passes his break-even point and only after that prices competitively? Using this approach to pricing, the chances are good that he may never reach his break-even point! A seller's customers are not going to be tolerant about their supplier's need to reach his break-even point before getting competitive prices. Customers are not interested in their suppliers' costs, cost systems, pricing systems, break-even points or this book. All other things being equal, they are interested in getting the lowest price they can. In a manner of speaking, realistic, flexible, rational pricing must start on the first day of the operating year, setting acceptance or rejection levels based on the unit contribution of the transaction, the state of the accumulated contributions pooled to date and the way they stack up against fixed expenses prorated for the same period, the economical use of capital, the state of facility loading, inventory, and space commitments, etc. The inference that profit is earned only on the last sales made is fallacious, since contribution must be as vigorously pursued in January as in June or December!

The Break-even System

The break-even system* is a simple and easily understandable method of picturing to management the effect of changes in prices and volume on profits. Detailed analysis of break-even data will reveal to management the effect of alternative decisions that convert costs from variable to fixed or vice versa, the effect of decisions which reduce or increase costs and those which increase sales volume and income, and, most important for our use, the effect of decisions to change selling prices. The break-even system is a device which portrays the effects of any type of forward planning by evaluating alternative courses of action.

The break-even *point* can be defined as that sales revenue at which losses cease and profits begin or vice versa, or it can be described as that level of sales revenue at which profits are zero. For our purposes, the break-even point is better thought of as that amount and type of sales revenue which generates contributions equal to the period fixed expenses. Thus it follows that many companies can have the same break-even point for a certain period, even though their operating characteristics are vastly different. Contributions in a period are generated through the infinite interplays of differing costs, volumes, and prices, and thus the same break-even point may be reached in myriad ways by totally different companies. This, of course, is a function of the specific cvp characteristics of each company.

Finding the break-even point itself is an operation that dwindles to

* Spencer A. Tucker, *The Break-even System: A Tool for Profit Planning*, Prentice-Hall, Inc., Englewood Cliffs, N.J., 1963.

insignificance once the data produced by developing it become available. Surely every company wants to do more than break even. However, it is in the analyses leading to the determination of break-even that we learn about the economic character of the company from which point management can then plan its actions. As we shall see, it is possible for many companies to have the same break-even point and yet respond to proposed changes in sharply differing ways.

Pricing decisions can be made using the break-even approach in arithmetic or formula form. But equally important for some is a graphic portrayal which pictures the effects of pricing decision.

Unlike the traditional approach to break-even, which assumes a constancy between costs, volume, revenue, and profit, the break-even system (a modified concept) is able to cope with the ever-changing facets of the business enterprise–the interplay of costs, volume, prices, and profit–all within the constantly changing product mix.

Break-even Applications

To build a firm foundation for using the break-even system, we shall start by being very basic, using first a small business where few variables interfere with the basic concept and gradually building the concept to the point where it can give answers to pricing and operating problems encountered in the typical multiproduct business. The simple formulas will be presented as needed.

EXAMPLE: Using the small retail store operation (candy bars) mentioned earlier in this chapter, the break-even formula and the break-even point is:

$$\text{Break-even (in unit quantity)} = \frac{\text{fixed expenses}}{\text{unit contribution}}$$

$$= \frac{\$1,000}{\$.02}$$

$$= 50,000 \text{ bars} \qquad (1)$$

$$\text{Break-even (in revenue)} = \frac{\text{fixed expenses}}{\text{PV}} \qquad (2)$$

$$\text{PV} = \frac{\text{unit contribution}}{\text{unit price}} \qquad (3)$$

or

$$\text{PV} = \frac{\text{total contribution}}{\text{sales revenue}} \qquad (4)$$

Using Eq. (3)

$$\text{PV} = \frac{\$.02}{\$.10}$$

$$= .20$$

and substituting in Eq. (2)

$$\text{Break-even} = \frac{\$1,000}{.20}$$

$$= \$5,000$$

(Of course, the reader recalls that Unit contribution = unit price − unit out-of-pocket costs; or Total contribution = sales revenue − total out-of-pocket costs.)

PROBLEM A: If the man increases his fixed expenses to $1,500 per year, what is the effect on the break-even point? *Solution:*

$$\text{Break-even} = \frac{\$1,500}{.20}$$
$$= \$7,500 \text{ (increase of } \$2,500) \tag{2}$$

PROBLEM B: If he raises his price per bar to 11 cents, what is the new break-even point? *Solution:* The PV is now 3 cents/11 cents or .273, and

$$\text{Break-even} = \frac{\$1,500}{.273}$$
$$= \$5,500 \text{ (approx.)} \tag{2}$$

PROBLEM C: If fixed expenses remain at $1,500, but instead of raising prices, he is able to buy candy bars from his supplier for 7 cents each instead of 8 cents. What is the new break-even? *Solution:* The PV is now 3 cents/10 cents or .30, and

$$\text{Break-even} = \frac{\$1,500}{.30}$$
$$= \$5,000 \text{ (the original break-even point)} \tag{2}$$

Comment: Certain guideposts emerge from even these simple problems at this point:
a. A change in just the fixed expenses changes only the break-even point.
b. A change in the price and/or the out-of-pocket cost changes both the break-even as well as the PV.
c. An increase in prices and/or a decrease in out-of-pocket costs can offset a rise in fixed expenses.

PROBLEM D: Comparing the conditions in the original example where the break-even point is $5,000 with those in Problem C where the break-even point is identical, compute profits in both cases when sales reach $8,000. *Solution:* For this problem, other formulas have to be presented:

$$\text{Profit} = (\text{sales revenue} \times \text{PV}) - \text{fixed expenses} \tag{5}$$

or

$$\text{Profit} = \text{profitable range of sales} \times \text{PV} \tag{6}$$

substituting in Eq. (5) for *Original Case:* Profit = ($8,000 × .20) − $1,000
$$= \$600$$
substituting in Eq. (5) for PROBLEM C: Profit = ($8,000 × .30) − $1,500
$$= \$900$$

Comment: This leads to additional guideposts:
d. Two companies can have the same break-even point but will earn profits or losses at their own PV rate above and below that point.
e. Above or below the break-even point, the differences in the PVs of two different companies will be proportionate to their differences in profits or losses.

PROBLEM E: What is meant by the "profitable range of sales"? *Solution:* The range of these sales extends from the break-even level of sales up to the operating sales level. For both the Original Case as well as the case of Problem C, this range would be from $5,000 to $8,000, or $3,000. Using Eq. (6) for the Original Case, Profit = $3,000 × .20, or $600; and for the case in Problem C, Profit = $3,000 × .30, or $900.

Comment: And an additional guidepost:

f. Above or below the break-even point, profits or losses are generated at the PV rate.

PROBLEM F: What must the bars be priced at to generate a profit of $1,450 at a $9,000 sales level if out-of-pocket costs are $.078 each and fixed costs are $1,700 per year? *Solution:* This calls for new formulas:

$$PV = \frac{(\text{target profit} + \text{fixed expenses})}{\text{sales revenue}}$$

$$= \frac{(\$1,450 + \$1,700)}{\$9,000}$$

$$= .35 \tag{7}$$

$$\text{Unit price} = \frac{\text{out-of-pocket costs}}{(1 - PV)}$$

$$= \frac{\$.078}{(1 - .35)}$$

$$= \$0.12 \text{ each} \tag{8}$$

Comment: Another rule:

g. If it is desired to establish a price to produce a target PV, divide the oop costs by the complement of the PV.

Constructing Break-even Charts

Basically, there are three lines on a break-even chart. One shows the fixed expenses over the volume range, another shows the total cost line, and the third is the revenue line. The point at which the revenue line intersects the total cost line is the break-even point. In order to draw the various lines, it is necessary to have a scale of values for each.

1. *Break-even chart for the candy store:* In the simplest form of chart, the sales revenue is shown on the *x* axis or horizontal scale and the expenses are plotted on the *y* axis or vertical scale. Both are expressed in identical dollars on the identical scale; therefore any point on the diagonal 45-degree revenue line will produce the same value when referred to either the vertical or horizontal scale. When the total cost line intersects this revenue line at any point, at that sales volume costs and revenue are equal–the break-even point.

Exhibit 10-1 shows the break-even chart for the candy store operation in the original case. The data for this chart are given as $1,000 annual fixed expenses, unit selling price of 10 cents, and unit oop cost of 8 cents. The dollar values on both horizontal and vertical scales are identical. The dashed line parallel to the horizontal axis shows the values of the fixed expenses with changes in volume. Of course, this value remains the same over the operating year. The revenue line is drawn as a 45-degree diagonal as explained above. The total cost line starts at the fixed expense level at zero sales volume (because the total cost at zero volume are the fixed expenses) and requires another point before the line can be drawn. To find another point, simply calculate what the total cost is for a corresponding sales revenue. For example, at a volume of 80,000 bars the total cost and revenue would be:

oop cost ($0.08 × 80,000)............ $6,400
Fixed cost......................... 1,000
Total cost..........................$7,400
Total sales ($0.10 × 80,000).......... $8,000

Therefore, the second point through which the total cost line must pass is a point on the chart where a revenue of $8,000 corresponds to

EXHIBIT 10-1. BREAK-EVEN CHART: SMALL RETAIL STORE

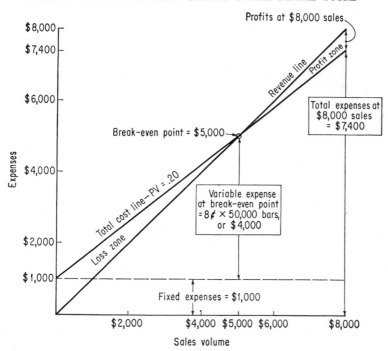

total cost of $7,400. When this total cost line is drawn, it intersects the revenue line at $5,000—the break-even point.

2. *Dynamics of cvp:* Profit and loss can be measured directly on the chart for any volume level. Since profits or losses occur between cost and revenue, the wedges enclosed by the total cost and revenue lines are the profit or loss areas or zones. The amount of profit or loss at any volume is the perpendicular distance between the cost and revenue lines.

Things are not so uniform in typical business enterprises. This type of chart assumes that each dollar of revenue will have the same cost, the same PV, and, ultimately, the same profit. The dynamics of practical operating would have these effects on the chart:

a. A decrease in the oop cost, with no change in the fixed expenses, would lower the slope of the total cost line, thereby reducing the break-even point and widening the profit wedge (because of the increase in PV). In this kind of a situation, not only do profits start earlier (at a lower break-even) but when they do start, they are generated at a higher rate of profit (the PV rate). A reverse condition would produce opposite effects.

b. An increase in prices for the same volume, with no change in fixed expenses, would reduce the oop content in the sales dollar (increase in contribution), which would lower the slope of the total cost line (increase in PV), causing a lower break-even and a greater angle of wedge with similar effects as above.

c. Increasing or decreasing the fixed expenses, with no other change taking place, would increase or decrease the break-even point accordingly, thereby causing profits to start earlier or later, but at the same PV rate.

As can be seen, the interplay of changes in any or all of the price, volume, cost ingredients of the profit structure can be displayed on the break-even chart or may be calculated by formula. Proposals which would affect any of these profit ingredients always should first be tested to make sure they are compatible with the goals of management.

3. *Testing a proposed expansion of facilities:* The following are the data of a company before it makes any changes in facilities:

Expenses	Fixed	Variable	Total
Direct materials.........................	....	$300,000	$ 300,000
Productive labor........................	....	300,000	300,000
Factory overhead.......................	$ 50,000	80,000	130,000
Administrative overhead................	30,000	70,000	100,000
Selling overhead.......................	20,000	50,000	70,000
	$100,000	$800,000	$ 900,000
Sales....................................	....	....	$1,000,000
Pretax profit............................	....	....	$ 100,000
Contribution ($1,000,000 − $800,000)....	....	....	$ 200,000
PV ($200,000/$1,000,000)...............	....	....	.20

The break-even point would be

$$\text{Break-even} = \frac{\text{Fixed}}{\text{PV}}$$
$$= \frac{\$100,000}{.20}$$
$$= \$500,000 \qquad (2$$

Now management is considering modernizing their equipment at an additional cost of $100,000, bringing the total fixed expenses to $200,000 in the hope of saving $200,000 in oop costs. This would have the effect of reducing the variable costs to $600,000. The condensed operating data for this decision would be:

Sales.................	$1,000,000
Variable costs.........	600,000
Fixed costs............	200,000
Total costs..........	$ 800,000
Pretax profit...........	$ 200,000
Contribution..........	$ 400,000
PV...................	.40

And the new break-even point would be

$$\text{Break-even} = \frac{\$200,000}{.40}$$
$$= \$500,000 \tag{2}$$

The break-even points for both the original condition and the proposal are the same, but as can be seen, the profit structures are entirely different. The original situation earns 20 cents on every dollar of sales revenue above the break-even point, whereas in the proposed change, 40 cents would be generated. Exhibit 10-2 shows the effect on the profit wedges.

EXHIBIT 10-2. PROPOSED REPLACEMENT OF FACILITIES

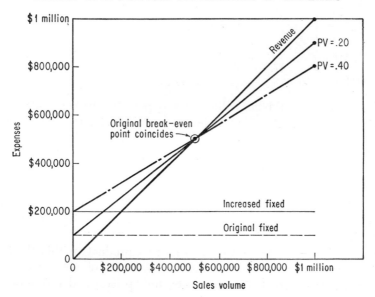

This proposal can be characterized as one in which the proposed increase in equipment is offset by operating savings and produces a double profit over the same profitable range of sales (without raising the break-even point).

The Break-even Chart in PV Form

As we have said earlier, not all sales dollars produce the same PV in multiproduct businesses. Even the small retail operator discussed earlier could have a product mix. Besides the candy bars which have

EXHIBIT 10-3. PV BREAK-EVEN CHART: BASIC FORM

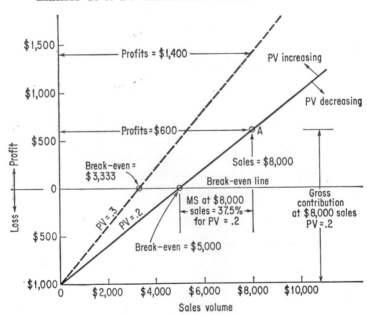

a PV of .20, he could be selling newspapers for 10 cents at a PV of .10, cigars at a PV of .25, and toys at a PV of .40. He would have to sell twice as many newspapers as candy bars to gross the same contribution that the candy bars alone did. He would have to sell only one-half as many toys as candy bars to generate the original contribution of the bars.

Thus, it would be possible to earn a greater profit on fewer sales and a smaller profit on more sales, as the product mix swings from a more favorable to a less favorable mix.

Because the contribution rates of different products within the typical multiproduct firm are different and the amounts of volume each generates are also different, the oop costs, unit prices, and revenue figures are all different and changing. Because the cost line on a conventional break-even chart assumes no changes, it is limited for making pricing decisions. What is needed is a chart on which the effect of different PVs of products can be seen and measured simply. In the PV chart, a single line or multiple lines are drawn (each indicating a certain PV) which show directly the variation in profit with volume and a variation in prices on PV and profit. Exhibit 10-3 shows a PV chart for the candy

EXHIBIT 10-4. PV BREAK-EVEN CHART: SMALL RETAIL STORE

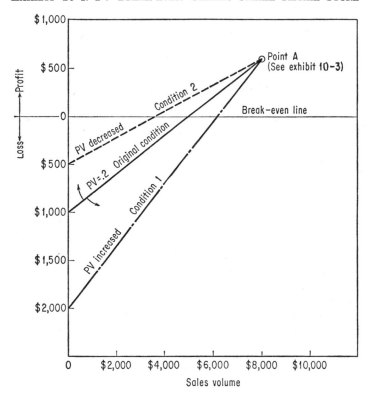

store operation. The PV = .2 line is produced when candy bars are bought for 8 cents each and the unit contribution is 2 cents. In the dashed PV = .3 line, bars are bought for 7 cents each. The PV line can be visualized as hinged at the fixed expense point and swinging about the break-even horizontal line changing as the specific PV changes. Profit at any volume is the distance between the break-even line at the desired sales volume and the specific PV line.

1. *Increase in PV to offset increase in fixed expenses:* In Exhibit 10-4 it is desired to maintain a profit of $600 at $8,000 in sales under changing

conditions of costs and revenue. The desired profit corresponding to the target sales is shown by Point A. Condition 1 shows the increased level of fixed expenses that can be tolerated with an increase in PV. Condition 2 shows how much fixed expenses must drop because of a poorer PV. Since the fixed expense vertical scale can be read directly, we can solve for the required PV very simply:

$$\text{For Condition 1:} \quad PV = \frac{\text{(target profit-fixed expenses)}}{\text{sales revenue}}$$

$$= \frac{(\$600 + \$2,000)}{\$8,000}$$

$$= .325 \tag{7}$$

$$\text{For Condition 2:} \quad PV = \frac{(\$600 + \$500)}{\$8,000}$$

$$= .1375$$

Referring again to the candy store situation, if the man wished to add fixed expenses of \$1,000 annually to modernize his store, then, in order to continue making the same profit of \$600 at \$8,000 sales, he would have to buy his candy bars at 6.75 cents instead of 8 cents. If the cost of candy bars rose from 8 cents to 8.625 cents, he would have to cut his fixed expenses in half (to \$500) in order to continue making the \$600 profit at \$8,000 sales.

2. *Price-volume sensitivity:* PV charts are convenient for observing the effect of volume and prices on contribution. As we mentioned in an earlier chapter, before the pricing decision is made, management should be in intimate touch with the reactions of the market to proposed changes in prices, particularly to evaluate how an increase or decrease in price will affect volume and gross contribution. The following is a tabulation which shows the likely effect of a decision to increase or decrease prices. Decision B is the data for normal pricing; Decision A involves a reduction in price but an increase of 30 per cent in volume; Decision C details the increase in price and a 20 per cent decrease in volume.

Item	Decision A	Decision B	Decision C
Unit selling price..............	\$7	\$8	\$9
Unit oop cost....................	6	6	6
Unit contribution..............	\$1	\$2	\$3
PV.............................	.143	.250	.333
Volume of units sold...........	1,300,000	1,000,000	800,000
Revenue generated..............	\$9,100,000	\$8,000,000	\$7,200,000
Fixed expenses.................	\$1,000,000	\$1,000,000	\$1,000,000

Exhibit 10-5 is a PV chart which shows the profit available from the three decisions. Obviously, if the response of the market to increased prices is expected to follow this pattern, the wisest course of action would be to follow Decision C.

3. *Pretesting pricing decisions:* Often management is confronted with the question of maintaining prices, lowering them, or increasing them. Let's take a company which is presently earning a profit of $500,000 on one of its products. The market research department estimates that if prices were reduced, the company's territorial penetration would be

EXHIBIT 10-5. PV BREAK-EVEN CHART: PRICE-VOLUME COMBINATIONS

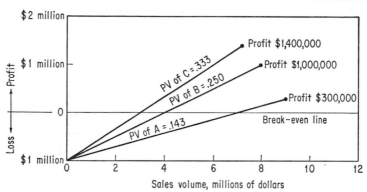

increased and new markets generated to provide a higher sales volume. Others in management believe that prices should be raised to a point where the lower resulting volume at the higher price would still provide more contributions than the price reduction.

Obviously, the selection of either one of these alternatives will produce risks and will impose pressures on the company. Before either step is taken, the wise course would be to test their respective effects on the PV chart. For purposes of illustrating the method, we shall assume the following data:

Item	No price change	Decrease prices 5%	Increase prices 5%
Unit selling price..........	$0.60	$0.57	$0.63
Unit oop cost..............	0.45	0.45	0.45
Unit contribution..........	$0.15	$0.12	$0.18
PV......................	.250	.210	.286
Fixed expenses............	$750,000	$750,000	$750,000

To find the sales revenue required to attain the desired profit of $500,000, use the following formula: Sales revenue = (target profit + fixed expenses)/PV (9) and the required sales revenues and unit volumes are:

Sales revenue required to attain de- sired profit.....................	$5,000,000	$5,950,000	$4,375,000
Unit volume required.............	8,333,333	10,438,000	6,944,000

Exhibit 10-6 shows the effect on profits of the two price changes. To accomplish the same desired profit with a price decrease of 5 per cent, the sales volume would have to increase by 19 per cent and the unit

EXHIBIT 10-6. PV BREAK-EVEN CHART: ALTERNATIVE
PRICING DECISIONS

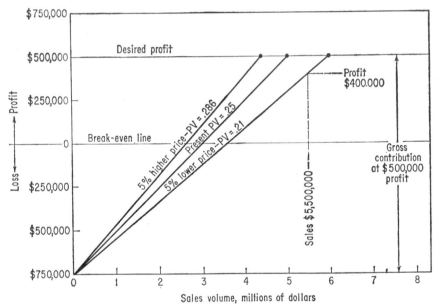

volume by 26 per cent. Had the market analysts persuaded management that a 5 per cent cut in price would boost volume 10 per cent and management believed (without testing) that the 10 per cent increase would justify the price reduction, it would have earned less than the target profit, since actually 19 per cent is the offsetting sales increase required. The actual profit earnable at a 10 per cent sales increase is shown in dotted lines on Exhibit 10-6. On the other hand, if information on the market's elasticity of demand is such that it will produce $4,375,000 of business at the higher price, this would appear to be the more favorable move. Obviously, if business in excess of this figure can be booked, the move toward higher prices is to be preferred.

While all products and markets do not have a proportionate relationship between the amount of price change and the amount of revenue change, there still are some which do, and it is possible under these circumstances to find that the same profits can be generated with different price-volume combinations. In these cases, the lower volume decision is usually to be preferred because it generally involves the seller in less working capital, space, facility loadings, transaction costs, etc.

4. *Pricing and product-mix decisions.* Even though selling prices for several products in a company's line may be equitable or at the level targeted by management, the profit results may be severely affected by an unpoliced product mix. It is desirable to use the break-even system as a detection device as well as a tool for pretesting other internal decisions. The following are the data for a multiproduct company:

Product	PV	Total planned volume, %
A	.30	50
B	.20	30
C	.10	20

Annual fixed expenses are $500,000. It is now desired to compute the break-even point and to determine profits at various sales levels. Obviously, before the break-even point can be found, the proper PV must be used, following the formula, Break-even = fixed expenses/PV. Three PVs are given in the above tabulation; which one is to be used? No one PV can be used by itself. A large PV generated at a small volume of product can have as little impact on the profit structure as a small PV produced from a large volume of product. Therefore, what must be considered in determining the PV to use is the integration between PV and volume, as this is what generates the contribution. In multiproduct companies, the PV is obtained by weighting the PV of each product by the volume each generates or by relating each product's PV to its percentage of the total volume of all products.

Finding the composite PV by weighting the product-volume mix produces:

Product	Weighted PV for three products
A	.30 × 50% = .15
B	.20 × 30% = .06
C	.10 × 20% = .02

Total of weights = the composite PV = .23

And the break-even point is

$$\text{Break-even} = \frac{\text{fixed expenses}}{\text{PV}}$$
$$= \frac{\$500,000}{.23}$$
$$= \$2,173,913$$

Profit at, say, \$4,000,000 sales may be obtained from (2)

$$\text{Profit} = (\text{sales} \times \text{PV}) - \text{fixed expenses}$$
$$= (\$4,000,000 \times .23) - \$500,000$$
$$= \$420,000$$

EXHIBIT 10-7. PV BREAK-EVEN CHART: THE COMPOSITE PV

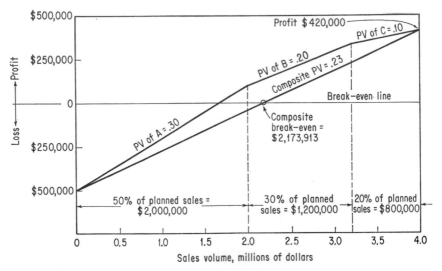

Exhibit 10-7 shows the profit structure of this condition in PV chart form. The horizontal scale shows only the increase in sales volume and should not be interpreted to mean an increase in time. Product A is not necessarily being produced and sold first and Product C last. The reverse may actually occur, or all three products may be transacted simultaneously. Therefore, do not draw the inference that Product A has its own break-even point since its PV line crosses the break-even line. This would be true only if Product A did not require common fixed expenses, for, in that case, Product A would have its separate break-even or PV chart.

Now let's solve the following problems if the volume mix of the three products is allowed to change to:

Product	Total planned volume, %
A	20
B	30
C	50

a. Compute the break-even point.

b. Compute profit at $4,000,000 sales point.

c. Compute the level of sales required at this volume mix to generate a profit of $420,000, the profit available from the original mix at the same sales volume.

We can solve these problems by following the above procedure.

a. The composite PV is .17, and the break-even is:

$$\text{Break-even} = \frac{\$500,000}{.17}$$
$$= \$2,941,176 \tag{2}$$

b. The profit is

$$\text{Profit} = (\$4,000,000 \times .17) - \$500,000$$
$$= \$180,000 \ (43\% \text{ of the original profit}) \tag{5}$$

c. To find the sales level that will restore the original profit of $420,000, it must be realized that whereas each sales dollar generated 23 cents of contribution under the original conditions of mix, the changed mix only produces 17 cents per sales dollar. The new sales level that must be found must be high enough to produce $420,000 of profit and must overcome the $500,000 of fixed expenses:

$$\text{New sales} = \frac{(\text{desired profit} + \text{fixed expenses})}{\text{PV}}$$
$$= \frac{(\$420,000 + \$500,000)}{.17}$$
$$= \$5,411,765 \tag{7}$$

The change in the product-volume mix which dropped the composite PV from .23 to .17 had a marked effect on profits, reducing them from $420,000 to $180,000. If the company markets this mix, it will have to increase planned sales from $4,000,000 to $5,411,765 to maintain the $420,000 profit target. In other words, the drop in profit of $240,000 will have to be made up by an additional sales volume of $1,411,765 at a composite PV of .17, viz., $1,411,765 \times .17 = $240,000.

In an attempt to correct for this poorer PV, management decides to raise prices 10 per cent on all three products. This change produces the following data:

Product	Original PV	New PV	New total planned volume, %	Weight
A	.30	.364	10	.0364
B	.20	.273	30	.0819
C	.10	.182	60	.1092
				.2275 (Composite PV)

In summarily raising prices, management tries to force the external factors of competition and market demand to support its internal needs for profit. While the PV is substantially restored to the original .23, the effects of price-volume sensitivity caused a drop in sales to $2,500,000, thereby generating a gross contribution of $568,750 and a profit of

EXHIBIT 10-8. THE EFFECT OF PRODUCT MIX ON PROFITS

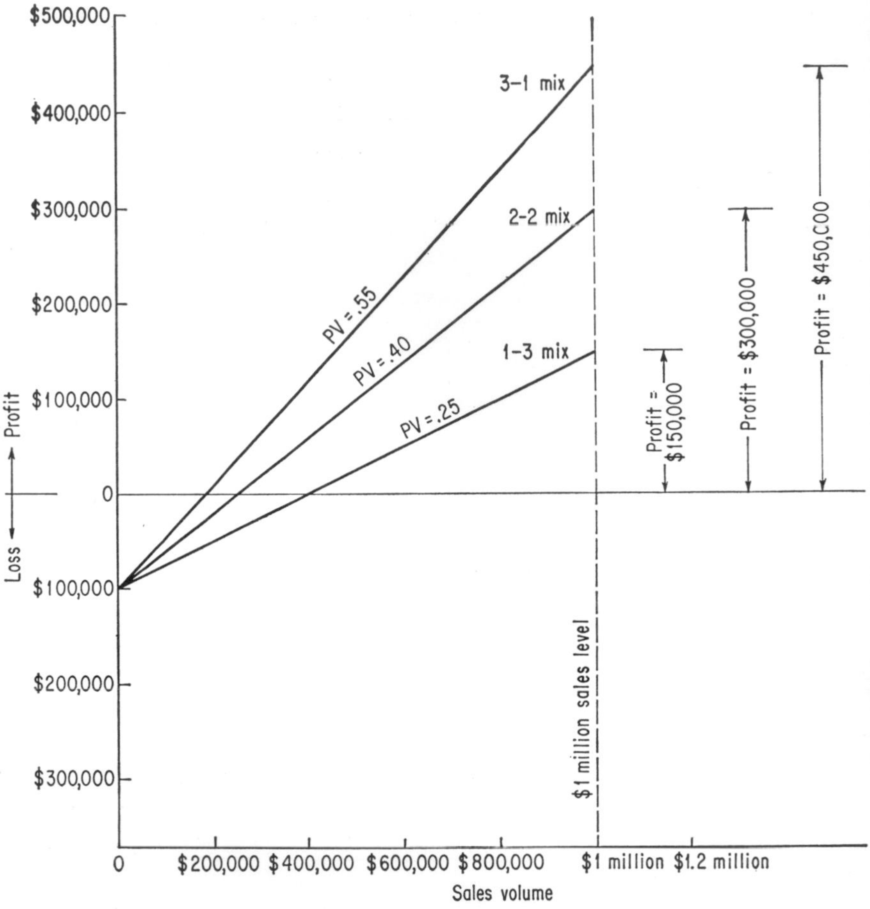

$68,750, barely one-third of the previous condition and only 16 per cent of the original profit of $420,000.

Where there is a large difference in PVs among various products in a company's line, a favorable revision in product mix is usually more effective than an increase in price. The following example discusses a situation in a company which makes only two products. Annual fixed

expenses are $100,000 and the two products are sold under three condi-
tions of changing product mix: a 2:2 proportion, 1:3 proportion, and
a 3:1 proportion—all for the same sales level of $1,000,000:

Product	Volume mix	PV	Weight
A	½	.70	.35
B	½	.10	.05
			.40 (Composite PV)
A	¼	.70	.175
B	¾	.10	.075
			.25 (Composite PV)
A	¾	.70	.525
B	¼	.10	.025
			.55 (Composite PV)

Exhibit 10-8 shows the effect that the three different mixes have on
profits. It is clear to see that the slope of the PV line, which determines
the profit at any sales level, is a function of pricing, volume, and product
mix.

Section 4

RATIONAL PRICING METHODS

CHAPTER 11 *Contribution Pricing*

When we think of price, we are naturally thinking about the dollars to be asked for a product. At the same time, we may be thinking about the price that others are selling it for. Therefore, since the asked price and the final price may be different, management must measure what contribution it would get if it met the competitive, market, or "going" price. If this contribution is acceptable to management, it will book the order at that "going" price.

A knowledge of costs is important and a knowledge of the costs of related products in a product line is essential in establishing relative values. But using these costs routinely to price by formula is unrealistic. In the final analysis, the customer determines the price, and his decision is based on his notion of value. The customer decides by comparing a product price with the prices of others available to him, even if it means product substitution. As we have seen, no two companies have the same actual costs; this fact would eliminate formula pricing from having any practical value. Since cost accounting is not a precise science because of the various allocation methods employed, there is no way to predict the spread between the asking price and the final price.

As we have discussed, the out-of-pocket (oop) cost is the floor on prices. Out-of-pocket costs are considered incremental because, if the product is not made, the oop costs can be saved. If the product is made, the increment in cost incurrence is the oop cost. However, a company does not stay in business very long selling its products below oop costs, except when such sales help to sell other products which make a large enough contribution to offset the below-oop prices. On the other hand, the recovery of fixed costs in selling prices presents a complex problem because most of the fixed costs usually cannot be specifically identified with products or orders. The reason for this fact is that facilities (production, sales, administrative, technical, etc.) may be shared in common by the entire mix of product. So when a company accepts an order below

121

oop cost, it is left with fewer dollars than it would have had if the order had not been produced. Whereas, if an order is priced above oop costs, it is making a contribution to the payment of the fixed expenses and leaves the company with more dollars than it would have had without the sale.

PV Characteristics of Profit Segments

Products and orders can contribute differently to the pool out of which fixed expenses are paid and profit made available, and these differences may change from time to time. The reasons for these differences lie in the differences in customer demand, competitive intensity, local attitudes towards certain types of products, local availability of substitute products, feelings of status, etc. Thus, neglecting the direct product costs, such as freight delivery costs to point of destination, enables one product to produce a different contribution rate in each of four sales territories in which it is sold because of the aforementioned reasons. If this is the case, then sales territories should be considered a separate profit segment for evaluation. When a seller's product is used by several different end-user markets, that same product can yield different PVs in each of those markets because of the specific characteristics of the end market itself. Thus, it would be rewarding also to establish the end-user market as a profit segment.

Obviously, in computing PVs, we are interested in the percentage that the contribution bears to the selling price. Contribution requires only that the oop costs and selling price be known. Adding an allocated fixed cost to profit-segment analyses only distorts the inherent PV characteristic of that profit segment and could mislead management into making wrong decisions. An allocation of fixed cost is based on a calculation of the proportionate benefits a product receives from its use of the common period costs (which may be true theoretically), but it may in no way correspond to the ability of that product to contribute to the common pool of period costs which is determined by market factors. Thus, there cannot be any predictable relationship between the product's ability to contribute and its fair share of common fixed costs which it ostensibly uses up. Therefore, a product which receives a large share of fixed cost because it is produced on expensive facilities and requires costly technical services will not and cannot contribute in proportion to this share if it is sold into a territory or to customer classes in which the market price is low and contributes a small amount over oop cost. An attempt to equate this allocated share with a proportionate amount of contribution can price the product out of its markets. If the contribution from a "going" price is inadequate to management, means should be sought to reduce its oop cost, withdraw the product from the market, or investigate other alternatives.

In those rare circumstances where a uniform selling price is acceptable in various territories, then the PV of the product will vary only to the extent of the specific oop costs associated with each territory. These are usually the selling and the freight costs. However, there are some interesting variations that could take place. One Midwest manufacturer set up stock programs for his many products which he sold to jobbers located all over the United States. Several times a year, jobbers placed their orders with this manufacturer, and orders were shipped at prices which included all delivery costs. The mix of products and volume levels of each product ordered by jobbers were all substantially different and reflected the market served by the individual jobber. Until a product-mix and profit-segment analysis was made, the management thought that because it had to absorb the delivery costs, the contribution of the jobber located 2,000 miles away was less than the contribution of a jobber located in the same city as the manufacturer. What the manufacturer overlooked was the composite contribution that was generated by the specific product mix ordered by an individual jobber. The differences in the PVs of the various mixes were much greater than the delivery cost differences, so it was entirely probable for the combination of the contribution of the mix and the diluted contribution caused by prepaying freight cost to give a higher net contribution from jobbers who were located at great distances. From this analysis, jobbers were set up as profit segments and ranked according to their net PV—after the consideration of all contribution factors. Thus, management had a basis for future pricing, negotiating, and concession making, which was keyed to the realistic appraisal of its individual jobbers. Exhibit 11-1 shows how a comparative analysis was made between two jobbers, one located 200 miles from the manufacturer and one located 2,000 miles away.

Product-line Profitability

The calculation of contribution as the difference between the seller's oop costs and the competitive prices makes it easy to measure the relative profitability of products and other profit segments of the business, such as markets, customers, territories, etc. This knowledge of the relative rates of contribution among the various segments helps the company to decide which segments need emphasizing, which ones need attention for profit improvement, which ones yield a low return on capital, which ones can advantageously be replaced. While there is no defensible method of obtaining the net profit of each segment because of the arbitrary allocation of common fixed costs, it is possible to determine the rate at which each segment contributes to the net profit from all segments combined. As long as the common fixed costs are not changed by a pricing decision, these common fixed costs have no bearing on such decisions and need not be allocated to the products being priced. However, contribution and PV are relevant to pricing decisions because both oop costs and revenues do change with changes in prices and unit volume.

The reader will recall in an earlier chapter discussion of the various classifications of period costs. The classifications reflect the rankings of

EXHIBIT 11-1. COMPARATIVE CONTRIBUTION: PRODUCT MIX
VERSUS TERRITORY

Product	Contribution each unit	Jobber located 2,000 miles from plant		Jobber located 200 miles from plant	
		Quantity purchased	Contribution generated	Quantity purchased	Contribution generated
A	$ 4	40	$ 160	0	
B	11	0	. . . . . .	10	$ 110
C	17	60	1,020	25	425
D	3	100	300	200	600
E	7	50	350	0	
F	2	20	40	100	200
G	14	0	. . . . . .	5	70
Gross contributions.			$1,870	. . .	$1,405
Delivery costs.			175	. . .	25
Net order contribution.			$1,695	. . .	$1,380

managerial decisions in terms of whether or not these fixed costs are separable, discontinuable, inescapable, or incurred in common. Where certain fixed costs have been incurred specifically for the exclusive benefit of product lines—specific programmed costs—these costs may be directly assigned to product lines in the determination of profit. Other period fixed costs which are shared in common with other lines cannot be validly apportioned because of the necessity of using arbitrary allocation methods. Thus, the inherent PV of product lines may be modified to include this specifically programmed period cost, and management is able to narrow the gap between a relative contribution figure and a true net profit figure.

Exhibit 11-2 shows a typical statement of product-line profitability combining both the results of pricing and operating. First, the inherent

PV of each product line is calculated by subtracting the respective oop costs. This PV typically shows the gross amount of contribution in each product-line's sales dollar before the application of programmed period costs which are directly associated with, and traceable to, each. If there were no specific period costs necessary to support annual activity in each line, Product line B would rank highest with Product line C second and Product line A last. (Note this ranking is not in proportion to sales revenue.) However, after the $3 million specific programmed costs are assigned to each product line on the basis of the specific use of these

EXHIBIT 11-2. ANALYSIS OF PRODUCT-LINE PRICING AND PROFITABILITY

Profit structure	Annual total	Product lines		
		A	B	C
Sales revenue.............	$9,000,000	$2,700,000	$3,000,000	$3,300,000
oop costs................	5,000,000	1,900,000	1,300,000	1,800,000
Gross contribution......	$4,000,000	$ 800,000	$1,700,000	$1,500,000
Operating PV............	.444	.296	.567	.454
Specific programmed period costs................	3,000,000	200,000	1,200,000	1,600,000
Adjusted contribution...	$1,000,000	$ 600,000	$ 500,000	$ (100,000)
Adjusted annual PV.......	.111	.222	.167	(.030)
Common period costs......	500,000			
Pretax profit...........	$ 500,000			

costs, the ranking is changed. Now Product line A, which ranked last, is first, with Product line B second and Product line C last. Not only is Product line C last, but it shows a direct loss of $100,000; even if an attempt was made to arbitrarily allocate the common period costs, Product line C could not improve its profits and could only make the situation worse. So while a PV of .454 is indeed a rapid rate of contribution in this company, an inordinately excessive amount of specific programmed cost is required to support it, thereby making it a candidate for elimination. (Again this ranking is out of proportion to sales revenue.) Notice that there is no attempt to distribute the common period costs because they are shared in common with all lines and would not change with activity in any of the lines.

When the allocation of fixed expenses is made to product lines, the results can be most misleading. The usual practice is to distribute these expenses on the basis of sales revenue. If this distribution were attempted with the $3,500,000, the results would be as follows:

Item	Product lines		
	A	B	C
Gross contribution........................	$ 800,000	$1,700,000	$1,500,000
Fixed expenses distributed on the basis of sales revenue........................	1,050,000	1,166,667	1,283,333
Pretax profit........................	$ (250,000)	$ 533,333	$ 216,667

This approach would mislead management into believing that Product line A, which is really its most profitable line, is producing a large loss and that Produce line C, which is actually a direct loss before the application of common costs, is generating almost one-half the profits of the enterprise. Any decision based on this wrong information could actually deprive the company of profits if the company eliminated Product line A and retained Product line C. In addition, decisions involving future planning of these lines would most probably further limit the company's profits. Some of these actions could involve increasing prices of Product line A to improve its profit, reducing prices of Product line C in the expectation of more volume, spending more for advertising and distribution for the wrong product lines, expanding into markets where distribution costs are higher, offering additional services to customers, etc.

The product-line profitability statement may be used as the format for projecting the expected product mix. Mix is as important as volume when it comes to selective selling. Rarely will all of a company's lines earn the same profit on sales and the same return on invested capital. When the PVs become known, as afforded by this type of analysis, the company can engage in special promotion and/or greater sales emphasis to attain the desired return.

Pricing for Desired Contribution

1. When capital and period fixed costs are directly associated with a specific product, the price can be determined based on a given rate of return. In the following data:

Unit oop cost..................... $12
Specific fixed cost................ $75,000
Specific capital employed.......... $200,000
Desired rate of return............. 30%
Number of annual units............ 20,000

Gross annual contribution desired from this line of products is $75,000 + .30 × $200,000, or $135,000. To obtain the target selling price, we must find the unit contribution. Obviously, this is $135,000/20,000 or $6.75. Price is the addition of oop cost and contribution, and the target selling price would be $12.00 + $6.75, or $18.75. Note that this would give a PV of $6.75/$18.75, or approximately .35.

If it is desired to price other products in the line (for which the period costs and capital employed are still specific), simply divide the oop cost of the product by the complement of the PV:

$$\text{Price to yield a desired PV} = \frac{\text{oop cost}}{(1 - \text{desired PV})}$$
$$= \frac{\$12.00}{(1 - .35)}$$
$$= \$18.75$$

2. Basically, in pricing for a target rate of contribution, the same formula applies, namely, price equals the oop cost divided by the complement of the desired PV. Most of the time in pricing, there are oop cost factors which are not known or applied until the selling price becomes known. Typical examples of these factors are sales commissions, various discounts to dealers and distributors, royalties, and the line. Since the PV is a direct rate on selling prices, these price-based additives can be anticipated and included in advance to provide for the seller his net desired contribution if he books the order. For example, let's assume that the seller wishes to net a PV of .35 on an order after paying a 5 per cent sales commission. The seller's oop costs are $15 each. The procedure is to add to the net PV desired the additional costs, which are expressed as a percentage of the unknown selling price. Thus,

$$\text{Target selling price} = \frac{\$15}{(1 - .35 + .05)}$$
$$= \frac{\$15}{.60}$$
$$= \$25$$

Testing this price:

Selling price	$25.00
oop cost	15.00
Gross contribution	$10.00
Less: 5% sales commission	1.25
Net contribution	$ 8.75

$$\text{Seller's net PV} = \frac{\$8.75}{\$25} \text{ or } .35$$

It should be borne in mind that this approach to target pricing, based on obtaining a target PV, uses the oop cost as a base without considering what may be very different elements which constitute the oop cost. For example, one product's oop cost may be dominated by a heavy raw material content—perhaps one which is made by hand and doesn't require the use of expensive facilities. Such an oop cost turns over material investment in which there is typically less at stake than the capital represented by expensive capital facilities. Another product's oop cost may have a much smaller material content, but the product may be made on expensive equipment. Such a product uses more of the company's capital investment. Yet the oop costs for both products could be the same.

This method of target pricing does not recognize the varying contents of the oop cost and the price which is based on the target PV. In effect, this method marks up material cost as much as conversion costs, putting the seller in the unrealistic position of asking the customer to pay dearly for a converting service simply because the materials may be high; at the other extreme, it does not price high enough because of the lower material content. Neither one makes good business sense, does it?

Pricing for desired PV on total oop should be used only when the relationship between materials and conversion costs remains rather fixed throughout the company's product lines. In this case, if the materials-to-conversion cost ratio is high, the PV is targeted uniformly lower than if the materials-to-conversion cost ratio is low.

Pricing for Target Profit

In some businesses, it is possible to hold a given target selling price over much of the range of the company's capacity. This pricing situation is true in some industries that make standard products where competitors are few. Yet some of these businesses are often confronted with proposals for "special price" volume. Especially in these cases, special-price business should never be allowed to crowd out regular-price business. However, when this possibility exists, management must have the means to deal with these proposals properly and profitably.

Suppose, in the following example, management sets its profit goals as follows:

Plant capacity	1,000 units
Fixed costs	$100,000
Unit oop costs	$200
Normal volume	800 units
Target profit	$30,000

At normal volume:

Fixed cost	$100,000
oop cost (800 × $200)	160,000
Total annual cost	$260,000
Total unit cost	$325.00

Unit selling price to attain target profit:

$$
\begin{array}{lr}
\text{Unit profit (\$30,000/800)} \ldots\ldots\ldots\ldots & 37.50 \\
\text{Normal unit selling price} \ldots\ldots\ldots\ldots & \$362.50
\end{array}
$$

Obviously, if the 800 units were booked for sale early in the operating period, 200 additional units could be sold during the year at any price over the $200 unit oop costs for a profit. Since the mixture of regular-price and special-price business may start at the very beginning of the period, management must have current information to guide its pricing decisions. Specifically, it must know what mixture of target-price and special-price business will meet the profit requirement of $30,000 for the period.

If all 1,000 units can be sold, the normal unit selling price can be reduced:

$$
\begin{array}{lr}
\text{Fixed costs} \ldots\ldots\ldots\ldots\ldots\ldots\ldots\ldots\ldots\ldots\ldots\ldots\ldots & \$100,000 \\
\text{oop costs (1,000} \times \$200) \ldots\ldots\ldots\ldots\ldots\ldots\ldots & 200,000 \\
\hline
\text{Total annual costs} \ldots\ldots\ldots\ldots\ldots\ldots\ldots\ldots\ldots & \$300,000 \\
\text{Total unit cost (\$300,000/1,000)} \ldots\ldots\ldots\ldots\ldots & \$\quad 300 \\
\text{Desired unit profit (\$30,000/1,000)} \ldots\ldots\ldots\ldots\ldots & 30 \\
\hline
\text{Unit selling price at maximum capacity} \ldots\ldots\ldots & \$\quad 330
\end{array}
$$

To find quickly the average unit selling price versus the required amount of units that have to be sold, use the following formula:

$$
\text{Required volume} = \frac{\text{fixed cost} + \text{target profit}}{\text{average price} - \text{unit oop cost}}
$$

Thus, an average selling price (representing the mixture of regular-price and special-price business) of $350 would require a volume of

$$
\frac{\$100,000 + \$30,000}{\$350 - \$200} = 866.67 \text{ units}
$$

to provide the target profit. The reader will recognize the denominator in the above formula as the unit contribution figure.

Pricing Specific Orders

Pricing starts at the point where a cost estimate is available for a product or order and management is getting ready to quote a price. More often than not, management is aware of the range of the "going" market price and can then set about measuring the contribution it would get by meeting that price. The basis for that measurement is management's estimate of what the oop costs of the order are likely to be when it is booked and run through the plant.

1. Exhibit 11-3 shows how an estimate is prepared in a commercial printing company. Estimated costs are separated to show the total oop as well as the "full" costs of producing this order.* If the "going" price for this work is $450, the contribution available to this printer would be $450 — $390.85, or $59.15—a PV of $59.15/$450, or .131.

EXHIBIT 11-3. ESTIMATE SHEET: APPLICATION OF TWO-PART
MACHINE-HOUR RATES

Production Center	Conversion				
	Hours Required	MHR		Conversion Costs	
		oop	"Full"	oop	"Full"
Prep:					
Art and paste-up............	*4.0*	*$ 4.20*	*$ 6.10*	*$ 16.80*	*$ 24.40*
Step and repeat.............	*1.5*	*4.40*	*14.70*	*6.60*	*22.05*
Strip and lockup............	*2.5*	*4.50*	*6.30*	*11.25*	*15.75*
Plate making...............	*0.5*	*7.20*	*11.50*	*3.60*	*5.75*
Press:					
Makeready.................	*4.0*	*9.20*	*29.20*	*36.80*	*116.80*
Run......................	*8.0*	*14.60*	*34.60*	*116.80*	*276.80*
Guillotine..................	*2.0*	*3.90*	*8.40*	*7.80*	*16.80*
Fold......................	*4.0*	*5.60*	*9.00*	*22.40*	*35.00*
Collate and stitch...........	*10.0*	*4.40*	*8.10*	*44.00*	*81.00*
Pack......................	*3.0*	*3.40*	*5.10*	*10.20*	*15.30*
Total Conversion Costs.................................				*$276.25*	*$610.65*
Total Materials Costs*.................................				*114.60*	*114.60*
Total..				*$390.85*	*$725.25*

* Not derived in this example.

If the "going" price is not known and the printer knows that his customer has been paying him prices which have averaged a PV of .22, (or where the work is going to a market that has a characteristic PV of .22), the price he may quote can be derived from the formula:

$$\text{Price to yield a desired PV} = \frac{\text{oop}}{(1 - \text{desired PV})}$$
$$= \frac{\$390.85}{.78}$$
$$= \$501.03$$

* The mechanics of establishing the two-part machine-hour rate are shown in Chap. 16.

2. Exhibit 11-4 shows in condensed form a cost estimate for 60,000 fabricated parts. From the data given, the seller would receive a unit contribution of 4 cents by meeting the "going" market price of 15 cents. The customer is supposed to be charged separately for the $4,000 of tooling, which is satisfactory to him, and he is about to agree to the price when the customer demands that the seller pay for the tooling himself at no increase in unit price. Should the seller agree to do this?

EXHIBIT 11-4. ESTIMATE SHEET (CONDENSED)

Part No. *HJT-002*

Quantity *60,000 units* Delivery *FOB plant*

Summary of oop Costs

Direct material....................	$5,740.00
oop conversion cost setup..........	210.00
oop conversion cost: run...........	650.00
Total oop costs................	$6,600.00
Unit oop cost.....................	$0.11
Competitive unit SP...............	$0.15

(Tooling cost = $4,000.)

The first thing the seller should do is to calculate the minimum order quantity which will pay at least all of his oop costs. Then he can figure what his net order contribution will be on any remaining balance. Since tooling is considered a one-time constant cost for the order (even though it is an oop cost), he can approach the solution of this problem by using the break-even technique. The $4,000 is the "fixed" portion of the formula, and the 4-cent contribution on each unit is the rate of gain:

$$\text{Break-even quantity point} = \frac{\text{fixed expenses}}{\text{unit contribution}}$$
$$= \frac{\$4,000}{\$0.04}$$
$$= 100,000 \text{ units} \qquad (1)$$

Thus, the seller would have to book a minimum order quantity of 100,000 units *just to get back his out-of-pocket costs.* If he took the order for 60,000 units and paid for the tooling costs out of his own pocket, he would incur a cash loss to the extent of the negative contribution on 40,000 units, or $1,600.

Knowing this information, the seller can go back to his customer to try to get some sort of compromise. While he realizes that he probably cannot get as high a PV for a larger quantity, he is willing to book the order *at the same unit price* providing the quantity is high enough to spread his setup and tooling costs so he can get a PV of at least .20. How does he calculate this higher quantity? He uses a modified form of Eq. (8):

$$\text{Revenue} = \frac{\text{oop costs}}{(1 - \text{PV})}$$

Revenue is the product of the unit selling price, which is known to be 15 cents, and the volume, which is unknown at this point. Therefore, let x equal the unknown quantity, and

$$\$0.15x = \frac{\text{oop costs}}{(1 - .20)}$$

To get the total oop costs, one must realize that they consist of the constant order costs of setup and tooling as well as the running and material costs. The former will remain the same regardless of quantity, but the running and material costs will vary directly with the unknown quantity:

Constant order costs

Setup...........................	$ 210
Tooling........................	4,000
Total......................	$4,210

Variable order costs

Run 60,000 units................	$ 650
Material for 60,000 units.........	5,740

$\$6,390 \div 60,000 = \$0.1065$ per unit

Therefore, the total oop costs will be the addition of the constant order costs of $4,210 plus the variable costs of $0.1065 per unit times the unknown quantity, thus:

$$\$0.15x = \frac{\$4,210 + (\$0.1065)x}{.8}$$

$$\$0.12x = \$4,210 + \$0.1065x$$

$$\$0.0135x = \$4,210$$

$$x = \frac{\$4,210}{\$0.0135}$$

$$= 311,852 \text{ units}$$

A worked-out formula, set up for solving directly for the unknown quantity is

Target unit volume

$$= \frac{\text{constant order oop costs}}{(1 - \text{PV}) \times \text{unit selling price} - \text{variable order oop costs}}$$

The Market Price List

In many industries, leading manufacturers issue a published, catalog-type price list for their products. Most of these lists give varying prices for a given product for different quantities, or one price is published and discounts are given for higher quantities. Buyers usually purchase from these lists; if competing sellers wish to quote these buyers, they are generally asked to follow the price schedule on these lists. While it is recognized that a given product will not make the same contribution to all companies capable of producing it, it is important to realize that there are contribution variances which the *same product* can make to the *same seller* by virtue of the quantity of the order booked.

EXHIBIT 11-5. DIFFERENT CONTRIBUTIONS FROM SAME PRICE LIST

Published price list product no. 4372		Company X			Company Y		
Order size	Price each	oop cost each	Contri-bution each	PV	oop cost each	Contri-bution each	PV
1,000	$40.00	$25.00	$15.00	.375	$48.00	$(8.00)	(.200)
2,000	30.00	23.00	7.00	.233	35.00	(5.00)	(.167)
5,000	24.00	22.00	2.00	.083	26.00	(2.00)	(.083)
10,000	20.00	21.50	(1.50)	(.075)	19.50	0.50	.025
20,000	18.00	21.25	(3.25)	(.180)	15.00	3.00	.167
50,000	17.00	21.20	(4.20)	(.247)	11.50	5.50	.324
100,000	15.00	21.18	(6.18)	(.412)	9.00	6.00	.400

Thus, while a given quantity of Product X contributes at a certain PV rate at a certain quantity, the contribution of the same product at a different quantity can be considerably different because of the change in the published selling price for that quantity and the effect of the seller's preparatory costs. Exhibit 11-5 shows the effects which published prices of the identical product have at varying quantities for two competing companies.

Company X is a company with older equipment, requiring less time to set up but more time to run each unit. Because of the relatively inexpensive setup cost, the unit oop cost ranges from a high of $25 at the 1,000 quantity to $21.18 in lots of 100,000. On the other hand, Company Y is a more modern company. It uses high-speed equipment and has a lower unit running cost, but the setup on its equipment takes longer and is much more costly. Therefore, its unit oop cost ranges from $48

EXHIBIT 11-7. INTERRELATIONSHIPS OF PV,
CONTRIBUTION, AND REVENUE

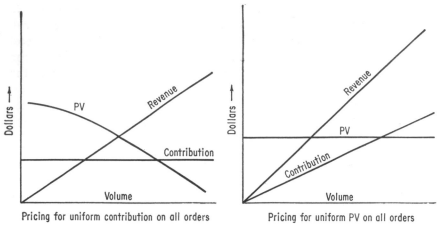

Pricing for uniform contribution on all orders   Pricing for uniform PV on all orders

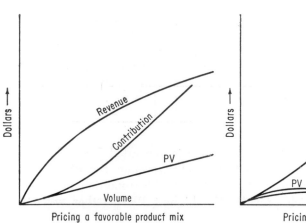
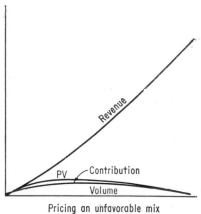

Pricing a favorable product mix   Pricing an unfavorable mix

EXHIBIT 11-8. ORDER SIZE FOR MAXIMUM CONTRIBUTION

Order size	Contract unit price	Contract selling price	Seller's oop cost	Seller's contribution	Seller's PV
1,000	$1.00	$ 1,000	$ 600	$ 400	.40
5,000	0.88	4,400	2,900	1,500	.34
10,000	0.74	7,400	5,600	1,800	.24
20,000	0.645	12,900	11,100	1,800	.14
40,000	0.5925	23,700	22,100	1,600	.067
100,000	0.555	55,500	55,200	300	.005

EXHIBIT 11-9. SELECTING THE MOST PROFITABLE ORDER QUANTITY

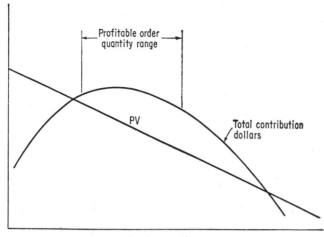

Total order quantity

Control of Contribution

Product mix means more than the existence of several products made by one firm. The mixture of products and their effects on profits refer also to the different prices at which each is sold, the typical order quantities for each member of the product line, the characteristic PVs available for each at different volumes as reflected by both the internal out-of-pocket costs to make and sell, the characteristics of the markets and territories into which each is sold, the varying use of facilities needed for producing and selling, and the variations in the invested capital levels of each.

In pricing, management must first measure what contribution is available from meeting a competitive price or from its own set price and then relate that proposal against the use of facilities and capital which must be committed in filling the order. At the same time, management must have a control of what contributions have been booked to date and what contributions are expected to develop in the future. Then it must stack up period contributions generated in a period against what period fixed expenses have to be covered in the same period. When contributions for a period have equaled the prorated (not allocated) fixed expenses for the same period, the company is at the break-even point for that period.

As indicated earlier, the profit formula in pricing is

$$\text{Period profit} = \text{period contribution} - \text{period fixed expenses}$$

The period contribution is that amount which has been "deposited" in the imaginary contribution pool by the different orders booked in that period. To guide management in policing the build-up of that pool and as an aid to it in its future pricing, a Contribution Log is used. An example is shown in Exhibit 11-10. A Contribution Log is a record of pricing transactions during a period. Since entries are made at the time of booking the orders, the data are necessarily estimated rather than actual. As such, the Contribution Log reports on the *results of pricing* and acts as an advance heralding of profits if actual operating performance is at least as good as the estimate.

EXHIBIT 11-10. CONTRIBUTION LOG

Month of *May*   Product Line A-2?

Order No.	Booked SP	Total oop	Contribution	PV	Cumulative Contribution
6706	$ 9,120	$6,170	$2,950	.324	$ 2,950
6707	5,150	3,080	2,070	.402	5,020
6708	4,970	4,230	740	.149	5,760
6709	10,510	5,860	4,650	.442	10,410
6748	8,740	8,020	720	.082	79,818
6749	11,360	7,115	4,245	.374	84,063
6750	7,390	6,112	1,278	.173	85,341

Summary

Total sales booked in month	=	$404,873
Booked contribution	=	$ 85,341
Average PV	=	.21
Less: prorated period expenses*	=	55,000
Pricing profit	=	$ 30,341

* Annual fixed period expenses = $660,000.

The conventional operating statement reports profit without being able to trace its sources—it reports profit as a mixture of the results of operating meshed in with the results of pricing.* Management must have crystal-clear indication of where its profits are coming from. Low profit in a period can be the result of excellent pricing and poor performance or vice versa.

If each entry in this chronological log is codified and identified with other information relating to each transaction, such as codes for customer, location, end market involved, facility, salesman, product, product line, channel of distribution, lot quantity, etc., contribution data may

* See Chap. 15.

be sorted according to each of these profit segments. When enough data have been collected and summarized, the relative profitability of each of these segments is ranked and exposed for managerial emphasis and action.

Besides showing the contribution rankings among the various profit segments of the firm, these data are useful for establishing future prices of these segments by pricing for a target PV as previously discussed.

How Much Contribution Is Adequate?

The acceptance of an amount of contribution available from meeting a competitive price is a highly personal matter to the seller. The pricing problem depends on finding for each product in the line the most profitable combination of volume and price—actually volume and unit contribution. When a seller agrees to a price after measuring contribution, he is really saying that the price of that product together with its unit volume (gross order contribution), plus the gross contributions of previous bookings in the operating year to date, plus the expected gross contributions of expected future work, will pool together to cover period fixed expenses and will leave over a profit equivalent to the target return on capital.

This approach could be highly academic since a competitor's capital base and desired return may combine to a target return much smaller than the seller's. The competitor's lower requirements for gross annual contribution may result in a lower price. In this case, there are other guideposts open to the seller: he may employ the technique of attempting to price by maintaining a PV consistency of similar work, a PV consistency to the specific customer, a PV consistency to the class of customer of which the immediate customer is a member, or a PV consistency in the contribution the seller obtains from the use of his facilities; or he may mark up his materials and conversion costs separately for a desired return. These methods will be discussed later.

One point to watch is that while a seller's price provides adequate contribution for *his* goals, it is not so low as to provoke price retaliation from competitors. This, in the eyes of competitors, is price-cutting, regardless of the motives of the seller; this inadvertent price-cutting is as bad as purposeful price-cutting in its effect on spoiling the market.

Limitations of the Method

This chapter has discussed the relative contribution figure as one tangible piece of pricing information. Contribution is developed from subtracting the total out-of-pocket cost from the selling price. No means were used to qualify or analyze the specific ingredients of the oop cost, whether it consisted largely of materials cost or of conversion cost. Thus, the contribution could not be related to the invested capital supporting the oop cost. Surely a given amount of contribution on a specific selling price is not enough basis for evaluating the equity of a price. If that same contribution was for an order which required little invested capital to produce, the judgment of price must be necessarily different than if that contribution applied to an order in which the invested capital was high. Thus, once a target price based on the return desired on the various elements of invested capital is established, then, besides the measurement of order contribution, management has the additional yardstick of measuring how far below or above booked contribution deviates from target contribution.

Additionally, the measurement of contribution alone as a basis for evaluating the quality of pricing is shallow unless there is some reference to the use of facilities required in generating the contribution. While the booked contribution of an order may be considered high, the number of facility-hours required to produce it may also be high. Booking this kind of work continually will cause the company to run out of available capacity before it can generate contribution sufficient for its desired target earnings.

The following two chapters will discuss facility-hour pricing and pricing for return on product investment. The chapter following those two will discuss criteria for selecting the most appropriate method to suit specific conditions.

CHAPTER 12 *Facility Pricing*

Industrial facilities used by manufacturers are those which convert a raw material into a salable state. Often joint or common facilities are employed to produce various product lines. Thus, many different products may pass through some or all of a manufacturer's machines on their way to completion. Facilities are not restricted to machines or equipment alone. Often common facilities refer to creative or design functions, to selling and administrative services, to warehousing, and, in some cases, to special critical materials which are necessary in the manufacture of products.

Not all products make the same use of facility time per dollar of revenue or oop cost. In accepting or agreeing to meet competitive prices, manufacturers must give consideration to the degree to which such orders will use up available facility time in a period. Otherwise the manufacturer might find that, in order to obtain a desired level of contribution, he is short of the necessary facility capacity. In setting target prices, a seller may aim for a specified amount of return for each facility-hour he commits; this can be done effectively even though the PV of a given order may be below what he otherwise thought was acceptable.

Order Contribution versus Facility Time

The acceptance or pricing of orders solely on their gross order contribution or PV may ultimately load facilities to the point where there are not enough facility-hours available in which to obtain the target annual contribution. For example, the following two orders have the same revenue, contribution, and PV, but there the resemblance ends:

Item	Order A	Order B
Selling price....................	$5,000	$5,000
oop cost.......................	4,000	4,000
Contribution.................	$1,000	$1,000
PV............................	.20	.20
Facility-hours required..........	10	50
Contribution per hour..........	$100	$20

If management depends solely on contribution pricing and aims at a minimum PV of .20, it will randomly book orders like A and B without evaluating contribution per hour. If by accident the bookings trend toward the Order B type, then, irrespective of PV, this company can easily require five times the amount of facility time to produce the same contribution than the Order A type of work demands. In this event, and if the company does not have enough capacity to meet these requirements, the overall annual contribution will be considerably reduced. For example, if the company can only accommodate one-half the capacity that the Order B type of work requires, the annual contribution generated will not exceed one-half of what Order A type of work could generate. Under these circumstances, the PV could still remain at .20!

PV, Contribution, and Facility Time

As we see, the PV does not provide a clue to the loading of facility time, as the following example demonstrates:

Item	Order C	Order D
Selling price....................	$10,000	$10,000
oop cost.......................	8,000	6,000
Contribution.................	$ 2,000	$ 4,000
PV............................	.20	.40
Facility-hours required..........	20	50
Contributions per hour..........	$100	$80

Even though Order D contributes twice as much as Order C to the "pool," it requires a disproportionately greater number of hours to generate. Where facility-hours are in very short supply, measurement of *contribution per hour* becomes an important pricing yardstick. For example, if both Orders C and D are competing for the same slot of facility time in a period where facilities are almost fully loaded, it is possible that

Order C should be taken in preference to Order D, even though the latter can provide twice the order contribution. If, under these conditions, there are only 20 hours available, management would want to book Order C and get the $2,000 of contribution. If management mistakenly took Order D and was permitted to produce only a portion of its order, the contribution generated would be 20 × $80, or $1,600. If 50 facility-hours were available, management might want to book Order D and obtain the $4,000 of contribution. However, if management was allowed to take a portion of Order D, its best course of action would be to

EXHIBIT 12-1. CHRONOLOGICAL ORDER BOOKINGS

Inquiry no.	SP	Contri-bution	PV	Facility-hours required	CPH
4212	$15,000	$3,000	.20	100	$30
4213	8,000	3,000	.375	150	20
4214	9,000	3,000	.333	250	12
4215	12,000	3,000	.250	75	40
4216	7,000	1,500	.214	100	15
4217	10,000	2,500	.250	50	50
4218	3,000	800	.266	20	40
4219	11,000	3,500	.318	70	50
4220	6,000	1,500	.250	50	30
4221	13,000	4,500	.346	50	90

book all of Order C and 30 hours of Order D. The total contribution under those circumstances would be:

$$
\begin{array}{lll}
\text{Order C:} & \text{20 hours} \times \$100 & = \$2,000 \\
\text{Order D:} & \text{30 hours} \times \$80 & = \$2,400 \\
& \text{Total contribution} & = \$4,400
\end{array}
$$

Maximizing Profit at Full Capacity

Exhibit 12-1 is an inquiry log of all orders which could have been booked by a company in a month. The capacity of its facility on which all these orders may be run is 500 hours per month. Where a company does not state its contribution in terms of its short-run limiting factor (in this case, facility time), it would book orders chronologically, providing the PV was acceptable. Thus, the company would book the first three orders (4212, 4213, 4214), obtain the contribution of $9,000 and fully load its facility to 500 hours. However, a *selective selling* of facility time would result in the following bookings and gross contribution:

Inquiry no.	Contribution	Facility-hours required
4212	$ 3,000	100
4215	3,000	75
4216	1,500	100
4217	2,500	50
4219	3,500	70
4220	1,500	50
4221	4,500	50
Total	$19,500	495

Selecting orders based on facility time, when such time is limited, results in this case in a contribution of $19,500 for a facility loading of 495 hours. This figure is more than double the performance of the previous practice of booking orders randomly.

Selling the Scarce Factor

When the volume of products that can be sold exceeds the productive capacity of the firm, the largest contribution (and therefore the greatest profit) results from using the capacity to produce those products and orders which generate the greatest contribution per facility-hour. As was shown previously, this method doesn't necessarily mean selling those products which have the greatest PV. This is especially true when various products made on the same equipment have to be processed at different rates of speed. Usually the most common factors which cause bottlenecks or limit output are machines and equipment, but other factors in the company may be considered scarce. In some companies, insufficiency of highly skilled labor may be a limiting factor; the most profitable course of action in this case would be to use the available skilled labor to produce only those items which generate the highest contribution per hour of skilled labor. In other companies where critical materials are in short supply, management may elect to produce only those items which generate the highest contribution per unit of material.

In most industrial applications, the scarce factor is usually *time*. To illustrate the point a little differently, suppose an individual was permitted to enter a room in which the following coins were lying on the floor:

$1,000 in pennies
700 in nickels
400 in dimes
300 in quarters
200 in half dollars
100 in silver dollars

He was told that he could keep whatever coins he could pick up *in one minute.* Obviously the man would first pick up the silver dollar pieces, irrespective of the fact there were fewer of these coins than of any other. He knows that he would wind up with more money at the end of the minute pocketing the silver dollars than if he started to pick up the pennies just because there was ten times the amount of money in pennies. Of course, if he was permitted unlimited time, he would pick up all the coins. But when time is the limiting or scarce factor, he necessarily will pick up those coins which maximize his money intake per unit of time.

This example is analogous to the comparison between gross order contribution and contribution per facility-hour. The largest amount of contribution is the pennies, which can be obtained only if there is enough time. The smallest amount of contribution is the silver dollars, but more value from these can be obtained per unit of time.

Pricing the Scarce Factor

In manufacturing, it is not unusual for different products to be fabricated on the same machine, each requiring a different cycle time and carrying a different rate of contribution. Under these circumstances, the unit contribution of the product must be adjusted by the speed of output. Suppose there are two products in the line which run through the same machine:

Item	Product X	Product Y
Unit selling price............................	$3.30	$5.80
Unit oop cost...............................	2.80	4.90
Unit contribution........................	$0.50	$0.90
PV...	.151	.155
Output speed per hour......................	100	50
Contribution per machine-hour..............	$50	$45

If it is desired to increase the price of Product Y so it provides the same contribution per hour of Product X, we must calculate as follows:

Product Y

Desired contribution per hour............ $50
Output speed per hour.................. 50

Desired unit contribution ($50/50).............. $1.00
Unit oop cost................................. 4.90
   New unit selling price........................ $5.90

Pricing to equalize contribution per hour is also demonstrated in the following example:

Item	Order E	Order F
Selling price............................	$19,000	$16,000
oop cost................................	15,000	13,000
Gross order contribution................	$ 4,000	$ 3,000
PV......................................	.21	.19
Facility-hours required..................	100	60
Contribution per facility-hour (CFH).......	$40	$50

Order E has the higher revenue, gross contribution, and PV, but since the facility-hours it requires are disportionately higher, the contribution return it obtains per hour is not as attractive as that provided by Order F. In effect, Order E, compared to Order F, requires a ⅔ increase in facility time to obtain a ⅓-increase in contribution money. This fact is not important if excess capacity is available and if the bookings of large order commitments will not displace more profitable work in the future. When no consideration is given to the selective selling of facility time, the annual contribution level attained is usually less than what could be obtained, as it represents the unplanned cumulative total of all orders booked solely on a gross contribution or PV basis.

The contribution per facility-hour (CFH) approach can be very effective in target pricing in establishing an acceptable and consistent return for the use of facilities. For example, management might wish to accept Order E, provided it yielded the same return per hour as Order F. Using the basic pricing formula

$$\text{Selling price} = \text{contribution} + \text{oop costs}$$

and amending it to

$$\text{Selling price} = (\text{facility-hours} \times \text{CFH}) + \text{oop costs}$$

and using the CFH of Order F, we produce the target selling price of Order E

$$\text{Selling price of Order E} = (100 \times \$50) + \$15,000$$
$$= \$20,000$$

Exhibit 12-2 shows four situations; in each, management has to choose between two orders when capacity is scarce. In Situation 1, the pair of orders has equal revenue, equal contributions, and equal PVs. In Situation 2, revenue is equal but contributions and PVs are different. In Situations 3 and 4, revenues are unequal and the larger contribution

EXHIBIT 12-2. PRICING TO EQUALIZE CPH

Item	Situation 1		Situation 2		Situation 3		Situation 4	
	A	B	C	D	E	F	G	H
Selling price................	$10,000	$10,000	$5,000	$5,000	$18,000	$12,000	$ 8,000	$7,000
oop costs..................	8,000	8,000	4,000	4,500	16,000	9,000	7,000	5,000
Contribution...............	$ 2,000	$ 2,000	$1,000	$ 500	$ 2,000	$ 3,000	$ 1,000	$2,000
PV........................	.20	.20	.20	.10	.111	.25	.125	.286
Facility-hours required.....	50	20	30	10	25	60	40	20
CPH......................	$40	$100	$33.33	$50	$80	$50	$25	$100
Selling price of order of lower CPH to equal selling price of order of higher CPH:								
(1) Hours required........	50		30			60	40	
(2) Higher CPH..........	$100		$50			$80	$100	
(3) (1) × (2)............	$ 5,000		$1,500			$ 4,800	$ 4,000	
(4) Plus oop costs........	8,000		4,000			9,000	7,000	
(5) Equalizing SP........	$13,000		$5,500			$13,800	$11,000	

147

and PV are produced from the smaller revenue. For each situation, the facility-hours required sometimes follows the contribution and at other times is opposite to the contribution. Regardless of these variables, the order to take when capacity is limited is the one with the greater CPH.

The bottom of this exhibit shows the target selling price for the order with the smaller CPH, which would equate its CPH with the other order in each situation.

Pricing for Specific CPH

Even when a company is not operating at its maxiumum capacity, the use of the CPH approach is valuable in establishing price consistency to customers, for setting up minimum target prices for product lines made on the facilities, for targeting into certain end markets or territories, etc. Some examples of various applications follow:

1. *CPH on list prices:* As was mentioned in an earlier chapter, published list prices in an industry cannot possibly make the same contribution to all competing companies which are able to produce the work. Even for one specific type of product, there can be great variations from quantity to quantity, from company to company. That is, each company can find the lot quantity range which is best for it because of the published quantity differential prices, which do not make the same contribution to each company at each given lot quantity. In most of these cases, it is helpful to the company to find out the extent to which taking uneconomical quantities can deprive it of needed facility time. This can have the effect of displacing facility time for more profitable work in the future.

In the following case, a company measures the effect on CPH which list prices have on three different lot quantities for the same item:

Item	Lot size		
	500	5,000	50,000
Unit selling price.............	$10.00	$9.00	$7.00
Unit oop cost.................	8.00	7.75	6.75
Unit contribution............	$2.00	$1.25	$0.25
Lot contribution.............	$1,000	$6,250	$12,500
Facility-hours required........	20	200	2,000
CPH.........................	$50	$31.25	$6.25

While the seller may wish to take orders in the 5,000-lot quantity, he certainly should think twice about committing his equipment to lots which provide a return barely more than a tenth of what the 500 lot generates. Strategically, taking the 50,000-lot quantity is equivalent to loading up one machine for one year on a one-shift basis. Devoting this time to work which produces a $50 CPH would provide annually for that machine a contribution of $100,000 instead of $12,500. Perhaps the answer, if capacity was not fully loaded, would be to take the 5000-lot order which would provide $6,250 of contribution. This solution would leave a balance of 1,800 hours open for other work which could produce more than a CPH of $6.25.

A price for the 50,000 lot which would give the same CPH as the 500 lot and which would recognize the savings in oop costs due to higher quantity runs would be

$$
\begin{aligned}
\text{Selling price} &= \frac{(\text{facility-hours} \times \text{CPH}) + \text{oop costs}}{\text{lot quantity}} \\
&= \frac{(2,000 \times \$50) + (50,000 \times \$6.75)}{50,000} \\
&= \frac{\$437,500}{50,000} \\
&= \$8.75
\end{aligned}
$$

2. CPH pricing of quantity differentials: A suggested way of pricing inquiries for various quantities of the same product is to maintain a uniform CPH. This method still recognizes the customer's valid expectation that he receive lower prices for higher quantities because of the spread of certain constant preparatory and transaction costs. But this method does not dilute the target or desired CPH required by seller.

In the following example, a manufacturer has quoted a unit price of $9.25 for a 400-piece lot and is now being asked to quote a unit price for an 800-piece lot. He first prepares his estimate on the 400 pieces and then by employing the same CPH, he obtains the unit price for the 800-piece lot:

For 400 pieces

Material cost at $3.25 each.................	$1,300
Equipment setup cost (12 hours)...........	67
Machine running cost (111 hours).........	416
Total oop cost........................	$1,783
Revenue at $9.25 unit selling price........	3,700
Order contribution....................	$1,917
CPH ($1,917/123 hours).................	$15.58

To make sure that he prices the 800-piece lot quantity to get the same return for the usage of his equipment and recognizes the valid price break which the customer expects, the manufacturer applies the hourly contribution of $15.58 to the larger quantity as follows:

For 800 pieces

Desired CPH..	$15.58
Facility-hours required for 800 pieces (12 + 2 × 111)........	234
Order contribution required: (234 × $15.58)...............	$3,645.72
oop costs: Material at $3.25 each......................	2,600.00
Conversion ($67 + 2 × $416).................	899.00
Selling price of 800 pieces............................	$7,144.72
Unit selling price....................................	$8.93

This price does not ensure that the customer will find it attractive nor does it say that the manufacturer couldn't get more. The price of $8.93 is simply the price which will provide the same CPH as the 400-piece quantity—considering the more effective use of preparatory costs.

EXHIBIT 12-3. ANALYSIS OF PRODUCT PROFITABILITY AND FACILITY USAGE

Product line B	Total	Products		
		1	2	3
Sales revenue.............	$3,000,000	$500,000	$1,000,000	$1,500,000
oop costs...............	1,300,000	200,000	350,000	750,000
Gross contribution.......	$1,700,000	$300,000	$ 650,000	$ 750,000
Operating PV.............	.567	.60	.65	.50
Specific programmed period costs................	1,200,000			
Adjusted contribution...	$ 500,000			
Adjusted annual PV.......	.167			
Machine-hours...........	17,800	3,600	8,000	6,200
CPH....................	$95.51	$83.33	$81.25	$120.97

3. *CPH product profitability and pricing:* Exhibit 12-3 is an analysis of the three products which comprise Product line B of Exhibit 11-2 of the previous chapter. Notice that the analysis for each product is not carried below the operating PV point. Since the specific programmed period costs cover such expenses as advertising, research and development, etc., and are incurred for the entire line in total, no defensible allocation among products is possible. The operating PV shows the speed at which each product's sales dollar generates contribution money, but, again, it is no indication of how each product loads the manufacturing facilities.

Product 2 with the highest PV provides the lowest CPH, and Product 3 with the lowest PV yields the highest CPH. Management's job in pricing is to sell its facilities selectively to provide a realistic balance between the loading of its facilities and its needs for contribution.

The characteristic CPH shown for each product may be used in pricing of future orders if management wishes to adopt each CPH as a target. For example, suppose management is quoting on an order for Product 2 as follows:

$$\text{Estimated oop cost of order} \dots\dots\dots\dots \$3,653$$
$$\text{Estimated facility-hours required} \dots\dots\dots 15.3$$

then

$$\text{Selling price} = (\text{facility-hours} \times \text{CPH}) + \text{oop costs}$$
$$= (15.3 \times \$81.25) + \$3,653$$
$$= \$4,896.13$$

This pricing technique is most valuable when management has limited knowledge of the "going" or competitive market price. If these data were available, it could measure what contribution would be provided by meeting that price and then could reduce the information to CPH and make its decision. For example, if the "going" price on the above order was found to be $3,956, the contribution generated by meeting that price would be $3,956 — $3,653, or $303. For 15.3 facility-hours, this figure would provide a CPH of only $19.80, far below the average annual CPH for Product 2. However, where competitive prices are not known, management may use the product's average annual CPH as a yardstick for pricing.

CPH Pricing of Profit Segments

As was stated earlier, profit is not a single-faceted function of time or revenue. Every business consists of a number of profit segments, each of which has a characteristic PV and each of which contributes to the "pool" from which profits ultimately develop. Thus, profit is multifaceted and is the result of the pooled contributions flowing in from all profit segments. Profit segments constitute management's knowledge of its sources of profits and are developed by segregating total sales by customers, customer classes, geographic territories, end-market users, salesmen, machines, products and product lines, channels of distribution, etc.

Once this sorting has been accomplished, a characteristic PV will emerge. In much the same way, it may be possible to identify and rank profit segments in terms of their characteristic use of facility time. This information is valuable for specific pricing for a particular profit segment.

Exhibit 12-4 shows a sorting of the activity of Product 2 into three profit segments: territories, end markets, and customers. Territorially, the analysis shows that both Cleveland and Dallas provide the highest CPH in spite of the fact that Cleveland has the lowest PV and Dallas the highest. Because of the relative closeness of the variations in CPH, it would be difficult to consider that territories actually had a characteristic CPH for the selling company.

EXHIBIT 12-4. PROFIT SEGMENTS AND CPH PRICING

Item	Total product 2	Territories			
		New York	Chicago	Cleveland	Dallas
Sales revenue.........	$1,000,000	$200,000	$300,000	$300,000	$200,000
oop costs............	350,000	75,000	100,000	125,000	50,000
Gross contribution..	$ 650,000	$125,000	$200,000	$175,000	$150,000
Operating PV........	.65	.625	.667	.584	.75
Machine-hours.......	8,000	1,600	2,500	2,100	1,800
CPH................	$81.25	$78.12	$80.00	$83.33	$83.33

Item	Total product 2	End markets			
		Food	Hardware	Cosmetics	Gift
Sales revenue.........	$1,000,000	$250,000	$100,000	$350,000	$300,000
oop costs..........	350,000	75,000	50,000	75,000	150,000
Gross contribution..	$ 650,000	$175,000	$ 50,000	275,000	$150,000
Operating PV........	.65	.70	.50	.786	.50
Machine-hours.......	8,000	2,000	700	2,800	2,500
CPH................	$81.25	$87.50	$71.43	$98.21	$60.00

However, in the end-market sorting, there are some definite CPH patterns which are generated as a function of the end-user specifics. Sales to the cosmetic market provide the highest PV as well as the highest CPH, indicating that up to this point new sales to the cosmetic market can be targeted around the $100 CPH level with possibly some slight modification for territory. However, data by market are a composite contribution of all customers within that market and, therefore, it would be helpful to know the rankings of customers. These rankings are shown in Exhibit 12-5, which is a sorting of all customers sold in the cosmetic market.

While the dynamics of the PV variations are not great among the six customers, the large variances in the CPHs indicate the characteristic mix purchased. Even though this analysis still applies to a portion of

EXHIBIT 12-5. CPH BY CUSTOMERS IN SPECIFIC END MARKET

Item	Total Cosmetic Market	Customers in Cosmetic Market					
		A	B	C	D	E	F
Revenue	$350,000	$40,000	$45,000	$50,000	$65,000	$70,000	$80,000
oop costs	75,000	6,000	12,000	10,000	12,000	18,000	17,000
Contribution	$275,000	$34,000	$33,000	$40,000	$53,000	$52,000	$63,000
PV	.786	.85	.733	.80	.816	.743	.787
Machine-hours	2,800	400	360	580	580	350	580
CPH	$98.21	$85	$91.67	$68.96	$100	$148.57	$108.62
PV ranking		1	6	3	2	5	4
CPH ranking		5	4	6	3	1	2

Produce 2's annual sales, it must be remembered that there are variations in mix within the same product. This variation is in terms of order quantity, size and shape of product, etc. So while Customer A has the highest PV ranking, he ranks fifth in CPH. And while Customer E ranks highest in CPH, he ranks fifth in PV. As discussed in the pricing criteria chapter (Chapter 14), when facilities are limited, Customer E's work is to be preferred.

Once such an analysis is prepared, management is in an enviable position to direct its pricing and profit-planning. When quoting an order to Customer E which might constitute a slight modification of Product 2 and for which no market price can be determined, management's safest course of action is to price based on a target CPH which is related to experiences with that customer. Thus, if an inquiry for price from Customer E (for a similar product as Product 2) has an estimated oop cost of $2,317 and the machine time for processing is estimated to be 10 hours, the target price is

$$\text{Selling price} = (\text{facility-hours} \times \text{CPH}) + \text{oop costs}$$
$$= (10 \times \$148.57) + \$2,317$$
$$= \$3,802.70$$

Pricing the Annual Profit Plan with CPH

Once management has sufficient data on CPH from all its profit segments, it can use this information in designing a future profit plan. Unlike the classic variety of profit-planning which starts with unqualified sales revenue, this type of planning targets a desired CPH by product lines, products, or other profit segments and then builds the supporting costs up to the planned revenue as the last step. A profit plan which starts with revenue dollars unqualified by the specifics of contribution and facility usages is shallow and usually becomes a fact only by accident.

Exhibit 12-6 shows how a profit plan is built up by using desired CPH and expected hours of usages. Actually the revenue figures need never be inserted in such a plan unless the company wishes to show the PV by product lines, which are purposely omitted in this exhibit. This profit plan is built on the product-line segment, although if the costs are more closely identified with another segment, such as end market or classes of customers, then that segment should be the basis for the plan.

In forward pricing, management can then develop variances from the plan based on booked-to-target CPH and can continually police the loading of hours together with the build-up of cumulative contribution so that necessary remedial action can be taken while the facts are alive rather than after they have become ancient history.

Expanding the Contribution Log

Exhibit 12-7 shows the Contribution Log originally shown in Exhibit 11-10 and now expanded to include information about the use of facilities. This supplementary information is used to guide management in the build-up of contribution as it relates to the loading of facilities. When

EXHIBIT 12-6. PRICING THE PROFIT PLAN WITH CPH.

Item	Product lines				Total
	1	2	3	4	
Target CPH...............	$30	$40	$65	$95	
Planned activity hours.......	6,000	12,000	2,000	4,000	
Planned contribution........	$180,000	$ 480,000	$130,000	$380,000	$1,170,000
Budgeted programmed period costs....................	$ 80,000	$ 170,000	$100,000	$120,000	470,000
Budgeted common period costs	....	....	....	....	200,000
Target pretax profit..........	....	....	....	....	$ 500,000
Budgeted oop costs..........	$420,000	$ 520,000	$270,000	$120,000	$1,330,000
Planned sales revenue........	$600,000	$1,000,000	$400,000	$500,000	$2,500,000

Summary

Planned sales revenue...............................		$2,500,000
Budgeted oop costs.......................	$1,330,000	
Budgeted programmed costs...............	470,000	
Budgeted common costs..................	200,000	
Total costs.......................................		$2,000,000
Target pretax Profit...............................		$ 500,000

more than one facility is involved in the production of orders, the facility used is the major facility or the one within which bottlenecks are likely to occur to cause the primary scarce factor to emerge. As in Exhibit 11-10, the Contribution Log may be designed for the entire company, for major product lines, or for major facilities irrespective of product lines. The criterion for segmenting a Contribution Log is generally the degree to which oop costs and major facility-hours can be identified with the chronological transactions.

A Refinement of the Technique

Many converting businesses will find it worthwhile to employ the CPH method, but with a refinement which will make the information more meaningful. Before we explain this method, a rationale of the contribution approach is in order: When we speak of the contribution money in an order, we mean the difference between the selling price and the oop costs specifically identified with that order or product. However, with what do we identify the contribution money itself? Until now we have identified contribution money only with the revenue. Obviously, though, the contribution is also identified with the oop costs but only on a total oop cost basis. If the total oop costs are divided between oop material costs and oop conversion costs, how much of the total order contribution is attributable to each?

EXHIBIT 12-7. EXPANDED CONTRIBUTION LOG

Month of ___May___   Product Line ___A-22___

Order No.	Booked SP	Total oop	Contribution	PV	Cumulative Contribution	Facility Utilization		
						Hours	CFH	Cumulative CFH
6706	$ 9,120	$6,170	$2,950	.324	$ 2,950	52	$57	$57
6707	5,150	3,080	2,070	.402	5,020	29	71	62
6708	4,970	4,230	740	.149	5,760	24	31	55
6709	10,510	5,860	4,650	.442	10,410	48	97	68
6748	8,740	8,020	720	.082	79,818	31	23	49
6749	11,360	7,115	4,245	.374	84,063	93	46	48.50
6750	7,390	6,112	1,278	.173	85,341	38	34	48

Summary
Total sales booked in month	=	$404,873
Booked contribution	=	$ 85,341
Average PV	=	.21
Less: Prorated period expenses*	=	55,000
Pricing profit	=	$ 30,341
Facility-hours committed	=	1,780
Average CFH	=	$48

   * Annual fixed period expenses = $660,000.

In a converting business, the primary function of that enterprise is to convert raw materials and to add conversion skills and the associated capital invested in those converting facilities which increase the values of these materials to the ultimate purchaser. A converting enterprise is in the business to sell the time of its facilities profitably and not to act as a jobber of someone else's raw materials. Therefore, the removal of the material cost figure from CPH calculations can provide a more sensible comparison among orders, products, customers, end markets, etc.

Exhibit 12-8 shows the regular as well as the refined CPH approach applied to three orders, all of which have the same revenue, oop costs, and contribution. In the regular CPH method, Order B provides the highest CPH because that order turns over mostly materials rather than conversion costs and therefore uses a minimum amount of facility time. The fact that it has such a high CPH is more a function of the market price level than it is the low conversion cost. In other words, the company is in business to generate as much contribution as possible in a period, within the limits of its invested capital and therefore it doesn't necessarily follow that a lot of facility usage produces contribution. Because of the little facility time and the large contribution generated by Order B, Order B may be said to be well priced. Order C, which requires

EXHIBIT 12-8. THE "CONVERTED" CPH

Method	Orders		
	A	B	C
1. Regular method:			
Selling price	$2,000	$2,000	$2,000
oop costs:			
Materials	400	1,200	800
Conversion	1,200	400	800
Total	$1,600	$1,600	$1,600
Contribution	$400	$400	$400
Facility-hours required	20	8	10
CPH	$20	$50	$40
Ratio: $\dfrac{\text{contribution}}{\text{conversion}}$	0.33	1.00	0.50
2. Refined method:			
Conversion contribution	$800	$1,600	$1,200
Refined CPH	$40	$200	$120

25 per cent more facility-hours, incurs twice the conversion cost and shows a CPH of only 20 per cent less than Order B. This CPH comparison of $50 versus $40 is not sufficient to show the positive price effect of Order B, shown by the ratios of contribution to conversion costs. Order B obtains a dollar's worth of contribution for every dollar of conversion cost, three times what Order A gets and twice what Order C obtains. This ratio is obtained separately from the consideration of hours. However, when differences in facility-hours are included together with differences in the contribution-conversion ratios, the results are CPH figures based on conversion-contribution alone without the presence of materials cost.

The $200 CPH of Order B gives effect to both the facility-hours required as well as to the contribution money generated per dollar of conversion cost and also bears a more sensible comparison to the CPHs of the other two orders.

Limitations of the Method

This chapter has discussed the use and loading of facilities caused by the booking of order contributions. As such, it provided one more dimension in the task of analyzing the equity of a price. Gross order contribution and usage of facilities solely give the impact that pricing has on the operating structure, but they do not evaluate or consider the capital employed in orders. Thus, while management may be satisfied with the selling price of an order based on the level of contribution it provides and the reasonableness of the amount of facility time committed to it, it really cannot evaluate how equitable that price is until it knows the specific capital invested in that order and what return on that capital the selling price will provide.

Once these data are available, management can police its pricing in terms of the target return on capital as well as providing a target price when no market price is in existence. The latter use of the technique is especially valuable when the selling company is an innovator. Such is the subject of the next chapter.

CHAPTER 13

Pricing for Return on Product Investment

The ultimate objective of a business enterprise is to earn a satisfactory rate of return on all the capital employed in its operations. This objective is the basic reason for the formation of the enterprise and for the confidence which creditors place in its management. Stated goals of a return on sales or a profit on total costs are not significant until the profit has been compared with the amount of capital resources that is required to generate it. While profit on sales may be considered high, it cannot be accepted as satisfactory unless the profit percentage on total capital is adequate and at least higher than what management could get if it invested its capital in another enterprise.

A 10 per cent profit on sales of $2 million may not be considered an adequate return for the use of capital if $10 million is the total capital employed in the company. The pretax return on capital in this case would be 2 per cent, far less than what could be earned by the capital if it was invested in a blue-chip security or even in a savings account.

The pricing function should consider the desired rate of return on capital as it applies to how products make different uses of the various elements of capital employed in their manufacture. Especially in market-product situations where no competitive price level exists, the target return approach will at least state a more rational price than one which is set by the classic "10 per cent markup." Its use provides a more logical ranking of prices among the various product lines of the company. This approach is also helpful when introducing a brand-new product.

Composition of Capital

Capital can refer to one or several elements on the balance sheet. First we must understand some basic facts. Total capital is composed of current assets, also known as current, circulating, or variable capital, and fixed assets or fixed capital. Total capital employed is comprised of vari-

159

able plus fixed capital. These are the assets which keep the enterprise moving and show the present location of the borrowed and owned capital. On the other side of the balance sheet are the liabilities and net worth amounts. Liabilities are borrowed capital; the net worth shows the owned capital or the equity of the stockholders, or where the money came from that financed the fixed and variable (assets) capital. The capital equation can be expressed in several ways:

1. Total capital employed = liabilities + net worth
2. Variable + fixed capital = borrowed capital + owned capital
3. Total assets = creditors' interests + stockholders' interests
4. Where the money is now = where the money came from

Fixed capital represents the value of the machinery, equipment, land, and other capital facilities which are used in producing the company's output. These do not vary with changes in output but decrease by time period to the extent of the depreciation. Variable capital, on the other hand, represents cash in bank, accounts receivable, and the inventories involved in the operation of the business. These elements do change with changes in output, hence the term "variable capital."

Selecting the Capital Base

Many refer to return-on-capital pricing as *return on investment*. We avoid this term because it implies that profits are being compared with equity instead of with total capital employed. The return on equity is primarily a guide for investors and serves more as a measure of financial management than of operating management. The ultimate measure of management accomplishment requires the total capital base. Investment in the broad sense must include all assets used in making and selling a product, irrespective of whether they were provided by equity or by debt. A company should use a dollar of credit just as effectively as it uses a dollar from a stockholder. A business which borrows money should increase its operating profit from the use of these funds to get a return which is greater than the cost of interest on this borrowed money.

The use of equity as the base for return-on-capital measurements can be quite deceptive. For example, let's assume the following operating and financial data in a company at the end of an operating period:

Pretax profit............	$100,000
Total liabilities..........	$600,000
Net worth..............	$400,000
Return on equity........	25%

During the next period, the quality of financial management weakens; profits are also somewhat off:

Pretax profit............ $80,000
Total liabilities.......... $800,000
Net worth.............. $200,000
Return on equity........ 40%

In this weakening of financial management during the second period, there was no change in the total capital employed—it remained at $1 million, but the mix of the capital sources changed and became more highly leveraged. That is, a smaller amount of equity now controlled the total assets. Relating profit to equity could mislead some into believing that this second period showed an improvement. But whereas the return on equity showed an increase from 25 to 40 per cent, the return-on-total-capital approach showed a decrease from a return on 10 per cent to a return of 8 per cent in the second period.[*]

Investment in Product

In Chapter 5 we showed some of the traditional approaches in pricing for return on capital. In Method A, the desired rate of return was translated into a markup on annual total cost and then applied to various products. No consideration was given to variable and fixed portions of total capital and the flat markup did not recognize the investment differences in the various cost elements of the product. In Method B, the fixed and variable capital portions were separately treated but the markup was developed in one total irrespective of how each product's investment level differed.

A plan which recognizes the different fixed and variable capital elements which different products may have is shown below. While this plan apportions capital more equitably among products or product lines, it is still not free from deficiencies.

Markup on Different Product Costs for Separate Returns on Variable and Fixed Capital

Where it is possible to clearly apportion fixed capital to different products or product lines, the return-on-capital pricing approach can be used to provide prices which, while differing in markups on the products' costs, can still provide the same return on capital. In order to provide such differing markups, we must know the specific characteristics of each

---

[*] For additional financial ratios see Spencer A. Tucker, *Successful Managerial Control by Ratio-analysis*, McGraw-Hill Book Company, New York, 1961.

products' employment of variable capital. The following shows the different cost and capital data for two product lines:

Item	Product line A	Product line B
Unit cost..........................	$20	$30
Annual quantity..................	30,000	40,000
Annual cost.......................	$600,000	$1,200,000
Variable capital employed (VCE):		
Cash...........................	5% of sales	4% of sales
Receivables....................	18% of sales	11% of sales
Inventories....................	38% of sales	24% of sales
Total VCE..................	61% of sales	39% of sales
Specific fixed capital employed:		
Fixed assets....................	$650,000	$750,000
Desired return on total capital employed, %..................	20	20

1. To obtain the selling price which will provide a 20 per cent return on the total capital employed in Product line A, we start with the basic profit formula

$$\text{Revenue} = \text{profit} + \text{cost}$$

and amending it to read

$$\text{Revenue} = \text{return on total capital employed} + \text{cost}$$

and then substituting the known values, letting x equal the unknown revenue, we have

$$x = \text{desired return (fixed capital} + \text{variable capital)} + \text{cost}$$
$$x = .20(\$650,000 + 0.61x) + \$600,000$$
$$x = \$130,000 + 0.122x + \$600,000$$
$$0.878x = \$730,000$$
$$x = \frac{\$730,000}{0.878}$$
$$\text{Revenue} = \$831,435$$
$$\text{Price/unit} = \frac{\$831,435}{30,000}$$
$$= \$27.71$$
$$\text{Return on sales} = \frac{\$7.71}{\$27.71}$$
$$= 27.8\%$$
$$\text{Markup on cost} = \frac{\$7.71}{\$20.00}$$
$$= 38.5\%$$

Thus, the cost of products in Product line A would have to be marked up 38.5 per cent to arrive at a selling price which would provide a 20 per cent return on the specific elements of capital invested in it.

To prove this method:

$$
\begin{aligned}
\text{Variable capital employed (61\% × \$831,435)} &\ldots\ldots\ldots \$\ \ 507,175 \\
\text{Fixed capital employed} &\ldots\ldots\ldots\ldots\ldots\ldots\ldots\quad 650,000 \\
\hline
\text{Total capital employed} &\ldots\ldots\ldots\ldots\ldots\ldots\ldots \$1,157,175 \\
\text{Desired return (20\% × \$1,157,175)} &\ldots\ldots\ldots \$231,435 \\
\text{Return} = \text{revenue} - \text{cost} & \\
= \$831,435 - \$600,000 & \\
= \$231,435 &
\end{aligned}
$$

2. To obtain the selling price which will provide a 20 per cent return on the total capital employed in Product line B, we use the same basic formula and make the appropriate substitutions:

$$
\begin{aligned}
x &= \text{desired return (fixed capital} + \text{variable capital)} \\
&\quad + \text{cost} \\
x &= .20(\$750,000 + 0.39x) + \$1,200,000 \\
x &= \$150,000 + 0.078x + \$1,200,000 \\
0.922x &= \$1,350,000 \\
\text{Revenue} &= \$1,464,208 \\
\text{Price/unit} &= \$36.61 \\
\text{Return on sales} &= 18.1\% \\
\text{Markup on cost} &= 22\%
\end{aligned}
$$

Comparing these data on both product lines:

Item	Product line A	Product line B
Unit cost	$20.00	$30.00
Unit selling price	$27.71	$36.61
Return on sales, %	27.8	18.1
Markup on cost, %	38.5	22
Return on capital, %	20	20

The basic fallacies of this method are:

1. While distinctions are made for the specific capital employed in each product line, all products within each line are assumed to carry capital investments in the same proportions.

2. It is assumed that the mix of the two products, used as the basis of obtaining balance sheet data will remain as indicated, ignoring the market acceptance of the respective formularized prices.

3. No distinction is made in cost for materials and conversion.

4. *The markup was based on total or fully allocated costs,* introducing the distortion that may possibly result from a shift in the activities of

the various facilities within each line. No oop cost was developed and thus contributions resulting from a price lower than target cannot be measured.

Pricing for Contribution and Capital Return

Measuring gross contributions of booked orders for "go or no-go" pricing decisions are vital for planning profits in a period; cumulative contributions compared to period fixed expenses show the profit trend. Relating gross order contributions to facility time is valuable for showing the effectiveness with which the converting facilities are being marketed. However, neither of these methods gives consideration to what return on capital is being provided by the selected prices. So while we may have an order for $10,000 at a PV of .30 or a total order contribution of $3,000, we are also able to determine that the order would provide a CPH of $30 if it takes 100 facility-hours to produce. Questions to be answered are: Is the PV of .30 acceptable? Is the contribution of $3,000 enough? Does the CPH of $30 represent a fair return on the capital we have invested in the different cost elements of the order?

The ultimate goal in pricing is to establish a selling price for an order or product that returns an amount of contribution which produces a desired return on the specific capital invested in that order. Such a selling price is a *target selling price* representing both the seller's specific investment levels and his concept of what a fair return should be for him. Since this target is an expression of a specific figure and a desire for return, a target price is no guarantee of market acceptance—as is no other formula price. Just as the Contribution Log measures the cumulative period flow of contributions against period expenses, the target selling price provides a yardstick which tells management the trend of its pricing in relation to its desired return on capital.

The decision involving meeting a competitive price integrates total order contribution, contribution per facility-hour, and the variance between the "going" price and the target price. Sound pricing involves a balancing among these three variables. When the company innovates a new product, or when no competitive price bench marks exist for a product, pricing for return on capital is the starting point. Then the strategic elements, such as skimming, penetrating, prestige, and demand pricing factors, are added.

As we have seen so far, pricing for return on capital is practiced in industry on the basis of "full" costs. This method is just as misleading as cost-plus pricing. The procedure simply shifts the base from the return on sales to the return on annual capital employed and applies it to orders on an average basis.

The following method shows how prices are established by separately marking up each major element of identifiable product cost in direct relation to its specific capital investment elements without the distorting effects of facility-hours or "full" cost.

Pricing for Investment in Product

Basically, manufactured products contain two major cost elements which can be separated and identified with capital investments. One is raw materials cost; the other is all other direct manufacturing cost. Raw materials cost generally represents a lower investment from the standpoint of risk than the operating facilities do. Raw materials turn over faster, are more liquid, and can be discontinued in low periods. Operating facilities costs consist of elements which cannot be readily adjusted to varying sales levels and represent a long-term investment which cannot be easily discontinued. This is why a dollar's worth of raw materials investment is not expected to earn as much return as a dollar's worth of operating facilities capital.

For example, here are two products, both of which have the *same out-of-pocket cost:*

Item	Product A	Product B
Materials cost...............	$10	$ 5
oop manufacturing cost.......	2	7
Same total oop cost........	$12	$12

Since both of these products have the same oop cost, each will provide the same contribution if both are priced the same. If Product A is priced at $14, the contribution will be $2. But pricing Product B at $14 because the oop cost is the same is tantamount to agreeing that the capital invested in Product B is the same as that invested in Product A. Even though Product B contains one-half the materials cost of A, the capital invested in Product B would generally be higher (in most industries) because it has three and one-half times the amount of facility cost of Product A. Discounting the competitive and market factors for the moment, if both products were priced the same because of their identical oop costs, Product B would be underpriced if Product A's price was right or Product A would be overpriced if Product B's price was right.

When orders are priced so that no distinction is made for the different capital elements, customers are being asked to pay very dearly for a manufacturing or converting service simply because the materials happen to be a high percentage of total oop cost (as in Product A), or customers are being given partial gifts of the manufacturing service when materials happen to comprise a lower portion of total oop costs (as in Product B). When no capital distinction is made, orders loaded with mostly material cost are difficult to sell, while highly converted products requiring a small portion of material move fast but provide a smaller return.

Even though the contribution concept must be maintained because of the necessity for knowing the cost floor and for measuring the benefits available if a price must be booked below the target price, the specific cost elements which comprise the oop cost must be separated and marked up individually to reflect the investment differences; that is, materials should be marked up separately from conversion cost and (generally) at a lower rate. If the selling prices are to reflect these differences in capital investment, Product B will be priced above Product A.

Developing the Markup Factors

Essential for developing separate markups is the projection of an annual profit plan. The profit plan is the foundation of operation in the progressive company and is designed to reflect the planned product mix, the PVs of each that are expected to develop, and the facility times for each. While such a plan may be adjusted during the operating year, a first rough projection sets the business ship on the right general heading and gives the markup tools to work with.

1. First is the statement of capital and desired return:

```
Total capital employed.........  $2,000,000
Desired return (pretax).........  15%
Target earnings................  $   300,000
Annual fixed expenses..........      400,000
       Target contribution*.........  $   700,000
```

2. Second, the operating plan:

```
Planned sales.............................  $3,000,000
oop costs:
   Direct materials..............  $1,200,000
   Direct manufacturing..........   1,100,000
       Total...............................  $2,300,000
       Contribution...........................      700,000
       Less: fixed expenses......................      400,000
       Planned profit.........................  $   300,000
```

To develop the markup on material cost and the markup on manufacturing or conversion cost, we proceed as follows:

* In multiproduct progressive profit management, the gross revenue approach to budgeting has given way to the use of budgeting annual contribution.

A. *Materials cost markup:* This markup is obtained by dividing the desired percentage return by the number of turns per year of capital employed for material. Assuming this turnover is three times, the markup on material would be 15 per cent/3, or 5 per cent. Thus, as each turn of material provides a 5 per cent return, the three turns during the year will provide the desired 15 per cent return.

Thus, the selling price of annual material cost would be $1,200,000 × 1.05 per cent, or $1,260,000.

B. *Manufacturing or conversion cost markup:* If the selling price of annual material cost is subtracted from the planned revenue, the difference would be the selling price of every other cost involved in the planned sales. This figure would be $3,000,000 — $1,260,000, or $1,740,000. In order to avoid the compounding distortion of marking up "full" costs and to provide a basis for marking up only the identifiable portion of order or product cost (the oop costs), the selling price of every other cost but materials is divided by the direct manufacturing or conversion cost to get the markup factor, as follows:

$$\frac{\$3,000,000 - \$1,260,000}{\$1,100,000} \text{ or } 158.2\%$$

Thus, the selling price of direct manufacturing cost would be $1,100,000 × 1.582, or $1,740,000. Note that the "selling price of everything else," the *markup margin* of $1,740,000 covers the fixed expenses on an annual basis, even though the oop cost is the only cost being marked up.

Marking up both elements by their respective factors would produce the planned sales level, viz, $1,260,000 + $1,740,000 = $3,000,000.

Pricing With Separate Markups

Applying these separate markups to the previous two Products A and B produces these selling prices:

PRODUCT A

Cost element	Cost	× Markup	= Selling price of cost element
Materials	$10.00	1.05	$10.50
oop manufacturing	2.00	1.582	3.16
Selling price to provide a 15% return................			$13.66

PRODUCT B

Cost element	Cost	× Markup	= Selling price of cost element
Materials	$ 5.00	1.05	$ 5.25
oop manufacturing	7.00	1.582	11.07
Selling price to provide a 15% return................			$16.32

These are the target selling prices which will provide for the seller a 15 per cent return on the specific elements of capital invested in each product in spite of the fact that at these target selling prices, the contribution levels and PVs of each are considerably different viz.:

Product A		Product B	
Target selling price.............	$13.66	Target selling price.............	$16.32
oop cost.....................	12.00	oop cost.....................	12.00
Contribution................	$ 1.66	Contribution................	$ 4.32
PV..........................	.122	PV..........................	.265

Clearly, Product A earns the same return on total capital employed as B at a lower contribution and PV.

PV and CPH Not Controlling

Generating a high PV, a large amount of order contribution, and/or a large CPH is no guarantee that the selling prices producing those data are near, at, or above the target selling prices, because these factors of measurement do not include the consideration of the measurement of the desired return on the two major elements of capital invested in the order. Thus, it is possible to achieve the desired return on capital from a selling price which has a low PV, contribution, and CPH. Conversely, it is possible for a high PV, contribution, and/or CPH from an order to provide considerably below the return on capital.

In the first instance, a low-PV priced order of, say, .06 can provide the desired return on capital if the converting costs are low and production equipment used on an order is at a minimum. In this event, the return would be generated by the presence of a large amount of material cost, in which case the .06 PV is acceptable. In the second instance, an order priced to provide a PV of .43 can provide less than the desired return on capital if the converting costs and usages of production equipment are large but the price is not proportionately high enough for the amount of conversion applied.

In the example of Product A and Product B, the contribution of Product B is more than two and one-half times that of Product A, and yet with the same oop costs, both products generate exactly the same return on the capital employed in their respective products. Let's say that Product B will be sold for $1 less than its target price, or $15.32. Its contribution is thus $3.32, exactly twice the contribution of A and yet, in spite of this greater contribution, Product B's selling price will not be earning as high a return on capital as Product A. This difference is obviously caused by the fact that in the Product A type of transaction, mostly material is being turned over, whereas Product B is the type of work which enables the manufacturer to merchandise effectively his manufacturing facilities, which is the fundamental function in his business.

Exhibit 13-1 shows the typical relationships among PV, contribution, and target selling prices that could exist for one converter-manufacturing company. The markup factors used are 10 per cent on materials cost and 50 per cent on oop conversion cost, or 1.10 and 1.50. Compare the first two orders, both selling at close to the same price and producing similar PVs and contribution amount. Order no. 6214 has been booked at a price below the target price and therefore is not providing the desired return on the capital employed in its order, whereas Order no.

EXHIBIT 13-1. COMPARISON OF CONTRIBUTIONS, PV, AND TARGET PRICES

Order no.	Booked SP	Established costs		Total oop costs	Contribution	PV	Target SP*	Revenue variance
		Material	Conversion					
6214	$ 4,300	$ 600	$2,500	$3,100	$1,200	.279	$4,410	$(110)
6471	4,400	2,000	1,200	3,200	1,200	.273	4,000	400
7318	7,860	1,300	4,100	5,400	2,460	.313	7,580	280
7340	7,800	5,000	1,800	6,800	1,000	.128	8,200	(400)
7460	10,400	8,600	600	9,200	1,200	.115	10,360	40
7753	7,520	300	4,840	5,140	2,380	.317	7,590	(70)
7872	6,840	†	4,560	4,560	2,280	.334	6,840	
Net pricing variance.								$ 140

* Markup on materials cost is 10 per cent, or 1.10; markup on oop conversion cost is 50 per cent, or 1.50, to obtain desired return.

† Job on which customer supplied material.

6471 has been booked at a price higher than its respective target price, thereby yielding a return above the desired return. While, from a contribution-flow standpoint, both orders are adequate, it seems obvious that the price of Order no. 6214 has not rewarded the company sufficiently for the large investment it has made in that order. This could be the result of the "going" market price which the company has decided to meet. On the other hand, the large contribution from Order no. 6471 can be the result of the market price, which, of course, does not necessarily have any direct relationship to the invested capital characteristics of this one particular seller.

In comparing the next two orders, we find a reverse effect. Here, Order no. 7318 is priced to recognize (and the market has permitted this to happen) the higher investment costs in the converting facilities. Order no. 7340, even though it turns over far more material than conversion cost, is booked at a price which fails to get the full return on this low-investment order.

In Order no. 7460 we have a PV which is far below Order no. 7340, but whose selling price provides a return above target and far above 7340. Even at a PV of .115, Order no. 7460 obtains more than the desired return on capital. Obviously, the answer is the fact that the return is being generated principally on the turnover of materials in which the company has a far lower investment than it has in its converting facilities.

Order no. 7753 has the highest PV logged to date, but still, because of the high proportion of conversion cost which is not fully reflected in the booked price, it has a small unfavorable variance to the target price. Order no. 7872 is typical in some converting operations in instances where the customer supplied the raw material to be converted. Since the company has no investment in the material portion of the order (all handling as well as converting being included in the oop cost), the markup applies only to the conversion cost.

At the end of a period, usually one month or one week, a net variance is shown which reports on the quality of the pricing function in the period and is not an indication of the results of operating. The results of operating are produced from the actual contribution figure less the period fixed expenses. The actual contribution figure is obtained by applying the different variances (performance, spending, material price and usage, etc.) to the estimated contribution amounts shown on this log. The revenue variance maintained on a cumulative basis shows the extent to which, and the likelihood of, the company's attaining its desired return on capital.

Testing the Pricing Structure

Competitive or market prices which exist for a given line of products represent simply the average of the prices of the supplying community of manufacturers. Often companies supply a given product line to the market in a wide range of prices due mainly to differences in size, capacity, function, etc. In order to make a comparison of the product line target prices to show the consistency which market prices bear to the actual manufacturing service performed by a manufacturer, it is desireable to convert the elements of product costs in ratios between material, conversion costs, and selling prices. This technique removes the differences in size, capacity, function, etc., and compares the various products in terms of the relative values stated by the foregoing ratios.

Such an analysis is shown in Exhibit 13-2. In this company five products in a given product line are separated into their material cost, oop conversion cost, target selling price, and competitive selling price. The five products chosen are those which the company believes are priced

EXHIBIT 13-2. TARGET-TO-COMPETITIVE PRICING ANALYSIS

Product	Material cost	oop conversion cost	Target SP*	Competitive SP	Ratios†		
					TS/ML	CC/ML	CS/ML
A	$18.00	$12.00	$40.50	$48.60	2.25	0.67	2.70
B	4.00	16.00	33.00	30.20	8.25	4.00	7.55
C	7.00	7.00	19.95	22.00	2.85	1.00	3.14
D	10.00	4.00	17.70	22.00	1.77	0.40	2.20
E	15.00	37.50	83.25	78.00	5.55	2.50	5.20

* Based on 1.05 markup on material and 1.80 markup on oop conversion cost.
† RATIOS:
    TS/ML = ratio of target selling price to materials cost.
    CC/ML = ratio of conversion cost to materials cost.
    CS/ML = ratio of competitive selling price to materials cost.

competitively. Three ratios are developed for each: target selling price to materials cost, conversion cost to materials cost, and competitive selling price to materials cost.

A chart showing the relationship between competitive and target prices for each of the five products is shown in Exhibit 13-3. The line

EXHIBIT 13-3. TARGET-TO-COMPETITIVE PRICING GUIDE

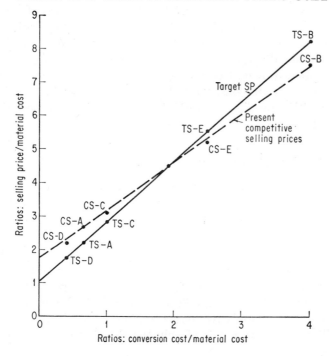

172

representing the target selling prices passes exactly through each target price for each product because of the consistent markup factors used. However, the line labeled competitive selling prices is drawn as closely as possible to the individual product's competitive selling prices to show the most accurate trend. From this line, it becomes possible to predict within reasonable limits what the competitive selling prices will be for the company's other products. The ratios are not guides to the level of selling prices, but rather predictive factors, which when multiplied by the material and oop conversion costs of a particular product will develop a price close to competitive levels. For example, if Product K has a target selling price-to-material cost ratio of 5.55, a conversion cost-to-cost ratio of 2.50, a material cost of $5 and an oop conversion cost of $12.50, a close competitive selling price would probably be 5.20 × $5, or $26.

The specific inference which can be drawn from this analysis is that the company's target selling price will probably be close to competitive levels when any one of its products has a conversion cost-to-materials ratio of 1.92 for a target selling price-to-materials ratio of 4.5. For the range of the conversion cost-to-material cost ratio up to 1.92, products which have a target selling price-to-materials cost ratio of less than 4.5 can be sold for more than their target selling price. For products above this 1.92-4.5 point, the company's target selling prices are uncompetitive.

Besides analyzing a company's pricing structure in terms of the market prices, this technique is valuable for testing the internal operating quality of the company and the way in which specific capital is employed. If wide unfavorable divergencies exist between target selling prices and competitive prices for most of a company's products, investigation could show that oop costs are consistently higher than competition and/or that too much capital (usually variable) is being used to support the company's output.

Expanding the Contribution Log

Exhibit 13-4 shows the Contribution Log, originally shown in Exhibit 11-10 and expanded for CPH in Exhibit 12-6, now further enlarged to show the target prices and the revenue variances between booked and target selling prices. In this form, the Contribution Log is the basis of management information reports regarding the quality of pricing and the results obtained in a period. Refinements can be made to this log which can improve its usefulness. For example, management can police the extent to which its pricing will attain the desired return by adding a column showing cumulative target selling prices versus cumulative booked selling prices or a pair of columns showing estimated contribu

EXHIBIT 13-4. EXPANDED CONTRIBUTION LOG: FINAL FORM

Month of ___ May ___   Product Line ___ A-22

Order No.	Booked SP	Total oop	Contribution	PV	Cumulative Contribution	Facility Utilization			Target SP	Revenue Variance
						Hours	CFH	Cumulative CFH		
6706	$ 9,120	$6,170	$2,950	.324	$ 2,950	52	$57.00	$57.00	$ 8,940	$ 180
6707	5,150	3,080	2,070	.402	5,020	29	71.00	62.00	5,970	(820)
6708	4,970	4,230	740	.149	5,760	24	31.00	55.00	6,210	(1,240)
6709	10,510	5,860	4,650	.442	10,410	48	97.00	68.00	8,190	2,320
6748	8,740	8,020	720	.082	79,818	31	23.00	49.00	8,960	(220)
6749	11,360	7,115	4,245	.374	84,063	93	46.00	48.50	10,980	(380)
6750	7,390	6,112	1,278	.173	85,341	38	34.00	48.00	7,210	180

Summary

Total sales booked in month	=	$404,873
Target sales revenue	=	416,942
Revenue variance	=	(12,069)
Booked contribution	=	$ 85,341
Average PV	=	.21
Less: Prorated period expenses*	=	55,000
Pricing profit	=	$ 30,341
Facility-hours committed	=	1,780
Average CFH	=	$48

* Annual fixed period expenses = $660,000.

173

tion versus target contribution. Of course, the basis for this evaluation is estimated oop costs, so while these data show the direction and speed of the profit trend, the final profit results cannot be obtained until the aforementioned variances are applied to the estimated oop costs.

As shown, the log is established for a particular product line. However, in some businesses, it may be more practical to set up the log for the entire company. In other cases, the log may be subdivided into individual products or individual facilities. The criteria for making these various segregations is *identifiability*. That is, if products are traceable to specific facilities and to specific elements of capital, characteristic CPHs, rates of return on capital, and revenue variances can be determined.

Notice that in all the logs shown so far, the fixed expenses are treated as a period amount and no attempt is made to show the recovery of fixed expenses which have been allocated to and carried by each order. If this were done, then, solely because of the accident of specific order bookings, the recovered fixed expenses allocated to each could be either above or below the prorated period amount. This variance could deceive management that its profit trend is either better or worse than it actually is, and the measurement of the results of pricing would be distorted by under- and over-absorption of fixed costs.

Developing Separate Markups for Individual Product Lines

Earlier in this chapter, we presented a method for developing separate markups for pricing materials and conversion costs. This method was developed from annual capital data as well as from annual operating data and was applied to all products manufactured by the company. When it is possible to identify portions of variable and fixed capital directly with individual product lines, separate materials and conversion markups can be developed for each product line. This method is useful when large variances exist in the use of various elements of capital for different product lines. One line of a company's products may be made entirely by hand, requiring little or no capital equipment. Another may be made entirely on expensive, fully automated facilities. Other distinctions between product lines are their characteristically different amounts of the elements of variable capital used. For example, one product may require large inventories and have fast collection characteristics. Another may be just the reverse. By reflecting the differences in these elements in a pricing plan, a set of specific markups can be developed for a product line which targets prices in conformity with the company's overall desire for a uniform return.

EXHIBIT 13-5. DEVELOPING SEPARATE MARKUPS FOR SPECIFIC PRODUCT LINE: PRODUCT WITH HIGH MATERIAL CONTENT

Cost and capital	Total	Applicable to:	
		Material markup	Conversion markup
Planned costs:			
oop: Material..........................	$300	$300	0
Conversion.........................	100	0	$100
Total oop costs....................	$400	$300	$100
Fixed: Selling..........................	40	0	40
Administration....................	20	0	20
R and D.........................	30	0	30
Total fixed costs.................	$ 90	$ 0	$ 90
Total costs...............................	$490	$300	$190
Planned capital:			
Variable:			
Inventory: Raw materials...............	$ 80	$ 80	$ 0
In process..................	40	30	10
Finished....................	30	20	10
Total inventory...........	$150	$130	$ 20
Accounts receivable....................	100	40	60
Fixed:			
Fixed assets..........................	40	0	40
Total investment.........................	$290	$170	$120
Desired return, %.........................	20	20	20
Target earnings............................	$ 58	$ 34	$ 24
Planned sales revenue....................	$548	$334	$214

1. Material markup $= \dfrac{\text{SP of material}}{\text{material cost}}$

$= \dfrac{\$334}{\$300}$

$= 1.11$

2. Conversion markup $= \dfrac{\text{SP of conversion}}{\text{oop conversion cost}}$

$= \dfrac{\$214}{100}$

$= 2.14$

Exhibits 13-5 and 13-6 show how separate markups are developed for two different product lines, each of which targets prices for a 20 per cent return on total capital employed. Exhibit 13-5 is a markup plan for a product with a high material content. We assume that there is nothing distinctive about raw material about to be converted; therefore,

Exhibit 13-6. Developing Separate Markups for Specific Product Line: Product with High Conversion Content

Cost and capital	Total	Applicable to:	
		Material markup	Conversion markup
Planned costs:			
oop: Material..........................	$100	$100	0
Conversion.........................	300	0	$300
Total oop costs....................	$400	$100	$300
Fixed: Selling...........................	50	0	50
Administration....................	30	0	30
R and D........................	40	0	40
Total fixed costs.................	$120	$ 0	$120
Total costs..............................	$520	$100	$420
Planned capital:			
Variable:			
Inventory: Raw materials...............	$ 30	$ 30	$ 0
In process..................	60	10	50
Finished....................	90	20	70
Total inventory...........	$180	$ 60	$120
Accounts receivable....................	190	30	160
Fixed:			
Fixed assets..........................	210	0	210
Total investment.........................	$580	$ 90	$490
Desired return.............................	20%	20%	20%
Target earnings............................	$116	$ 18	$ 98
Planned sales revenue......................	$636	$118	$518

$$\text{1. Material markup} = \frac{\text{SP of material}}{\text{material cost}}$$
$$= \frac{\$118}{\$100}$$
$$= 1.18$$
$$\text{2. Conversion markup} = \frac{\text{SP of conversion}}{\text{oop conversion cost}}$$
$$= \frac{\$518}{\$300}$$
$$= 1.73$$

we have attributed all of the fixed costs to the major function of the enterprise: conversion. The same is true of the way fixed capital is applied. The main characteristic of the product manifests itself in the employment of variable capital. Here the nature of the product shows that a fairly high level of raw materials inventory must be carried, which

EXHIBIT 13-7. BASIC DATA FOR TARGET CPH PRICING GUIDE

Data	Capacity			
	55%	70%	85%	100%
Fixed capital required.....	$ 800,000	$1,000,000	$1,000,000	$1,000,000
Variable capital required...	300,000	600,000	900,000	1,200,000
Total capital employed..	$1,100,000	$1,600,000	$1,900,000	$2,200,000
Target return on capital = 15%..................	$ 165,000	$ 240,000	$ 285,000	$ 330,000
Period fixed expenses......	150,000	180,000	180,000	180,000
Target contribution at 15% return..................	$ 315,000	$ 420,000	$ 465,000	$ 510,000
Facility-hours.............	8,000	11,000	13,000	15,000
Contribution per facility-hour at 15% return.....	$39.37	$38.18	$35.77	$34.00

NOTE: See Exhibit 13-8 for pricing guide showing contribution per facility-hour required for returns on capital between 1 and 15 per cent.

EXHIBIT 13-8. PRODUCT PRICING GUIDE

To earn return on capital of, %	Contribution required per facility-hour			
	55% capacity	70% capacity	85% capacity	100% capacity
15	$39.37	$38.18	$35.77	$34.00
14	38.00	36.73	34.31	32.53
13	36.63	35.27	32.85	31.07
12	35.25	33.82	31.38	29.60
11	33.87	32.36	29.93	28.13
10	32.50	30.91	28.46	26.67
9	31.13	29.45	27.00	25.20
8	29.75	28.00	25.55	23.73
7	28.37	26.55	24.08	22.27
6	27.00	25.09	22.62	20.80
5	25.63	23.64	21.15	19.33
4	24.25	22.19	19.69	17.87
3	22.88	20.74	18.22	16.40
2	21.50	19.29	16.76	14.94
1	20.13	17.84	15.29	13.47
Break-even.......	18.75	16.39	13.83	12.01

NOTE: See Exhibit 13-7 for derivative data for this pricing guide.

increases the variable capital investment for that product. Conversely, finished goods move rather quickly and collections are made promptly, making those variable capital elements lower in investment cost. For this particular product, a 1.11 markup on materials and a 2.14 markup on oop conversion costs are required to obtain the target 20 per cent return on the specific capital invested.

In Exhibit 13-6, a markup plan is shown for a different product which has a high conversion cost content compared to the previous one. Besides the specific identification of the fixed costs associated with the product, the variable capital characteristics of the product are shown to be different from those of the previous product. Here, for the same oop costs of $400 for both products, the variable capital is $250 for the first one and $370 for the second. Adding the fixed capital shows that the total investment for the second product is twice that of the first, thereby requiring double the target earnings at the same rate of return. For this product, a 1.18 markup on materials and a 1.73 markup on oop conversion costs are required to obtain the target 20 per cent return on the specific capital invested. Notice how different these markups are from the first product, and yet they are used within the same company.

The aim of this and the previous markup plan is to provide a way of distinguishing between the investment levels in a product's material and conversion cost to avoid overpricing items of high material content and/or underpricing products of low material content.

Integrating Capital Return with CPH

In some client companies we have installed pricing guides for different products which show what contribution per facility-hour is required at different levels of capacity to earn various rates of return on capital. This information is useful in helping management decide on the equity of a price at different conditions of machine utilization. Such a pricing guide for one product is shown in Exhibit 13-8. The derivative data for this pricing guide are shown in Exhibit 13-7.

CHAPTER 14 *Pricing Criteria for Specific Situations*

The pricer must be aware of all the pricing factors mentioned so far in this book if he expects to arrive at a balanced decision. The final pricing decision must be the result of balancing the objective internal factors and at the same time meshing them in with the subjective external factors. This approach is applicable to companies operating normally in reasonably-priced markets.

In many cases, however, companies cannot or do not operate under idealized conditions. In some firms, one product line may operate ideally, and another, which perhaps serves an entirely different market, may suffer from excess capacity, insufficient capacity, characteristically low PVs, and/or operations perennially below break-even. Then, again, as market conditions change, as dictated by shifting demand and competitive upheavals, a product line once thought ideal may gradually become a candidate for special pricing treatment.

Thus, pricing management may have to temporize the balanced approach recommended (either temporarily or permanently) by emphasizing one or more specific pricing methods to the exclusion of the others. Such manipulation requires a knowledge of the behavior and impact of each of these factors. Most importantly, the pricer's eye must never be removed from the competitive and market arena as he makes these special decisions.

As we have seen, there are several kinds of pricing measurements or methods available to the pricer. These data are generated when an order has been booked:

1. The PV
2. The contribution dollars
3. The contribution dollars per unit of the scarce factor, i.e., contribution per machine-hour, contribution per direct labor hour, etc.

179

4. The target selling price (or the target PV, target contribution, target contribution per unit of the scarce factor)

Normally, the pricing decision must come from a balancing of these variables, meshed in with the strategy of dealing with the forces of competition and market demand. This chapter outlines an approach to use in coping with certain times and conditions when management should use one of the pricing factors more than others. However, this suggested emphasis is to be used with care and only in special situations, as a total balancing of each facet of the pricing doctrine must be a prime objectives if long-term profitable pricing results are to be effective.

In the following discussion of special conditions, reference is made to work taken and work rejected by the company in order to illustrate the effects of the various pricing methods. In all these examples, the selling prices of the mistakenly rejected business refer to "going" market prices.

Which Method to Use When Activity Is Below Break-even

When a company is operating at a low level of capacity—or at some level below its break-even point—management's task in pricing is to fill the "pool of contributions" as quickly as it can so that it can reach and pass the break-even point. Only after this level has been exceeded are profits generated. Obviously, management must book work which provides *positive contribution dollars* and should not be concerned with targeting on the other three factors. Since this practice has the danger of booking work having only marginal contribution levels *it should be tempered with competitive and market considerations*. If such marginally priced work is below competitive levels, strategic judgment is required to ensure that such prices will not provoke competitive retaliation and will not spoil the general market levels. However, if such practice produces prices which are in line with competitive levels, management has everything to gain by the booking of such work because it provides contribution money which would not otherwise be available.

Pricing for any other factor in this instance can deprive the company of contribution money—perhaps when it needs it the most.

1. *The effect of PV pricing:* The following company divides its output among eight product lines, all of which are made on joint or common facilities. Its activity is considerably below capacity and the break-even point. Its annual fixed expenses are $600,000. It has established a policy that no work will be priced below a PV of .19. Following this practice, it books certain work for its product lines and turns down others:

Work taken	Product lines				Annual total
	A	Q	C	P	
Revenue............	$300,000	$400,000	$500,000	$600,000	$1,800,000
oop costs............	240,000	320,000	400,000	450,000	1,410,000
Contribution.........	$ 60,000	$ 80,000	$100,000	$150,000	$ 390,000
PV (higher than .19)..	.20	.20	.20	.25	.217
Less: fixed expenses...	....	....	....	....	$600,000
Operating loss......	....	....	....	....	$(210,000)
Work turned down	**B**	**R**	**D**	**S**	**Total**
Revenue............	$400,000	$500,000	$600,000	$700,000	$2,200,000
oop costs............	350,000	430,000	530,000	600,000	1,910,000
Contribution.........	$ 50,000	$ 70,000	$ 70,000	$100,000	$ 290,000
PV (less than .19)....	.125	.140	.117	.145	.132

While the work booked certainly provides an average PV above management's minimum goal of .19, it produces an annual contribution of $390,000 which fails to recover fixed expenses by $210,000. Therefore, clinging to a PV goal under these circumstances is academic, especially in view of the fact that management has a large reserve amount of facility time which can be devoted to other work, even though the PV of that work is not up to its PV .19 goal.

The work turned down shows varying PVs, all below the PV .19 level. The PVs are those produced if the company would meet competitive price levels; therefore, no undercutting of prices is involved. Imposing the company's minimum PV goals on these four product lines would have resulted in unsalable prices. The company has more than sufficient capacity to take this work in addition to what it had already booked. Therefore, had it taken this work, it would have required no more fixed expenses, it would not have disturbed market price levels, and it would have provided an additional $290,000 in contribution money. In that event, the operating results would have shown:

Revenue........................	$4,000,000
Contribution....................	$ 680,000
Less: fixed expenses.............	600,000
Operating profit..............	$ 80,000

2. *The effect of facility-hour pricing:* If this company used instead a target contribution per facility-hour in deciding which work to take

and which to turn down, the results could also be poor. In this same
company, management sets a minimum of $50 of contribution per ma-
chine-hour as a return for the use of its facilities:

Work taken	Product lines				Annual total
	B	A	R	Q	
Contribution..........	$50,000	$60,000	$70,000	$80,000	$ 260,000
Machine-hours........	800	700	850	1,500	
Contribution per hour, (above $50).........	$62.50	$85.71	$82.35	$53.33	
Less: fixed expenses....	....	....	....	....	600,000
Operating loss.......	....	....	....	....	$(340,000)
Work turned down	D	S	C	P	Total
Contribution..........	$70,000	$100,000	$100,000	$150,000	$420,000
Machine-hours........	1,900	2,300	3,600	4,000	
Contribution per hour, (below $50).........	$36.84	$43.48	$27.77	$37.50	

Again, as in the PV-pricing example, the work booked does produce
a contribution per hour (CPH) above the required $50 minimum, but
in this instance it causes a shift in product mix because of the specifics
of the machine usages required and produces a contribution of only
$260,000, which fails to recover fixed expenses by $340,000. Obviously,
as different product lines use facilities differently, the product mix will
shift, causing a corresponding change in contribution.

Pricing on the facility-hour basis, under conditions of excess capacity
availability, will victimize the management in accordance with the non-
significant relationships between gross order contribution and facility-
hours needed. Had it booked all the work available to it, without requiring a minimum CPH, it would have gained the additional contribution
shown under "Work turned down," and profits would have been $80,000
as in the previous case. Here, again, the prices on the work turned down
are at competitive levels as shown in the previous example.

3. *The effect of return on capital pricing:* If a company marks up
its material and conversion costs separately in order to obtain its desired
rate of return on the capital employed in each, it produces a price which
is based on its specific employment of capital and the return it desires.
The price in no way ensures that it will be attractive to buyers or will

be in line with competitive levels. In this same company, taking work which is priced above its target price is the procedure being followed, irrespective of the availability of a considerable amount of converting capacity:

Work taken	Product lines				Annual total
	R	D	S	A	
Booked revenue......	$500,000	$600,000	$700,000	$300,000	$2,100,000
Target prices........	$470,000	$550,000	$690,000	$300,000	$2,010,000
Contribution........	$ 70,000	$ 70,000	$100,000	$ 60,000	$ 300,000
Less: fixed expenses...	....	....	....	....	600,000
Operating loss......	....	....	....	....	$ (300,000)
Work turned down	**Q**	**B**	**C**	**P**	**Total**
Market prices.......	$400,000	$400,000	$500,000	$600,000	
Target prices........	$420,000	$460,000	$530,000	$510,000	
Contribution........	$ 80,000	$ 50,000	$100,000	$150,000	$ 380,000

Here, again, the booked work is sold above target prices and the product mix shifts accordingly. In this case, $300,000 in contribution money is generated, which still leaves a loss of $300,000. With excess capacity available in terms of equipment, skilled labor, ability to carry higher inventory loads, etc., management could have taken this rejected work, which would have provided an additional $380,000 in contribution and which would have produced an operating profit of $80,000.

Which Method to Use When Operating Near Maximum Capacity

When a company operates near or at its maximum capacity point, the pricer's task is to obtain a maximum amount of contribution per unit of the scarce factor. Generally, as was discussed in an earlier chapter, the scarce factor (or bottleneck factor) in manufacturing enterprises is usually the time of its manufacturing facilities. Nominally, we shall talk in terms of machine or equipment time, even though it is not always the scarce factor.

The principle underlying this concept is that if all machine time available generates a large amount of contribution per hour, the annual gross contribution will be a maximum. Orders which are selected solely because of their high PV, high gross contributions, or target prices do not consider the facility-hours required to generate these conditions and thus may result in ultimately committing to these orders more hours than available. If this overcapacity booking is backed down from the resulting contribution could be less than what would otherwise be generated.

Again, pricing for any other factor for this condition of maximum operating capacity could lower the company's profits, as shown by the following two alternative pricing methods:

1. *The effect of PV pricing:* The following company has eight product lines, all of which are processed on common or joint facilities. It normally is able to obtain enough work to keep all its machines busy full time and is unable to expand its capacity beyond this point without the acquisition of additional equipment. The company prices to obtain a minimum PV on all its work of .22. Its annual fixed expenses are $350,000:

Work taken	Product lines				Annual total
	1	2	3	4	
Revenue............	$350,000	$470,000	$520,000	$640,000	$1,980,000
oop costs...........	260,000	360,000	410,000	480,000	1,510,000
Contribution.........	$ 90,000	$110,000	$110,000	$160,000	$ 470,000
PV (above .22).......	.257	.234	.231	.250	.237
Facility-hours required	2,400	3,000	3,600	5,000	14,000 (maximum capital)
CFH...............	$37.50	$36.67	$30.51	$32.00	
Less: fixed expenses...	....	....	....	....	$350,000
Operating profit....	....	....	....	....	$120,000
Work turned down	5	6	7	8	Total
Revenue............	$480,000	$620,000	$760,000	$920,000	$2,780,000
oop costs...........	420,000	500,000	630,000	780,000	2,330,000
Contribution.........	$ 60,000	$120,000	$130,000	$140,000	$ 450,000
PV (below .22).......	.125	.194	.171	.152	.162
Facility-hours required	1,200	2,000	2,400	2,700	8,300
CFH...............	$50	$60	$54.17	$51.85	

Admittedly, the company satisfies its goal of obtaining more than a PV of .22 on all its booked work. This contribution came from four of its product lines and produced a contribution of $470,000 and a pretax profit of $120,000. In booking this work, it used up all its facility-hours at the maximum level of 14,000. However, the work that it turned down, while having PVs of less than .22, required an amount of facility-hours proportionately less than the lower PV. It is interesting to note that all the work it turned down required only 8,300 facility-hours but produced $20,000 less of contribution, or $450,000.

Since the company has a definite limit on facility-hours, it can select work based on its respective contributions per hour rather than on any other factor, with due consideration for market price levels:

Most profitable mix

Product line	Facility-hours required	Contribution	CFH	PV
Work originally rejected				
6	2,000	$120,000	$60.00	.194
7	2,400	130,000	$54.17	.171
8	2,700	140,000	$51.85	.152
5	1,200	60,000	$50.00	.125
Work originally accepted				
1	2,400	90,000	$37.50	.257
2	3,000	110,000	$36.67	.234

	13,700	$650,000
Less: fixed expenses........................		350,000
Operating profit........................		$300,000

Thus, if the company had booked work based on CFH rather than on PV, its contributions would have been $650,000 instead of $470,000 and profits would have been almost triple, or $350,000.

Using PV as the sole criterion, the company simply took whatever work was available to it as long as it was above a .22 PV, until it reached its maximum capacity point of 14,000 hours. While the total contribution level of what it booked per order was certainly greater than the work it turned down, this fact didn't mean that each slot of limited time contained a higher dollar *time contribution*. It should be realized also that this company could have booked work of a much higher PV than it did: if this work required a disproportionately higher amount of machine time to produce, even though all 14,000 machine-hours were filled, the profit results could have been below $120,000.

2. *The effect of return on capital pricing:* Using the target selling prices as the sole criterion without recognizing the usages of facilities in a maximum capacity operating situation can also deprive the company of profits. In this case, the same company uses the criterion of booking work only when it is priced at or above its target prices:

Work taken	Product lines				Annual total
	4	3	5	1	
Booked revenue......	$640,000	$520,000	$480,000	$350,000	$1,990,000
Target prices........	$630,000	$500,000	$450,000	$300,000	$1,880,000
Contribution........	$160,000	$110,000	$ 60,000	$ 90,000	$ 420,000
Facility-hours required	5,000	3,600	1,200	2,400	12,200
Less: fixed expenses...	....	....	....	....	350,000
Operating profit....	....	....	....	....	$70,000

Work turned down	2	6	7	8	Total
Market prices........	$470,000	$620,000	$760,000	$920,000	$2,770,000
Target prices........	$510,000	$670,000	$840,000	$990,000	$3,010,000
Contribution........	$110,000	$120,000	$130,000	$140,000	$500,000
Facility-hours required	3,000	2,000	2,400	2,700	10,100

The company, in this instance, turned down work simply because the market prices of that work were below that which the company established as its targets. Yet a simple inspection of the tabulation will show that had the company taken the work it turned down and rejected the work it booked, it would have generated an additional contribution of $80,000 and would have boosted profits to $150,000. The company could have accomplished this increase in profit with the use of 2,100 fewer facility-hours.

Which Method to Use in a Low-PV Business

Many manufacturing enterprises or specific product lines in a company are characterized by a high content of oop costs in the sales dollar and a consequent low PV. As we discussed earlier, a characteristic PV is contributed from two sources or a combination of both. The first factor is the natural high ratio in some businesses between oop costs and fixed costs. This ratio is true of hand-assembly industries where little use is made of capital equipment, and the element of fixed costs is low; a large percentage of total costs is the oop costs. The second factor is the market-contributed PV, in which the output is sold into markets where prices are relatively depressed.

Even here the earlier suggestions as to what method to use still apply: if such an effort is operating considerably below the capacity of its available pool of skilled labor, pricing for contribution will fill the pool faster than the use of the other methods. If the amount of business available exceeds the company's capacity, pricing the factor which limits the company's short-range output (labor in this case) will maximize contributions, i.e., contribution per productive labor hour.

However, regardless of which condition the company is in, a small change in the specific price of an order will have a dramatic effect on contribution in a typically low-PV business. For example, the following tabulation shows characteristic data for the five products of a low-PV manufacturing company:

Product	Usual SP	oop cost	Contribution	PV
A	$42	$38.98	$3.02	.072
B	37	34.48	2.52	.068
C	29	27.11	1.89	.065
D	27	25.05	1.95	.072
E	25	23.70	1.30	.052
Total....	$160		$10.68	.06675

From this tabulation, it is easy to see that a small change in the selling price (SP) will cause a large change in contribution and PV. To test the effect of price changes, we present the following schedule:

Increase in prices	Contribution increased to	Increase in contribution	Decrease in prices	Contribution decreased to
1% = $1.60	$12.28	15%	1%	$9.08
2 = 3.20	13.88	30	2	7.48
3 = 4.80	15.48	45	3	5.88
4 = 6.40	17.08	60	4	4.28
5 = 8.00	18.68	75	5	2.68
10 = 16.00	26.68	150	10	(5.32)

The sensitivity of a change in contribution to a change in selling prices is shown to be in the ratio of 15 to 1. That is, for every 1 per cent change in prices, the contributions are changed by 15 per cent. Another way to look at it is that for every 1 per cent that prices are increased, the speed with which contributions flow into the "pool" is increased 15 per cent. If the market is inelastic, that is, if small increases in price do not cause changes in volume, the seller runs no risk in shooting for higher prices. Even if the market has an elastic demand, the seller can estimate the probable drops in volume for an entire schedule of price increases. Then he can select the combination of volume and price which gives him the maximum contribution.

In the author's experience with client pricing engagements, he has seen a great deal of what may be termed "price rounding," the practice of rounding off a price calculation so that a neat, even number is quoted. This rounding off is poor customer psychology because the round number does not give the impression of a careful calculation. The customer may feel that the price was rounded *up* from a lower number and therefore he may believe that there is room for bargaining which the seller allowed for. Actually, the seller might have done the reverse and rounded *down*. Most important, though, in typically low-PV businesses every cent of price helps, as we have seen from the previous tabulation.

If a price calculation shows $27.36, don't round it off to $27. If you do this on all your work you may find that the speed of contributions is seriously reduced. Then, again, rounding it off to $28 in an elastic market may not produce enough volume to offset the volume drop. If your price on another item calculates to $48, consider changing it to $48.04 so that advantage may be taken of the careful-calculation psychology.

Many clients have believed that carrying "odd" numbers in pricing lengthened their transaction time in terms of invoicing and bookkeeping. While this might be true, the advantages to be gained from the smallest revenue increase in low-PV businesses usually make these cost factors dwindle to minor insignificance.

Which Method to Use in Companies Operating at Normal Capacity

In a company where the capacity exceeds the available business and the enterprise is operating above the break-even point, the measurement of operating performance is the ratio of the pretax profit generated to the total capital employed in the enterprise. The quantitive measure of this result is the net contribution remaining after all fixed expenses have been paid. However, pricing which aims simply at maximizing period contributions may involve high-volume selling of low-PV work, which would threaten the firm's working capital position because of the larger number of transactions and the greater short-term investments in labor and materials. High-volume selling of low-PV work for the sake of generating contributions could also bring the company to its limits of space, in terms of the greater warehousing required for raw and finished goods, as well as causing space and internal transportation difficulties for in-process work. In addition, an unselective drive for contributions may cause the company to reach the limits of its equipment capacity sooner than it ordinarily should. Strategically, of course, if prices are reduced solely for the purpose of attracting more volume, the reduced level could be below market and competitive price levels in which case the company cannot expect its competitors to remain passive.

1. *What factor to price for?:* When a cost estimate is placed on the pricer's desk, he is faced with deciding on the equity of a price. Should he aim for the highest PV, the greatest contribution dollars, the highest CPH, or the return-on-capital target selling price for the order? On a *period* basis, the goal is to maximize contributions because they determine ultimately the annual return on capital employed. But, order for order, maximizing contributions may not be the answer.

Because of the specific proportions between materials and conversion costs in a particular order, a high PV price does not necessarily yield the target return on capital. A selling price which provides the target return on capital may not result necessarily in a large amount of contribution. Similarly, a high CPH does not necessarily mean a high PV price.

Pricing of individual orders for high contribution dollars may be used providing the scarce factor is not involved, i.e., if the company is not operating near its maximum capacity point. However, this practice must be tempered with a knowledge of the build-up of machine loading, for as the loading increases, the strategy must shift emphasis to a measurement of CPH. In using contributions as the sole guide to pricing, consideration must be given to the variance between booked and target revenue to make sure that the company will come close to achieving its desired return on capital. Otherwise, the build-up of contributions will be achieved at the higher cost of working capital as the company gets involved more in greater activity in raw material turnover than in merchandising its converting facilities.

If the company expects that in the coming period it will be operating close to its maximum capacity point, the CPH tempering should start early in the year and pricing should be a balancing between gross order contributions and CPH so that facility time is not being overcommitted out of proportion to the build-up of contribution. If the company believes it will end the year with an excess of unused capacity, the emphasis should be placed on contribution dollars balanced against the turnover of raw material and conversion costs—variance between booked and target revenue.

Of course, it is possible to achieve an annual amount of contribution which appears to provide the annual target return on capital in comparison with the original profit plan. In the original profit plan, the two major ingredients of the total capital employed (TCE) were projected, viz., variable capital and fixed capital. At the time of the projection, the target contribution required was the desired percentage of the TCE plus the projected annual fixed expenses. However, if the company is operating below capacity and is booking work solely on a contribution basis without considering the target selling prices in each order transaction, it may generate a level equal to or above that of the original gross target contribution. But that really doesn't mean that it has achieved the target. If the attained contribution was of the low-PV variety, i.e., booked as a result of high selling prices in which individual order prices were far below target prices, the variable capital portion of the original TCE projection no longer applies and the actual or trending variable capital is greater than the original plan. This would make the actual TCE greater in amount, thereby requiring more gross annual contribution than originally stated. Thus, cumulative contribution must always be compared with the current TCE (usually the variable capital portion only) to evaluate pricing performance against target.

2. *Interplay of variables:* When a company does not expect to be limited during its operating year by capacity of its facilities, its goal should be the selective selling of work which produces the greatest amount of dollar contribution consistent with the use of variable capital. This goal will produce prices which will yield the annual return on capital or better because of the careful use of working capital and the smallest involvement in transaction costs.

Exhibit 14-1 shows the interplay of the various factors which may be used to guide pricing. From this tabulation, the quality of the pricing function can be evaluated. In the first four orders, A through D, the revenue, contribution, and PV are all the same. Yet, because of the specifics of facility usage and the proportions of materials and conversion costs, the target revenues are all different. While all four produce the same deposit of contribution into the "pool"—and this contribution is the one tangible result that determines the annual pretax profits—the four orders differ in quality of pricing. Orders A and C use 50 per cent more facility time than B and D. Order A, in addition, has a higher investment in its manufacturing costs than Order C because of its higher target price. Order C, while using 50 per cent more facility time, sells for $500 more than its target, indicating that its price obtains more than the target return on the specific capital invested in its costs. Orders B and D both use less facility time but, because of their respective cost ingredients, differ in obtaining their target price. Obviously, Order D is the best of the four because it obtains just as much contribution as the other three, uses fewer facility-hours, and provides a return on capital higher than target through its booked price.

In the second group of four orders, E through H, all are sold at the same revenue as the first four but at a higher dollar contribution and PV. The facility-hours correspond to those in the first group of four.

The same comments about the first four apply here, but now let's compare both groups. Even though the contributions, PV, and CPH are different from the first four orders, the target revenues and the revenue variances are the same. Thus, at no additional commitment in facility time, Group 2 provides a 50 per cent increase in contribution dollars at prices which have identical relationships with their target selling prices. Not only is Order H the best in its group, it is the best one in both groups.

EXHIBIT 14-1. INTERPLAY OF VARIABLES IN PRICING

Order	Booked SP	Contri- bution	PV	Facility- hours	CPH	Target SP	Revenue variance
Group 1							
A	$10,000	$2,000	.20	60	$ 33.33	$11,000	$(1,000)
B	10,000	2,000	.20	40	50.00	10,500	(500)
C	10,000	2,000	.20	60	33.33	9,500	500
D	10,000	2,000	.20	40	50.00	9,000	1,000
Group 2							
E	10,000	3,000	.30	60	50.00	11,000	(1,000)
F	10,000	3,000	.30	40	75.00	10,500	(500)
G	10,000	3,000	.30	60	50.00	9,500	500
H	10,000	3,000	.30	40	75.00	9,000	1,000
Group 3							
I	12,000	2,000	.167	50	40.00	13,000	(1,000)
J	12,000	2,000	.167	30	66.67	12,500	(500)
K	12,000	2,000	.167	50	40.00	11,500	500
L	12,000	2,000	.167	30	66.67	11,000	1,000
Group 4							
M	9,000	3,000	.333	50	60.00	10,000	(1,000)
N	9,000	3,000	.333	30	100.00	9,500	(500)
O	9,000	3,000	.333	50	60.00	8,500	500
P	9,000	3,000	.333	30	100.00	8,000	1,000

In the third group of orders, I through L, the contributions are all the same and equal to the dollar contributions booked by the first group. However, since this same contribution was generated on a higher level of prices, the PV is lower. Somewhat fewer facility-hours are used in this third group compared to the first group and so the CPHs are correspondingly higher. This fact, of course, does not change the speed of the build-up of the contribution pool. Interestingly enough, the variances from target prices are identical with those orders in the first group. If at the time the third group of orders was booked there was a trend towards full loading of facilities, pricing of the third group is of a higher quality than that of the first. However, if excess capacity is expected to be available, the quality of the pricing of the third group cannot be said to be as good as the first because of the greater booked revenue required to generate the same contribution, even though the revenue variances are the same.

In the fourth group of orders, M through P, the dollar contributions are the same as for the second group but the facility-hours correspond to the third group. This group represents the best pricing of all four groups because, in the fourth group, the largest amount of contribution is being provided from the smallest booked revenue and from the lowest use of facilities, with revenue variances similar to all previous groups. Order P would be considered the best priced of all sixteen orders.

An interorder comparison may be of interest. Which order is best, Order F or Order O? Both provide the same dollar contribution, but Order F, which obtains its contribution in fewer facility-hours, is priced below the target, whereas Order O, which requires more facility-hours, is priced above the target. Again, the target revenue is an individual company expression of invested capital and a personalized desired return on that capital, and it does not guarantee market acceptance. Thus, the CPH should be the next factor to evaluate if the contribution levels are equal. Taking Order F in preference to Order O doesn't disturb the pool and allows the company to obtain a return on additional facility-hours which are not committed to its manufacture. This point would certainly be the criterion if the company was approaching a maximum capacity point. The other point to consider is that the working capital levels are different. Order F has an oop cost of $7,000, and Order O, $6,000. This point works in favor of Order O if the working capital position of the company is not strong.

Successful pricing for companies operating at normal capacity involves a balancing of all factors previously mentioned and a shifting of emphasis among the factors as the trend changes during the operating year. As the reader can gather, pricing for any one factor to the exclusion of all others can lead from high-volume low-profit business to relatively inactive profitless operation.

Summary

Management does not necessarily adopt one set or combination of pricing criteria to the perpetual exclusion of others. Policing of internal and external factors and subsequent modification or adjustments of shifting economic conditions are often required.

Mechanical manipulation of pricing data is not the road to effective, profitable pricing. While those entrusted with submitting prices should be aware of each contributory factor, a total, all-embracing view of the company and its place in the competitive community must be constantly in sight.

The concepts and examples given in this chapter are presented to show the mechanics of approaching each condition, even though it is fully realized that the pricer does not always have the freedom of decision, action, and choice. Nor can he accurately predict the future, disregard past customer relationships, and be completely selective. Some managements will also abuse these methods, using the rationale of low activity, etc. The application of a sound pricing philosophy requires statesmanship consistently practiced.

Successful companies don't spoil the market; the failures do.

CHAPTER 15

Using the Results of Pricing

The performance which a company shows after a given period is the result of the performances which have occurred in all the company's activity areas. Not the least of these occurs in the pricing function and in the various evaluations and rankings of its profit segments. Unfortunately, when traditional data are used to report these performances, the result is a mixture of all contributing factors, making it impossible to separate data to determine the rankings of the profit contributors to find the real sources of profits. Often management is misled into acting contrary to the way it would have acted had objective information been available.

The purpose of this chapter is to suggest better approaches to the measurement of pricing results and to provide formats of management information to guide future pricing decisions.

Results of Pricing versus Results of Operating

The classical profit-and-loss operating statement shows (ostensibly) the profits which a company has earned in a past period. This profit result does not show the extent to which any one function or any one profit segment contributed to overall results. The bottom-line figure shows the averaging together of all factors and the net remainder. In controlling the pricing function, it is essential for management to see to what extent its pricing quality contributed to profit and to what degree its operating contributed. Obviously, if the pricing function performs well, it provides the company with a profit environment—a profit opportunity. This opportunity can be diluted by the operating function, enhanced, or carried through to final profit unchanged. That is, a company makes more or less profit by the admixture of pricing and operating performances: pricing can be lower than target and manufacturing performance can be above standard or vice versa—each can be present in varying degrees.

In the following estimate and price of an order, pricing quality and *estimated* operating costs are given:

Operation	Estimated production hours	oop MHR	oop conversion cost
107	80	$20	$1,600

Total oop conversion cost...............	$1,600
Direct materials cost....................	1,200
Freight out...........................	200
Total oop cost........................	$3,000
Booked selling price....................	4,000
Contribution.........................	$1,000
PV.................................	.25

Assuming that the price of $4,000 is considered excellent by the company, it must be understood that the $1,000 contribution shown is based on the anticipated performance of the 80 estimated production hours. If the production performance is poor and the actual hours taken are 120 (assuming good production time standards), then:

Estimated contribution........................	$1,000
Unfavorable hours............................	(40)
Cost of unfavorable performance = (40) × $20...	($ 800)
Actual contribution...........................	$ 200

Thus, the estimated contribution becomes diluted and reduced to one-fifth its value as the result of poor operating, and it is only that amount which is available for paying period fixed expenses and ultimately providing a period profit.

Conversely, if the $4,000 selling price is considered poor, this condition could be compensated for by performance in excess of that estimated. For example, if the actual production hours taken are 60 instead of 80, estimated contribution of $1,000 is increased by the amount of the favorable performance variance, up to $1,400.

Traditional operating statements combine the net effect of the pricing results with the operating results, thereby obscuring the targets for remedial action. That type of statement is composed of the pluses and minuses of both pricing quality and operating performance. Exhibit 15-1 shows a comparison between the traditional profit-and-loss operating statement and a contribution-type statement which is designed to separate the results of pricing from the results of operating. The traditional form simply matches up gross costs with gross revenue to show the net income. The contribution type shows first the contribution that was available from the revenue at the pricing point. That is, if the products represented by the revenue were produced for the same costs as the estimated costs, with no variances, the actual contribution would be the same as the estimated contribution. In this exhibit, however, the $350,000 of estimated contribution was diluted by unfavorable variances totaling $100,000, thereby reducing the actual contribution of $250,000. The net pretax profit is obtained after the application of the period fixed expenses.

EXHIBIT 15-1. REPORTING THE RESULTS OF PRICING

Conventional profit and loss		Contribution statement	
Billed sales..............	$1,000,000	Billed sales..............	$1,000,000
Material costs...........	$ 200,000	Established oop costs......	650,000
Direct labor.............	300,000	Established contribution...	$ 350,000
Factory overhead........	250,000	Established PV...........	.35
General and administrative		oop variances:	
expenses............	150,000		
Total cost............	$ 900,000	Material..............	$ (12,000)
Pretax profit............	$ 100,000	Performance...........	$ (80,000)
Target profit............	150,000	Spending..............	$ (8,000)
Profit variance..........	$ (50,000)		
		Actual contribution.......	$ 250,000
		Less: period fixed expense..	150,000
		Pretax profit............	$ 100,000
		Target profit............	150,000
		Profit variance...........	$ (50,000)
		Pricing variance $50,000 favorable Operating variance ($100,000) unfavorable	

The results of pricing are easily determined by this approach to profit reporting: If fixed expenses are $150,000 and the target profits are $150,000, pricing which provides at least $300,000 of contribution will be satisfactory. However, the pricing function provided $350,000 of contribution, thereby exceeding the profit requirements. Thus, the pricing quality can be said to have a favorable variance. However, in producing the billed products in that period, the company used up $12,000 more in material because of waste and rejects, performed below standard to the extent of $80,000, and spent $8,000 more for other items than called for, thus winding up with a net unfavorable variance of $100,000.* The

* Actually, many more items of expense in a company are subject to variance measurement and control than is shown in this condensed exhibit. This subject, though, is outside the scope of this book.

net variance between these two functions is an unfavorable $50,000, correlating with the unfavorable variance between actual and target profit.

If the pricing here is actually as good as stated, it may be unwise for the company to attempt to get even higher prices with the motive of compensating for the poor performance. This practice may lead to price resistance and a consequent worsening of profits. The fact that this type of analysis is available to management makes it possible to avoid the obvious pitfalls of this type of action and to direct its efforts to correcting the production performances. With only the traditional form of statement available, how does management determine what portion of profit is due to pricing quality and what portion due to operating performance? And if it usually doesn't think in these terms, isn't it about time it did?

In the data of Exhibit 15-1, the pretax profit of $100,000 shows that the company generated less than its target profit—a fact which may be the result of market and competitive pressures. Surely a company cannot expect to impose successfully its drives for profit on the marketplace simply for the sake of fulfilling its profit ambitions. Having only the traditional form of profit-and-loss statement, management does not know objectively where the pressures and the drains on the target profits are coming from. It could be that there is considerable market resistance coupled with a high degree of operating performance from production. However, this is not the case as shown by the contribution-type statement. For here, the pricing is to be praised for generating a higher profit opportunity than targeted. Production, in turn, is to be condemned for diluting it with poor performance. This separating of vital functions is essential for directing management into the proper areas for remedial action.

Management Information Reports

Management Information (MI) reports should give the manager hard-hitting, condensed facts on which he can take immediate action without painstaking analyses and prolonged explanations. MI reports relating to the activity and quality of pricing should show the direction which pricing is taking and should be used for evaluating the various profit segments in the company's profit structure. MI reports for the pricing function should answer questions such as these: How much contribution has been accumulated to date? Are we on target considering how much time has passed in the operating year? Do we have enough facility-hours available to attain our target? Which is our best customer? Our best salesman? Our best territory? Our best end market? Are the sales of an important customer in proportion to the contribution he provides and the capacity he requires?

1. *Pricing results company-wide:* Exhibit 15-2 shows the results of pricing in all the company's product lines during a certain period. All the basic information is shown: booked revenue, contribution, PV, target revenue, revenue variance, facility-hours sold, contribution per facility-hour, *prorated* (not allocated) fixed expenses, period pretax profit, target return on employed capital, and the actual return on said capital. The data shown are cumulative data from the start of the operating year. The total pricing results show that to date the company has

EXHIBIT 15-2. SUMMARY OF PRICING RESULTS
Period Ending *June 30*

Item	Line A	Line B	Line C	Total
Booked revenue..........	$2,611,224	$608,018	$265,520	$3,484,762
Contribution.............	$709,826	$100,522	$73,909	$884,257
PV.....................	.272	.165	.278	.254
Target revenue..........	$2,579,264	$622,396	$270,851	$3,472,511
Revenue variance........	$31,960	$(14,378)	$(5,331)	$12,251
Variance, %.............	1.2	(2.3)	(1.9)	.35
Major facility-hours sold...	12,690	7,638	2,587	
Contribution per hour of major facility..........	$55.94	$13.16	$28.57	
Period fixed expenses......	$312,786	$71,574	$84,684	$469,044
Period profit.............	$397,040	$28,948	$(10,775)	$415,213
Profit % to sales..........	15.2	4.7	(4.1)	11.9
Target return on capital employed*.............	$265,746	$59,166	$65,754	$390,666
Return % on capital employed................	22.4	7.3	(2.4)	15.9

* All lines have a target per cent return on total capital employed of 15 per cent.

accomplished .9 per cent more than its target of 15 per cent return on total capital employed. Whether this trend can be maintained is not only a function of the pricing quality but also a balancing between the available capacity remaining for the year and the amount of contribution necessary to achieve the year-end target. If capacity is not scarce, management need not intensively police the build-up of facility-hours committed, but instead it may devote its attention to booking contribution with a watchful eye on the commitment of working capital. This latter item of capital may become scarce as the company drives towards attaining its target.

2. *Pricing results by product line:* Exhibit 15-3 shows the details of the pricing results of Product line A shown first in the previous exhibit. Three products constitute this product line. Pricing results are shown for the period up to but not including the current month, the current

EXHIBIT 15-3. SUMMARY OF PRICING RESULTS:
DETAIL OF LINE A REVENUE DOLLARS
PERIOD ENDING June 30

Item	Year to Date through May			Month of June			Year to Date Ending June 30		
	Product 1	Product 2	Product 3	Product 1	Product 2	Product 3	Product 1	Product 2	Product 3
Booked revenue	$1,149,357	$854,925	$47,461	$371,527	$112,148	$75,806	$1,520,884	$967,073	$123,267
Contribution	$289,987	$261,281	$9,838	$101,422	$33,790	$13,508	$391,409	$295,071	$23,346
PV	.252	.306	.207	.273	.301	.178	.257	.305	.189
Target revenue	$1,109,211	$872,433	$45,421	$361,352	$115,528	$75,319	$1,470,563	$987,961	$120,740
Revenue variance	$40,146	$(17,508)	$2,040	$10,175	$(3,380)	$487	$50,321	$(20,888)	$2,527
Press hours sold	7,586	2,581	....	1,969	554	....	9,555	3,135	....
Contribution per press hour	$38.22	$101.23	....	$51.50	$60.99	....	$40.96	$94.12	....

SUMMARY OF ABOVE DETAIL

Item	Year to Date through May	Month of June	Year to Date
Booked revenue	$2,051,743	$559,481	$2,611,224
Contribution	$561,106	$148,720	$709,826
PV	.273	.266	.272
Target revenue	$2,027,065	$552,199	$2,579,264
Revenue variance	$24,678	$7,282	$31,960
Variance, %	1.2	0.8	1.2
Press hours sold	10,167	2,523	12,690
Contribution per press hour	$55.19	$58.95	$55.94
Period fixed expenses	$260,655	$52,131	$312,786
Period profit	$300,451	$96,589	$397,040
Profit % to sales	14.6	17.3	15.2
Target return on TCE	$221,455	$44,291	$265,746
Return % on capital	20.4	32.7	22.4

EXHIBIT 15-4. COMPANY-WIDE PRICING RESULTS

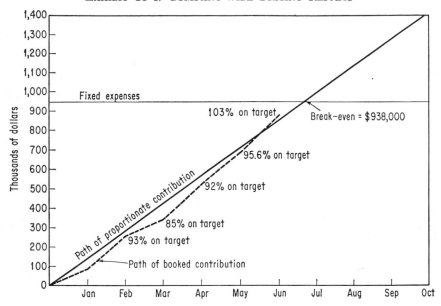

EXHIBIT 15-5. PRODUCT LINE A—RESULTS OF PRICING

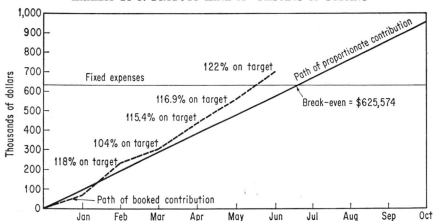

month, and finally, the year to date. Notice that fixed expenses are not allocated to individual products because of the use of joint facilities and common fixed expenses incurred by the product line as one total.

3. *Charting of data:* Exhibits 15-4 and 15-5 show the pricing performances company-wide and for Product line A, respectively. These charts show the cumulative comparison between the contribution booked to date against the target contribution prorated evenly throughout the year. This latter figure is represented by the "Path of proportionate contribu-

tion." As we have discussed throughout the book, no one period can be charged with generating a given amount of sales or contribution for this action would deny the pressures of the market and the presence of competition. The proportionate contribution line is provided as a yardstick against which the trend of cumulative booked contribution may be measured. The degree of target attainment can be realistically measured only at the end of the operating year. However, if the actual booked contribution departs too seriously from the path after a considerable portion of the operating year has passed, management should either question its original target set out in its profit plan or investigate the performance of the sales department or both. Again, these data have nothing whatever to do with production performance. This information shows what prices have been booked and what the revenue it represents is estimated to provide in contribution dollars.

4. *Pricing results by customer:* Exhibit 15-6 shows how pricing information is sorted to provide a ranking of customers by PV ratio as well as by contribution dollars. Because of the size of the typical sales transaction, only those customers which purchased a minimum of $4,000 in the period were used in this tabulation. The ranking by PV is valuable for evaluating the characteristic PVs of customers, owing to their purchasing habits, to the end market of which they are members, to the specific territory in which they are located, or to a combination of all three. While Mohaje Hardware has the largest booked PV and shows a most favorable PV variance compared to its target PV, the sales booked for it must be low as shown by its contribution ranking in the contribution tabulation. PV alone should not be the sole guide to customer quality. On the other hand, Beautycraft, which ranks low in PV and has an unfavorable PV variance, ranks on top of the contribution tabulation. The value of cumulatively showing the booked and target PV for each customer provides rough boundaries for future pricing.

However, some kind of additional analysis is required to evaluate the worth of a customer. In this analysis, it is important to include the relationship of booked contribution to committed facility-hours to ensure that the constant booking of low-PV, high-sales business will not cause the company to exhaust its capacity before the end of the operating year. Obviously, without an analysis, the seller would have a difficult task selecting the better of the following two customers:

Customer X: Provides 10 per cent of the firm's annual sales
             Gives only 2 per cent of the firm's annual contribution needs
             Uses up 30 per cent of the annual capacity of the firm
Customer Y: Provides 8 per cent of the firm's annual sales
             Gives 12 per cent of the firm's annual contribution needs
             Uses up only 9 per cent of the annual capacity of the firm

EXHIBIT 15-6. MANAGEMENT REPORT: CUSTOMER RANKING BY
PV AND CONTRIBUTION, (BOOKED SALES)
PERIOD ENDING *June 30*

Product Line A

Customer Ranking by PV (Minimum Sales of 4,000)			Customer Ranking by Contribution Dollars		
Customer	Booked PV	Target PV	Customer	Booked Contribution	Target Contribution
Mohaje Hardware......	.444	.314	Beautycraft............	$137,686	$154,478
Lestur................	.385	.355	American Hardware......	57,210	69,084
Weston-Smith.........	.347	.328	Associated Hardware.....	46,876	36,637
Helena Fox...........	.341	.308	Clyde Co..............	44,121	35,770
Clyde Co.............	.337	.292	Brill, Inc............	32,521	33,310
Femini...............	.324	.287	Dimilto-Star...........	30,259	24,632
Shaster..............	.321	.242	Shaster...............	29,829	20,155
Rontar...............	.318	.294	Lestur................	28,510	25,020
Industrial Brush........	.318	.297	Jontil Drug...........	25,589	25,589
Fern Leather..........	.307	.270	Lafe Pharmacy.........	22,227	16,681
Semple...............	.300	.306	Hartley Electric........	22,068	18,940
Ron Electric..........	.296	.233	V.S. Soap.............	19,937	16,984
Associated Hardware....	.293	.244	Frederick Electric.......	19,888	22,716
Dewar's..............	.290	.266	Femina...............	17,413	14,556
American Hardware.....	.287	.330	Bangor, Inc...........	16,744	13,568
V.S. Soap.............	.287	.255	American Enterprises.....	16,688	14,661
Bangor, Inc...........	.287	.246	Fern Leather..........	15,778	13,141
Testron..............	.283	.217	General Metals.........	15,013	19,270
Home Industries........	.280	.272	Helena Fox...........	14,160	12,165
Dimilto-Star...........	.279	.239	Weston-Smith.........	13,020	11,931
American Enterprises...	.276	.251	Home Industries........	11,270	10,790
S. W. and T...........	.269	.187	Mohaje Hardware......	7,648	4,398
General Metals........	.264	.316	Rontar...............	6,495	5,811
Albany Products........	.262	.222	S. W. and T...........	6,306	3,932
Jener Manufacturing....	.261	.236	Industrial Brush........	6,060	5,485
Associated Drug........	.261	.277	Dewar's..............	5,897	5,234
Beautycraft...........	.257	.280	Breton...............	5,102	4,521
Jontil Drug...........	.255	.255	Testron..............	3,374	2,370
Hartley Electric........	.253	.225	Beach Wear, Inc........	3,001	2,403
Lafe Pharmacy.........	.230	.184	Semple...............	2,985	3,067
Frederick Electric.......	.218	.242	Lockland.............	2,406	6,389
Beach Wear, Inc........	.215	.180	Albany Products........	1,975	1,591
Brill, Inc.............	.207	.211	Jener Manufacturing.....	1,926	1,686
Breton...............	.202	.183	Associated Drug........	1,859	2,015
Lockland.............	.087	.201	Ron Electric...........	1,782	1,285
			Total.................	$693,623	$660,265
			Favorable pricing variance	$ 33,358	

Exhibit 15-7 shows how such an analysis is prepared. Five customers
are used in this analysis, all of whom give the firm approximately the
same amount of business annually. Customer A reveals a reasonable degree of proportionality among the factors of sales, contribution, and facility usage. In other words, Customer A provides the firm with 19.7 per
cent of its annual sales, generates 16.3 per cent of its total supplied con-

tribution (slight negative proportionality) and uses up 15.3 per cent of its facility capacity (slight positive proportionality). Customer E provides the most sales, 21.2 per cent, but generates only 13.1 per cent of its supplied contribution and uses up 21.2 per cent of the facility capacity. This condition is a negative one in both measurements. Here

EXHIBIT 15-7. BALANCED CUSTOMER RANKING

Customer	Sales volume	Total sales, %	PV	Contri-bution generated	Contri-bution supplied, %	Facility-hours committed	Capacity used, %	CPH
A	$ 280,000	19.7	.24	$ 67,200	16.3	2,100	15.3	$32.00
B	270,000	19.0	.38	102,600	25.0	1,600	11.7	64.12
C	290,000	20.4	.25	72,500	17.6	3,700	27.0	19.59
D	280,000	19.7	.41	114,800	28.0	3,400	24.8	33.76
E	300,000	21.2	.18	54,000	13.1	2,900	21.2	18.62
Total........	$1,420,000			$411,100		13,700		

the booked sales are out of proportion to the contribution generated and the facility time used up. This condition is not necessarily true of all low-PV customers, for while the supplied contribution could be low the facility-hours required might be out of proportion low enough to make the customer a valuable one. Customer D, who has the largest PV, requires double the facility-hours of Customer B, making B the favored customer of the lot.

There are various ways of ranking customers in terms of their realistic economic value to the firm. These ways are shown in the following tabulation:

Ranking on the basis of:			
Sales	PV	Contribution	Balance
E	D	D	B
C	B	B	D
A and D	C	C	A
B	A	A	C
	E	E	E

The CPH column shown on Exhibit 15-7 follows the balanced ranking only because the sales levels of the five customers are so similar, also the reason the rankings by PV and contribution are the same. This analysis is most valuable when the question of customer replacement arises. The author has seen extremes in service to a customer simply because he had been on the seller's books for forty years, still provided the maximum sales, and was considered a prestige account. The customer in mind gave the client firm over 50 per cent of its annual sales, provided only 16 per cent of its annual contribution needs, and used up 42 per cent of its manufacturing capacity. An investigation of this customer's history showed that the seller had not increased his prices to this customer in the last fourteen years in spite of the steadily rising material and labor costs. At the time of developing the customer's price schedule fourteen years ago, the prices were set under the concept of getting the business to keep facilities occupied and for reasons of prestige.

5. *Pricing results by salesman:* Exhibit 15-8 shows how pricing data are sorted to give rankings by salesman. The tabulations show the data by PV and contribution. Here, again, one must be guided more by con-

EXHIBIT 15-8. MANAGEMENT REPORT: SALESMEN'S RANKING, BY
PV AND CONTRIBUTION DOLLARS
PERIOD ENDING *June 30*

Summary

Salesman	Booked PV	Target PV	Salesman	Booked Contribution	Target Contribution	Variance
Brown............	.284	.255	Thompson.......	$195,369	$167,361	$+28,008
Henry...........	.280	.322	Fuller..........	162,074	174,202	−12,128
Thompson........	.264	.234	House Accounts..	141,524	145,135	−3,611
Fuller...........	.263	.277	Hapway.........	118,064	117,575	+489
House Accounts...	.252	.257	Brown..........	103,290	89,330	+13,960
Hapway..........	.228	.227	Harlow.........	95,644	96,971	−1,327
Harlow..........	.227	.229	Henry..........	61,043	74,419	−13,376
Grant...........	.201	.183	Grant..........	5,102	4,521	+581
Myer...........	.099	.113	Myer..........	2,147	2,492	−345
			Total........	$884,257	$872,006	$+12,251

tribution than by PV. Of course, PV does show the type of work for which a salesman aims and can be used as some evaluation of his quality, but his productivity together with the PV of the work he gets determine the contribution results. So while Mr. Brown has the highest PV, he produces only one-half of the contribution which Mr. Thompson generates. Further evaluations are available from examining the degree to which each salesman gets the target prices. The chances are good that Thompson is a better salesman than Fuller over and above what the contribution and PV data show. Since their PVs are very close, Thompson's increase in contribution over Fuller's is more the result of aiming for better prices than for volume. The spread in revenue variance of $36,136 between these two men confirms this judgment.

In some cases, evaluation of salesmen is carried out to more detail. In the following example, who is the better salesman?

Item	Salesman A	Salesman B
Booked sales......	$400,000	$400,000
oop cost.........	200,000	200,000
Contribution....	$200,000	$200,000
Elements of oop:		
Material........	$150,000	$ 50,000
Conversion......	$ 50,000	$150,000

From just the standpoint of PV and contribution, both salesmen are equal. However, we would consider attaining a high PV on a large turnover of material and on a small turnover of conversion cost a feat and would therefore give the nod to Salesman A.

EXHIBIT 15-9. MANAGEMENT REPORT: RATING OF END USE
CLASSIFICATION BY PV AND CONTRIBUTION

Folding Unit

End Use	Booked PV	Target PV	End Use	Booked Contribution	Target Contribution
Miscellaneous......	*.290*	*.254*	*Cosmetics*.....	*$451,611*	*$440,655*
Sporting goods.....	*.285*	*.239*	*Medicinal*.....	*108,297*	*96,078*
Textiles...........	*.283*	*.257*	*Hardware*.....	*56,775*	*54,383*
Medicinal products.	*.280*	*.257*	*Sporting goods*.	*48,552*	*38,340*
Cosmetics..........	*.278*	*.274*	*Textiles*.......	*16,639*	*14,565*
Food-dry only......	*.264*	*.316*	*Food-dry only*..	*15,013*	*19,270*
Hardware..........	*.229*	*.221*	*Soap*.........	*7,063*	*7,370*
Beverages..........	*.194*	*.337*	*Miscellaneous*..	*4,081*	*3,408*
Soap..............	*.155*	*.161*	*Beverages*......	*1,795*	*3,797*
			Total........	*$709,826*	*$677,866*

6. *Pricing results by end market:* Exhibit 15-9 shows how pricing data are used to determine the sources of profit by end-use markets. Again, rankings are prepared both by PV and contribution. The PV measurement enables an evaluation of the PV characteristic of the marketplace. In many cases, this sorting is carried out to include the territories constituting each of the end markets. Even though cosmetics have a lower than maximum PV, the volume generated by the various customers in this classification is great enough to rate it highest by far in contribution over any other. Notice that the sales figure is not used in many of these measurements of pricing results because obviously that figure is meaningless unless we know the specific economic ingredients of the sale.

Section 5

MECHANICS OF PRICING PROGRAM INSTALLATION

Introduction

The purpose of this section is to show the reader how to develop the basic internal data necessary for a complete pricing program. Information will be presented in step-by-step form. For purposes of continuity, the data of one fictitious company will be used throughout this section in developing the basic information, although the data of other companies will be introduced to demonstrate how the information may be used differently in other situations.

The fictitious company used for illustrating the pricing program represents one of the most difficult segments of United States industry from the standpoint of cost-estimating, pricing, and profit-planning. The Nova Corp. is a member of the flexible-packaging converting industry. Its products are printed and unprinted polyethylene plastic bags used in the garment, hardware, food, and other industries. These products are made on web-fed flexographic printing presses and converted into bags on bag machines. Nova also produces a line of gravure-printed laminated stock, which is used to contain small individual pouches of sugar, shaving lotion, shoe polish, etc., as well as a line of extruded laminated plastic films. These items are made on expensive gravure printing presses, adhesive laminators, and film extruders.

Nova principally makes to order and not to stock under competitive price-bid conditions. In some cases, the industry has price lists established by the larger producers, which act as guides for individual converters. The markets Nova serves are widely varied and large in number. The facilities are used in common for many of its product lines and completely in common for the different markets it serves. Other variables which contribute to the task of profit-planning are the widely differing order sizes, the mixture of differing raw materials, the variety of preparatory and run times, the variety of colors and sizes, the number of images which can be run at one time, etc. In short, very little is predictable at the start of the operating year about the variables of Nova's future business.

These characteristics are similar to those of other converters, such as printers, folding-carton and envelope manufacturers, foundries, steel mills, machine shops, fabric mills and converters, furniture manufacturers, and the vast majority of United States industry—in terms of numbers of enterprises. By choosing a complicated converting industry to demonstrate the principles and methods in this book, the author hopes to prove that if these concepts and procedures are workable in this case, they are practical for use throughout all industry.

In presenting this complete pricing program for the Nova Corp., we are including many refinements in the basic concepts and methods presented in Sections 3 and 4 to show how the system may be adapted to serve a wide range of needs.

CHAPTER 16 *Developing the Basic Costs for Pricing*

As we have said throughout the book, sound costs start the pricing process and are the point from which many other vital day-to-day decisions are made. In a converting industry which uses joint or common facilities to produce its output—where the vagaries of the market and reactions of competitors are not precisely predictable, where the use of expensive facilities cannot be forecast in advance—the right type of cost information is crucial and critical. A converting industry can be characterized as one which is in the business of selling facility time rather than a product. The converting facility, in which so much capital has been invested, is the cornerstone of the converter's economy. If each hour of converting facility time is intelligently cost-estimated, rationally priced, and then used as a guide to an optimum product mix, the seller has the best chance of coping maturely with competition and can adjust his policy to keep pace with immediate conditions. A cost-estimating system which provides this flexibility is known as the *machine-hour rate system,* and this chapter outlines in condensed form the steps which lead to its development.

Machine-hour Rate System

A machine-hour rate is the cost of owning and operating one converting (or other) facility for one hour. The traditional machine-hour rate is an all-inclusive cost (except material and other costs incurred by the order transaction rather than by the facility) and includes fixed plus variable costs. These costs lead to an order or product "full" cost, which deprives the seller of a measurement of contribution.* A machine-hour rate system which develops both the out-of-pocket as well as the "full" cost is known as the *two-part* machine-hour rate system.† In this system,

---

* Discussed in Chap. 4.
† Spencer A. Tucker, *Cost-estimating and Pricing with Machine-hour Rates,* Prentice-Hall, Inc., Englewood Cliffs, N.J., 1962.

the machine-hour rate for each facility is developed in two parts, thereby allowing the order estimate to show total oop costs and the contribution against any prevailing price.

The remainder of this chapter is devoted to a presentation of the various developmental steps of the machine-hour rate supported by brief explanations of the purposes of each.

EXHIBIT 16-1. CONVERTING FACILITIES CLASSIFICATION SHEET (CFCS)
($3.2 MILLION SALES)

Production Center	No. of Units	Hp per Unit	Working Space Occupied	Present Machinery Value	Annual Assigned Hours*	Shifts per Unit	Hp-hr
45-in. Dilts extruder-laminator...	1	70	600	$ 350,000	5,100	3	321,000†
8-color 30-in. Champlain gravure press...	2	100	2,000	650,000	6,800	2	450,000†
Mosstype mounter-proofer........	1	...	350	3,000	1,700	1	
Acraplate-molder..	1	20	200	10,000	1,700	1	34,000
6-color 42-in. Hudson-Sharp Flexo..........	1	50	900	150,000	3,400	2	153,000†
5-color 30-in. Kidder-Flexo...	1	35	600	60,000	3,400	2	107,000†
Cameron-Duplex slitter-rewinder.	2	25	400	80,000	6,800	2	170,000
Stanford-slitter-rewinder.......	1	10	150	12,000	1,700	1	17,000
40-in. Schjeldahl sideweld bag machine.......	3	10	400	60,000	7,650	1.5	76,500
42-in. Beck sheeter	1	15	150	10,000	1,700	1	25,500
Total..........	...	...	15,750	$1,385,000	39,950	...	1,354,000

* Hours reduced 15 per cent to provide for nonchargeable time.
† Two-thirds of annual hours applicable to "Run" portion.
1. Miscellaneous nonproduction equipment = $115,000.
2. Full activity shift = 2,000 hours.

1. *Converting Facilities Classification Sheet (CFCS):* Exhibit 16-1 shows the CFCS for the Nova Corp. The CFCS is a marshaling of the converting facilities of the company which are to be the subject of later estimate. Facilities which will not be estimated should not be listed. The physical factors—space occupied, horsepower, present market

value—are to be used later as the basis for the final allocation of cost to each converting facility.

2. *Crew Composition Table (CCT):* Exhibit 16-2 shows the CCT for the Nova Corp. The CCT is a listing of the normal manpower requirements for manning the selected converting facilities listed in the CFCS. The hourly rate per unit is used as the standard hourly direct labor cost of the facility and is added (rather than allocated) to the overhead portion of the machine-hour rate in the presentation of the composite machine-hour rates. The column headed "Direct labor budget" is not a cost figure; it is to be used later as a factor in allocating costs to each facility.

EXHIBIT 16-2. CREW COMPOSITION TABLE (CCT)
($3.2 Million Sales)

Production Center	Standard Crew per Unit	Hourly Base Rate	Hourly Rate per Unit	Annual Assigned Hours	Direct Labor Budget
Extrudor laminator	2	$3.00	$6.00	5,100	$ 30,600
Gravure presses	2	3.00	6.00	6,800	40,800
Mounter-proofer	½	2.50	1.25	1,700	2,125
Molder	½	2.50	1.25	1,700	2,125
6-color Flexo	1½	2.80	4.20	3,400	14,280
5-color Flexo	1½	2.80	4.20	3,400	14,280
Large slitter-rewinder	1	2.50	2.50	6,800	17,000
Small slitter-rewinder	1	2.50	2.50	1,700	4,250
Bag machines	2	1.75	3.50	7,650	26,775
Sheeter	1	2.50	2.50	1,700	4,250
Total	...	.....	.....	.....	$156,485

It should be pointed out that in keeping with the concept of traceability and identifiability the CCT is frequently expanded to include the specific hourly costs of fringe benefits, nonchargeable time, overtime and incentive premium, payroll surcharges, prorated supervisory costs, etc. In the Nova example, such additives have been included in the Allocatable Budget.

3. *Direct Charge Budget (DCB):* Exhibit 16-3 shows the DCB for Nova. The DCB is a schedule of overhead costs directly incurred by, and traceable and chargeable to, specific facilities. Handling such costs in this manner avoids the convenient but improper blanket distribution to all facilities. In this blanket procedure, facilities which do not incur these costs are the recipients of unfair charges and the facilities which are directly responsible for these cost incurrences are not charged enough. As in the case of the standard hourly direct labor cost, the direct cost per hour is a direct additive in the development of the final rates.

Within the limits of traceability, it is most desirable in analyzing the company's various costs to identify them either with a facility, as on the CCT and DCB, or with an order transaction, such as sales commissions, direct material, royalties, freight out, etc. Then the remaining costs can be organized into a budget schedule composed of blanket costs which are to be allocated on the basis of cause-and-effect factors.

EXHIBIT 16-3. DIRECT CHARGE BUDGET (DCB)

Production Center	Annual Amount	To Provide for:	Annual Hours	Cost per Hour
Gravure presses..........	*$50,000*	*Re-etching cylinders at $0.001 per M sq in.*		
	1,400	*Gas cost for dryers*		
	9,000	*Repair parts and supplies*		
Total..............	*$60,400*		*6,800*	*$8.88*
42-in. H-S Flexo........	*600*	*Gas costs*		
	2,000	*Repair parts and supplies*		
Total..............	*$ 2,600*		*3,400*	*0.77*
30-in. Kidder-Flexo......	*400*	*Gas costs*		
	1,000	*Repair parts and supplies*		
Total..............	*$ 1,400*		*3,400*	*0.41*
Extrudor-laminator......	*4,200*	*Repair parts and supplies*	*5,100*	*0.82*
40-in. bag machine.......	*4,000*	*Repair parts and supplies*	*7,650*	*0.52*
Cameron S-R..........	*2,000*	*Repair parts and supplies*	*6,800*	*0.29*
Stanford S-R..........	*400*	*Repair parts and supplies*	*1,700*	*0.24*
Sheeter................	*200*	*Repair parts and supplies*	*1,700*	*0.12*
Total.............	*$75,200*			

4. *Allocatable Budget* (*AB*): Exhibit 16-4 shows the AB for Nova. The AB is the schedule on which every other expense except direct *order* charges is listed. These expenses are costs which cannot be defensibly identified with individual production centers in the Nova Corp. The various costs have been classified into separate categories for the purpose of applying a cause-and-effect allocation factor. For example, all those costs under "Space" are to be allocated on the basis of "Working space

Exhibit 16-4. Allocatable Budget (AB)
($3.2 Million Sales)

Expense Classification	Fixed	Variable	Total
Manufacturing Costs:			
Space:			
Rent..................................	$ 30,000	....	$ 30,000
Repairs to building......................	6,000	....	6,000
Heat.................................	8,000	$ 2,000	10,000
	$ 44,000	$ 2,000	$ 46,000
Power:			
Electricity............................	$ 5,000	$ 35,000	$ 40,000
Machinery:			
Depreciation...........................	$150,000	....	$150,000
Price-level adjustment on depreciation (8%)..	12,000	....	12,000
Insurance (equipment portion).............	3,000	....	3,000
Repairs and maintenance..................	7,000	$ 14,000	21,000
Supplies and tools.......................	....	20,000	20,000
Outside services.........................	....	12,000	12,000
	$172,000	$ 46,000	$218,000
Indirect costs:			
Plant manager..........................	$ 17,000	....	$ 17,000
Indirect labor (not specifically assigned to production centers)......................	8,000	$ 24,000	32,000
Idle time of production workers.............	....	17,600	17,600
Subsidy costs of substandard production workers...............................	....	12,000	12,000
Porter-sweeper..........................	3,500	....	3,500
	$ 28,500	$ 53,600	$ 82,100
Fringe benefits:			
Payroll surcharges.......................	....	$ 34,000	$ 34,000
Holiday and vacation pay..................	....	7,000	7,000
Overtime premiums.......................	....	3,000	3,000
Incentive bonus earned....................	....	2,000	2,000
	....	$ 46,000	$ 46,000
Total manufacturing cost...............	$249,500	$182,600	$432,100
Nonmanufacturing Costs:			
Warehouse and delivery:			
Rent.................................	$ 10,000	....	$ 10,000
Wages: shipping clerks....................	....	$ 8,000	8,000
truck drivers......................	....	5,500	5,500
Insurance on inventory....................	500	500	1,000
Truck depreciation.......................	1,500	....	1,500
Truck operating costs.....................	....	5,000	5,000
	$ 12,000	$ 19,000	$ 31,000

EXHIBIT 16-4. ALLOCATABLE BUDGET (AB) (*Continued*)

Expense Classification	Fixed	Variable	Total
Nonmanufacturing Costs (Continued)			
Selling:			
Sales manager's salary (no commission).....	$ 20,000	....	$ 20,000
Salaries of clerks and secretaries...........	....	$ 10,000	10,000
Estimator..............................	9,000	....	9,000
Auto expense...........................	....	8,000	8,000
Nonbillable artwork......................	....	15,000	15,000
	$ 29,000	$ 33,000	$ 62,000
Administrative:			
General manager's salary..................	$ 25,000	....	$ 25,000
Office expense...........................	2,900	....	2,000
Accounting salaries......................	9,000	....	9,000
Clerical salaries.........................	....	$ 5,000	5,000
Other.................................	20,000	10,000	30,000
	$ 56,000	$ 15,000	$ 71,000
Fringe benefits:			
Payroll surcharges.......................	$ 12,000	$ 7,000	$ 19,000
Warehouse and delivery: overtime premiums..	....	1,000	1,000
Hospitalization insurance..................	2,000	....	2,000
Christmas bonuses........................	15,000	....	15,000
	$ 29,000	$ 8,000	$ 37,000
Total nonmanufacturing cost..............	$126,000	$ 75,000	$201,000
From Part 1: Total manufacturing cost..........	249,500	182,600	432,100
Annual budgeted overhead cost.................	$375,500	$257,600	$633,100

occupied"—an allocation factor listed on the CFCS. "Power" costs are to be allocated on the basis of horsepower-hours, etc. Obviously, it would be illogical to allocate all expenses on the basis of one factor because of the individual nature and behavior of each cost.

Nonmanufacturing Costs: Fixed or Variable?

By definition, a variable cost is one which changes with changes in output or activity. Expanding a bit, we may also say that a variable cost is one which is directly identified with a facility or order in the sense that it would not be incurred without the order or without the operation of a facility. Thus, the direct labor cost on the CCT and all the costs on the DCB are considered variable. Both these costs may be called *direct* variable costs,* as are the direct order charges such as materials and commission. Then, in order to get a realistic oop machine-hour rate, we must consider the extent of the *period* variable costs†

* See Chap. 8, pp. 79–80.
† See Chap. 8, pp. 80–81.

shown in blanket form on the AB. By definition, a period variable cost does not vary at the facility or order point unit by unit, but rather it changes in total level with changes in the total activity of the firm. Thus, as a company increases its overall sales by 40 per cent, it may have to add more clerical people to handle the additional office transactions, increase the size of its sales service department, etc. However, the mere getting or losing of an order, while exerting a direct impact on, say, the direct materials cost, will usually not affect the period variable administrative staffing costs directly.

The classic approach to the separating of fixed and variable costs is to place the nonmanufacturing costs into the fixed category using the rationale of conservatism. This approach enlarges the total fixed expenses in the company's budget and gives the impression that much more expense has to be covered before there is any profit. What is usually overlooked is that when more expenses have been programmed into the fixed category the amount left in the variable or oop category is reduced, thus producing a higher PV and contribution figure. Sometimes the contribution figure is so distorted by this practice that it materially changes the rankings in each of the company's profit segments.

The author's position is that the more sensible and conservative approach to use (to support the pricing theses in this book) is to recognize the period variable components in nonmanufacturing costs, thereby increasing the annual variable costs and lowering the contribution figure. Purely from a psychological viewpoint, this practice has the effect of narrowing the gap between oop costs and revenue as management tries to understand and adjust to the difference between the contribution figure and the traditional gross profit figure on the estimate sheet.

Out-of-pocket Costs Dangerous?

Those who still favor traditional absorption costing for pricing purposes, who believe that the gross profit shown on an estimate is valid, maintain that a knowledge of oop costs and contribution is a dangerous tool which can be the excuse for price-cutting. The author maintains that if an honest and intelligent businessman is shown what his out-of-pocket costs are, he will not knowingly price below this level, unless he is in need of extensive psychiatric treatment. Granted that if a businessman does not understand what oop costs are, the contribution figure, which usually tends to be greater than the gross profit figure, might give him the impression that the order profit is really greater than it is. Thus, this misunderstanding might prompt him to reduce prices on occasion. It is assumed that the oop-cost and contribution concepts are properly explained so that they do not become dangerous tools. After all, a sharp knife or an automobile can be considered dangerous weapons in the hands of an idiot, but these are essential for cutting bread and providing transportation, respectively. Management should not be deprived of a crucial pricing tool just because there might be the chance that other people may misuse it.

Practical Separation of Fixed and Variable Costs

At this point we may say that the total oop-cost package consists of the following:

At the facility point:
1. Cost of direct labor, fringe benefits, premiums, etc.
2. Direct overhead costs incurred specifically at the facility, such as maintenance, supervision, electricity, etc.
At the order point:
3. Cost of direct materials, sales commissions, royalties, freight out, etc.
To support annual operations:
4. Period variable costs such as clerical, warehousing, sales service costs, etc.

The first three costs are readily separable by a proper analysis of cost behavior. The fourth type of variable cost is not that easily determined in many of the company's expense accounts and requires a practical approach. Some of the expenses listed on the AB, Exhibit 16-4, can be considered almost fully fixed, such as depreciation, or fully variable, such as manufacturing fringe benefits. In other expenses, the degree of fixedness or variability is not that apparent. If we assume that recognition is given to the presence of a variable component in a traditionally fixed cost, how much of the cost will be considered variable and how much fixed? The problem boils down to the question of how and where to peg the fixed amount in the mixed cost.

Where to peg fixed cost?: Attempting to select how much of a company's expense package is to be considered fixed requires an understanding of the background of the person doing the separating. One school of thought states that the amount of annual fixed expense should be only that amount required to "turn the key in the door" with everything else being variable. Thus, rent, real estate taxes, interest on mortgage, depreciation, etc. would all be fixed and the balance of company expenses would be variable. This concept selects only that amount of fixed expense which would be incurred at zero operating level. Under these circumstances, the president would be operating the telephone switchboard, the vice-president would be operating a production machine, and the treasurer would be the janitor.

Under another concept, (taught by a different academic institution), the fixed amount would represent the present operating fixed expense, with all executive, administrative, clerical, and sales considered fixed and the balance variable.

The author subscribes to neither one of these concepts because they are both impractical and could be highly distorting in pricing and in

EXHIBIT 16-5. WHERE TO PEG FIXED EXPENSES?

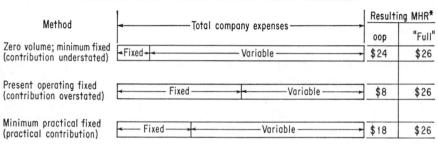

Effect on product–line[+] rankings

Product–line	PV		
	Minimum fixed	Present fixed	Practical fixed
A	.07	.28	.18
B	.08	.26	.24
C	.06	.27	.22
D	.07	.24	.14
E	.05	.25	.20
Relative range low-to-high	.03	.04	.10

[*]Conversion cost rate only. Does not include direct materials, sales commission, royalties, freight out and other direct order charges.

[+]Same comparative analyses may be developed for the other profit segments of the company.

analyzing the various segments of the profit structure. In the first case, that of pegging fixed costs to a zero operating level, fixed expense is small and variable cost is large, thereby making the PV and the contribution levels abnormally small. Besides, no company is actually in business at zero volume. In the second case, that of pegging fixed costs to the present operating level, fixed is a large amount and variable is too small, thereby making the PV and contribution excessively great. Using either one of these concepts distorts the measurement of the economic value of price, shifts the relative contribution values, and severely changes the interrankings among the various profit segments of the firm.

EXHIBIT 16-6. EXPENSE ASSIGNMENT WORK SHEET (EAW)

		Manufacturing							
Units	Production Center	Space		Power		Machinery		Indirect Costs	
		Fixed	Variable	Fixed	Variable	Fixed	Variable	Fixed	Variable
1	Extruder-laminator..	$ 4,591	$ 209	$1,189	$ 8,314	$43,463	$11,628	$ 3,638	$ 6,844
2	Gravure presses......	15,304	696	1,665	11,666	80,720	21,590	4,852	9,125
1	Mounter-proofer.....	2,679	121	......	....	373	100	1,213	2,281
1	Molder............	1,530	70	126	881	1,242	332	1,213	2,281
1	6-color 42-in. Flexo	6,887	313	566	3,963	18,630	4,980	2,425	4,562
1	5-color 30-in. Flexo...	4,591	209	396	2,771	7,452	1,992	2,425	4,562
2	Large slitter-rewinder	3,061	139	630	4,403	9,936	2,656	4,851	9,125
1	Small slitter-rewinder	1,148	52	62	446	1,490	398	1,213	2,281
3	Bag machines.......	3,061	139	283	1,981	7,452	1,992	5,457	10,258
1	Sheeter............	1,148	52	83	581	1,242	332	1,213	2,281
	Total..................	$44,000	$2,000	$5,000	$35,000	$172,000	$46,000	$28,500	$53,600
	Allocation factors........	Occupancy		Hp-hrs		Present Market Value		Annual Assigned Hours	
	Allocation fractions.......	$\frac{44,000}{5,750}$	$\frac{2,000}{5,750}$	$\frac{5,000}{1,354,000}$	$\frac{35,000}{1,354,000}$	$\frac{172,000}{1,385,000}$	$\frac{46,000}{1,385,000}$	$\frac{28,500}{39,950}$	$\frac{53,600}{39,950}$
	Allocation ratios..........	7.652 −	0.3478 −	0.0037 +	0.0259 +	0.1242 +	0.0332 −	0.7134 +	1.342 +

Minimum practical fixed level: Obviously, if identical firms used both of these impractical methods, the cost-estimating, pricing, and profit-planning results would be vastly different. Surely there must be one rational method which at least is more defensible than the two presented. The method of pegging fixed expense which the author has used for many years and which he recommends here is to find the level of fixed expense needed to support a *minimum* operating level below which the company would not *want* to stay in business. To approach this problem, determine first what the bare minimum return on total capital employed

Costs				Nonmanu-facturing Costs		Total Overhead Costs		MHR (Overhead Only)		Hourly Direct Charges	Hourly Direct Labor	Composite Machine-hour Rate	
Fringe Benefits		Total											
Fixed	Variable	Fixed	Variable	Fixed	Variable	Fixed	Variable	oop	Full	Variable	Variable	oop	Full
...	$8,990	$52,881	$35,985	$26,705	$14,780	$50,765	$130,351	$9.95	$25.48	$0.82	$6.00	$16.77	$32.30
...	12,005	102,541	55,082	51,786	22,626	77,708	232,035	11.42	34.12	8.88	6.00	26.30	49.00
...	625	4,265	3,127	2,154	1,284	4,411	10,830	2.59	6.37	.....	1.25	3.84	7.62
...	625	4,111	4,189	2,076	1,721	5,910	12,097	3.47	7.12	.....	1.25	4.72	8.35
...	4,195	28,508	18,013	14,397	7,398	25,411	68,316	7.47	20.09	0.77	4.20	12.44	25.06
...	4,195	14,864	13,729	7,506	5,639	19,368	41,738	5.70	12.25	0.41	4.20	10.31	16.86
...	4,995	18,478	21,318	9,331	8,755	30,073	57,882	4.42	8.51	0.29	2.50	7.21	11.30
...	1,250	3,913	4,421	1,976	1,816	6,237	12,126	3.66	7.12	0.24	2.50	6.40	9.86
...	7,870	16,253	22,240	8,2 8	9,134	31,374	55,835	4.10	7.30	0.52	3.50	8.12	11.32
...	1,250	3,686	4,496	1,861	1,847	6,343	11,890	3.73	6.99	0.12	2.50	6.35	9.61
...	$46,000	249,500	182,600	126,000	75,000	257,600	633,100						

Direct Labor	Budget		Manufacturing										
...	46,000	...	126,000	75,000									
	156,485		249,500	182,600									
...	0.294	...	0.505	0.4107									
	—		—	—									

would have to be as a requirement for staying in business. Then, starting with the present sales activity, tabulate the successive drops in sales volume and profits to lower and lower levels. In the same tabulation, show the changes in the total capital employed required to support each successively lower sales level, keeping in mind that this amount of capital does not change in direct proportion to sales. The fixed capital remains fixed, and only the variable capital portion (current assets) drops at a rate corresponding with sales. When the profit at each successively lower level is compared with its respective TCE, a rate of return percentage can be found. From these data, management can find its minimum practical operating level.

Exhibit 16-5 shows the three methods of pegging fixed expenses and the consequent effect of each on the PVs.

5. *Expense Assignment Worksheet (EAW):* Having planned the physical factors of the facilities (CFCS), planned the manning of those facilities (CCT), and planned the financing of those facilities (DCB and AB), we are now ready to combine these data into machine-hour rates for each facility. Exhibit 16-6 shows the EAW for the Nova Corp. The EAW is a sheet on which the various costs on the AB are allocated to each facility on the basis of selected cause-and-effect factors. Then, the additive costs (nonallocatable) shown on the DCB and CCT are added to get the composite machine-hour rate. The allocation factors selected for each budget category are shown on the bottom of the sheet. A ratio is then developed between the total cost to be allocated and the selected factor, and this ratio is used as the allocation factor by which the cost is assigned to the individual facility or production center. For example, $44,000 of fixed space cost (AB) is to be distributed on the basis of 5,750 square feet of working space (CFCS). This figure leads to a ratio of 7.652. This ratio means that it costs $7.652 in fixed space costs for every square foot of net working space occupied. When this ratio is multiplied by the specific working space occupied by each production center, the fixed space cost is the result. In the case of the extruder-laminator, it occupies 600 square feet, and its fixed space cost is 600 × $7.652, or $4,591. In a similar manner, all budgeted costs are allocated to all production centers. Note that in working this sheet, the budget totals are first inserted horizontally, and then the vertical figures above each total are generated by means of the allocation ratios.

Adding across for each facility gives the total overhead costs. Dividing by the annual assigned hours produces the overhead portion of the machine-hour rate. Then, when the two direct charges are added in on an hourly basis, the result is the composite machine-hour rate expressed in oop as well as in "full." The author has included provision for the "full" machine-hour rate, even though it has limited value in pricing and profit-planning. On client field assignments the "full" portion is carried for about one year to give doubting individuals a basis for comparison (as if that proves anything) and generally to give some feeling of security until no one pays any attention to it, and it can be dropped.

The machine-hour rate, though, is still a two-part system, as the "full" portion of the rate is replaced with the rate for the selling price of oop machine-hour rate. This topic will be discussed later in connection with the differential markup of facilities to target a desired rate of return on capital by individual facility.

EXHIBIT 16-7. RELATIONSHIP BETWEEN CONVERSION COST RATE AND ORDER ESTIMATE

	oop cost categories	How charged	Converted into order cost by	Order estimate	
Conversion costs converted into MHR	Allocatable budget: Overhead costs not identifiable with, and not incurred specifically by, production center or order	Statistically to production centers by Expense Assignment Worksheet	Multiplying MHR by hours of facilities required	Direct conversion costs	Total oop order costs
	Direct charge budget: Overhead costs traceable to, and directly identifiable with, production centers	Direct additive to overhead portion of MHR			
	Crew composition table: Direct labor, fringe benefits, and other charges directly associated with labor at production centers	Direct additive to overhead portion of MHR			
oop order costs	Direct materials				
	Other order costs: Costs specifically incurred by the order: freight out, sales commission, royalties, etc.	Direct additive to order estimate	Directly applied	Direct order costs	

Exhibit 16-7 shows the composition of the machine-hour rate and how these costs are transferred to the order estimate.

CHAPTER 17 *Application of Basic Costs in Pricing the Product*

Once we have developed the conversion cost rates (machine-hour rate) to allow an expression of order conversion costs in terms of both out-of-pocket as well as "full," we are ready to see how these data are applied in cost estimating and pricing. The machine-hour rate tells the rate of cost incurrence at each facility which Nova uses to process its output. Before these rates can be applied to cost-estimate a specific order, it is first necessary to determine the number of hours which is expected to be used by each facility or production center. To do this, estimated or standard production time must be determined. In effect, the company must be prepared to measure the work speed at each facility. These statistics are generally compiled into what are known as production standards, and the calculated standard hours are then used to convert a conversion cost rate into a conversion cost.

The Role of Production Standards

For a proper discussion of production standards, we should understand the meaning of the word "standard." A standard, used in the generic sense, represents a universally accepted unit of measurement of some physical characteristic. Thus, when 12 inches is used to define a foot, that measurement of length is a standard. The same is true of a unit of weight, such as the pound.

A production standard is a measurement of work. To develop this unit of work measurement, industrial engineers, motion study researchers, and industrial psychologists performed experiments over several generations. Their studies took them into areas of endurance, effort, fatigue, monotony, boredom, specific working conditions, various delays, and the physical factors constituting any given job. The result is the notion of a fair day's work pace. As labor unions became vitally interested in the application of production standards, there was insistence that the fair day's work pace be equated to a fair day's pay. The concept of a normal or fair rate of work is now defined as that rate of speed at which the worker fully earns his hourly pay rate, the pace at which he is delivering a fair day's work for a fair day's pay. At that pace, he is said to be performing at standard, or 100 per cent productivity. While there are many variations of this standard-hour plan in various forms of measured day-work and wage incentives in companies, the basic principles remain the same.

To develop a production standard for the large number of operations which generally are present at any facility, the industrial engineer or time study man will time the operation, breaking it down into certain specific motions which he can then analyze. He will next select the valid motions constituting the operation and choose which of the cycle times best fits the elements and methods being used. He then will take his observed stopwatch readings and will normalize them (also called speed rating or leveling) to indicate the extent his observed readings deviate from what he believes to be the normal, or 100 per cent, work pace. Having computed the standard times for each element of the operation, he will add time allowances for unavoidable delays, personal needs, and expected fatigue in order to arrive at the standard time for the job. Standard time for an operation may be presented in terms of standard hours per unit of quantity or in standard unit of quantity per hour.

Thus, a standard for an operation may be expressed in terms of 800 pieces per hour, or 1.25 standard hours per thousand (M). If an order of 10,000 pieces is being processed through a facility whose machine-hour rate is $23, the conversion time and cost through that facility is

$$10{,}000 \times 1.25 \text{ hr/M} = 12.50 \text{ standard hours}$$
$$\text{Conversion cost} = 12.50 \times \$23, \text{ or } \$287.50$$

Unlike the unvarying measure of a standard unit of length or weight, the production standard is qualified by the geographic area in which it is being developed. In some areas, the 100 per cent speed rating requires a higher rate of effort to attain; in other areas, the effort required is lower. These variances are a function of the historical work tempi of the specific area coupled with the local philosophy towards work. In small rural manufacturing communities down South, the 100 per cent concept is tighter than it would be in a large Northern city. Much of this difference is the result of union education of the rank and file membership and generally the degree of militance which unions bring to bear on wages and jobs. In addition, when jobs are scarce and workers plentiful, the 100 per cent rating tends to be pegged to a higher level of effort. In any event, production standards covering specific operations are usually valid neither country-wide nor industry-wide but generally are applicable only to the specific plant for which they are developed. Industry-wide standards do not account for individual differences in working conditions, machinery conditions, specific methods, skill levels, nor in the concept of the normal speed level.

It is up to management to recognize these differences and to have available proper production standards which reflect its expected output from each facility. Sloppy production standards cannot be compensated for by accurate machine-hour rates and vice versa. Obviously, since processing hours are multiplied by the machine-hour rate, errors in either factor will cause an error of the same magnitude in the stating of conversion costs.

Parameters of Production Standards

When many products pass through one given processing facility, it may be inequitable to have only one production standard figure for that facility. Generally, a converting facility is the place where many different orders are processed on their way to the next facility. Each of these orders may not be run through at the same speed because of its individual characteristics. Often, then, a group of production standards has to be developed for each facility to reflect the various classes of work expected to pass through the facility.

When production standards are developed, therefore, the variables of the operation which cause the basic time to change must be recognized and tabulated. This procedure sets the stage for the correct format of standards.

Exhibits 17-1, 17-2, and 17-3 show the production standards for three of Nova's facilities and the specific parameters and variables of each. Exhibit 17-1 is the production standards for the slitter-rewinder. The parameters are the "feet per set" and the "number of rolls per set." The variables reflect the ranges of each parameter. Obviously, as can be seen from these production standards, no one standard will serve as a proper unit of work measurement because the range of standards is from 1,801 to 8,475 standard feet per hour, depending on the specifics of the job being processed.

Cost-estimating

Proper machine-hour rates and production standards are vital for estimating the expected cost of an order or product. The multiplication of these two factors gives the oop conversion cost. When materials and other direct order charges are included, the result is the total oop order

EXHIBIT 17-1. FORMAT OF PRODUCTION STANDARDS:
REWIND AND SLITTING

Production standards						
Chart no. 148	Operation: Slit printed laminations					
Feet per set	Standard feet per hour and standard hours per thousand feet					
	Number of rolls per set					
	1	2	6	7	13	14
0–500	4,739	3,460	2,353	2,237	1,835	1,801
	0.211	0.288	0.425	0.447	0.545	0.555
501–1,250	5,587	4,329	3,106	2,976	2,488	2,451
	0.179	0.231	0.322	0.336	0.402	0.408
1,251–1,750	6,803	5,781	4,587	4,425	3,876	3,817
	0.147	0.173	0.218	0.226	0.258	0.262
1,750–2,250	7,194	6,289	5,181	5,051	4,484	4,444
	0.139	0.159	0.193	0.198	0.223	0.225
2,251–2,750	7,463	6,667	5,650	5,530	4,975	4,926
	0.134	0.150	0.177	0.181	0.201	0.203
2,751–3,250	7,634	6,944	5,988	5,882	5,348	5,319
	0.131	0.144	0.167	0.170	0.187	0.188
3,251–4,000	7,813	7,194	6,329	6,211	5,747	5,682
	0.128	0.139	0.158	0.161	0.174	0.176
4,001–5,000	7,937	7,463	6,711	6,579	6,135	6,098
	0.126	0.134	0.149	0.152	0.163	0.164
5,000–7,500	8,130	7,752	7,143	7,042	6,711	6,667
	0.123	0.129	0.140	0.142	0.149	0.150
7,501–10,000	8,333	8,000	7,519	7,463	7,143	7,143
	0.120	0.125	0.133	0.134	0.140	0.140
10,001–15,000	8,403	8,197	7,874	7,813	7,576	7,519
	0.119	0.122	0.127	0.128	0.132	0.133
15,000–20,000	8,475	8,333	8,065	8,065	7,875	7,813
	0.118	0.120	0.124	0.124	0.127	0.128

Limitations or other qualifying data:

1. Standard crew = one worker.
2. Standards based on 290 ft/min.
3. Standards applicable to machine number_____.
4. Standards for setup on pages_____.

EXHIBIT 17-2. FORMAT OF PRODUCTION STANDARDS: LAMINATING

Material and Operation	Gauge up through, in.	Range of lamination web width, in.	Nonoscillated			Oscillated		
			Standard speed, ft/min	Standard hr/M	Standard production, ft/hr	Standard speed, ft/min	Standard hr/M	Standard production, ft/hr
PE extrusion: First, second, and third lamination: Cello, mylar, acetate, and unsupported foil only..........	0.003	0-20	260	0.067	14,925	225	0.078	12,821
	0.0015	20-40	295	0.059	16,949	270	0.065	15,385
	0.001	40-65	285	0.061	16,393	270	0.065	15,385
All material and PE except	0.0005	0-60	350	0.050	20,000	350	0.050	20,000
Cello unsupported foil	0.00075	0-60	410	0.043	23,256	390	0.045	22,222
	0.001	0-45	400	0.044	22,727	370	0.047	21,277
All materials and PE not covered above	0.001	45-50	365	0.048	20,833	340	0.051	19,608
	0.001	50-55	335	0.052	19,231	315	0.056	17,857
	0.001	55-60	310	0.056	17,857	290	0.060	16,667
	0.0015	0-30	375	0.047	21,277	340	0.051	19,608
	0.0015	30-35	330	0.053	18,868	300	0.058	17,241
	0.0015	55-60	205	0.085	11,765	195	0.090	11,111
	0.002	0-22	360	0.049	20,408	315	0.056	17,857
	0.002	22-25	325	0.054	18,519	290	0.060	16,667
	0.002	25-30	280	0.063	15,873	255	0.069	14,493

1. Standard crew = two workers.
2. Standards applicable to machine number.
3. Standards for makeready on pages_____

EXHIBIT 17-3. FORMAT OF PRODUCTION STANDARDS: GRAVURE PRINTING

Product and operation	Web width, in.	Standards: 1, 2, or 3 colors			Standards: 4, 5, or 6 colors			Press no.
		ft/min	Production per hr, ft	Press hr/M ft	ft/min	Production per hr, ft	Press hr/M ft	
Print product 107Y....	to 27.5	315	17,200	0.058	315	17,200	0.058	12–22
Paper.................	all webs	298	16,667	0.060	298	16,667	0.060	10
Print (only) laminated foils (foil side).......	to 27.5	390	21,275	0.047	350	19,600	0.051	12 14–20
Print and emboss laminated foils (foil side)..	to 27.5	390	21,275	0.047	350	19,600	0.051	19
Print (only) laminated foils (foil side).......	over 27.5	335	18,180	0.055	...	......	.....	13

1. Standard crew = two workers.
2. Standards for makeready on pages_____.

EXHIBIT 17-4. SAMPLE ESTIMATE: PRINTED CELLO ROLLS
Quantity 20,000 lb.

Conversion

Production Center	Production Standard	Hours Required by Order	MHR		Conversion Cost	
			oop	"Full"	oop	"Full"
Prep:						
Mold plates........	*7 hr*	*7*	*$4.69*	*$8.35*	*$32.83*	*$58.45*
Mounter-proofer.....	*0.25 hr per plate*	*4*	*3.81*	*7.59*	*15.24*	*30.36*
MR-Kidder Flexo...	*5 hr*	*5*	*10.20*	*16.78*	*51.00*	*83.90*
Run:						
Kidder-Flexo.......	*350 fpm*	*57*	*10.20*	*16.78*	*581.40*	*956.46*

Conversion Cost............	$ 680.47	$ 1,129.17
Material Cost..............	15,800.00	15,800.00
Total Order Cost........	$16,480.47	$16,929.17
Cost per lb................	$0.8240	$0.8465
Booked SP — Per lb.........	$1.02	
Booked SP — Order..........	$20,400	
Contribution per lb..........	$0.196	
PV........................	.192	
CPH (Flexo)...............	$63.22	
Target SP* — Per lb.........	$0.882	
Target SP* — Per Order......	$17,651	
Pricing Variance (Order).....	$ 2,749	

* Markup on materials = 1.025. Markup on oop conversion cost = 2.14 (level markup).

cost. From this figure, expected contribution of the order, target selling prices, and a host of data to evaluate and guide every segment of the profit structure can be generated.

Exhibits 17-4, 17-5, and 17-6 show how Nova prepares three sample estimates of its different kinds of work. First, the production center operations are listed and separated for the preparatory and run segments.

EXHIBIT 17-5. SAMPLE ESTIMATE: PRINTED SIDEWELD POLY BAGS
Quantity 100,000 Bags (6 × 13 in.)

Production Center	Production Standard	Hours Required by Order	MHR		Conversion Cost	
			oop	"Full"	oop	"Full"
Prep:						
Mounter-proofer...........	*6 hr*	*6*	*$ 3.81*	*$ 7.59*	*$ 22.86*	*$ 45.54*
MR–H-S Flexo............	*3.5 hr*	*3.5*	*12.34*	*24.96*	*43.19*	*87.36*
MR–40-in. Bag Machine....	*1.0 hr*	*1.0*	*8.55*	*11.74*	*8.55*	*11.74*
Run:						
H-S Flexo................	*400 fpm*	*2.0*	*12.34*	*24.96*	*24.68*	*49.92*
40-in. Bag Machine........	*60 cpm*	*14.0**	*8.55*	*11.74*	*119.70*	*164.36*
Pack....................		*1.5*	*2.30*	*2.50*	*3.45*	*3.75*

Conversion Cost................	*$222.43*	*$362.67*
Material Cost.................	*334.10*	*334.10*
Total Order Cost............	*$556.53*	*$696.77*
Cost per Thousand Bags........	*$5.57*	*$6.97*

Booked SP	Per Thousand Bags..	*$7.50*
	Per Order.........	*$750.00*
Contribution per Thousand Bags..		*$1.93*
PV...........................		*.257*
Target SP†	Per Thousand Bags.	*$8.18*
	Per Order.........	*$818.45*
Pricing Variance (Order)........		*($ 68.45)*

* Two lanes.
† Same as on Exhibit 17-4.

This separation makes it convenient for the company to estimate different order quantities. To estimate for any other quantity besides the ones shown, the company holds the preparatory costs constant and varies only the run segment for the quantity. Then, referring to the production standards sheets, Nova inserts and extends the appropriate production standards by the order quantity. The machine-hour rates (two parts) corresponding to the selected production centers are then inserted, and the conversion costs are arrived at by multiplying the hours required at each production center by its machine-hour rate. Totaling both vertical columns gives the conversion cost in oop as well as in "full." Then the material cost, which is not derived in these examples, is added together with any other direct order cost to both columns, and the total oop and "full" order costs are developed.

When the booked selling price is added to this estimate, management is able to determine the economic value of this order. Obviously, the

EXHIBIT 17-6. SAMPLE ESTIMATE: POLY-COATED, ADHESIVE-LAMINATED
FOIL AND PAPER (8 COLOR)
Quantity 60 million sq. in.

Conversion

Production Center	Production Standard	Hours Required by Order	MHR		Conversion Cost	
			oop	"Full"	oop	"Full"
Makeready:						
Extruder-laminator.........	*3 hr**	*3*	*$16.62*	*$32.23*	*$ 49.86*	*$ 96.69*
8-color gravure press........	*6 hr*	*6*	*26.15*	*48.85*	*156.90*	*293.10*
Run:						
Extrudor-laminator.........	*250 fpm*	*14*	*16.62*	*32.23*	*232.68*	*451.22*
8-color gravure press........	*500 fpm*	*7*	*26.13*	*48.85*	*183.05*	*341.95*
Slitter-rewinder............	*150 fpm*	*23.3*	*7.15*	*11.24*	*166.60*	*261.89*
Wrap and palletize.........		*16*	*2.30*	*2.50*	*36.80*	*40.00*
		Conversion Cost................			*$ 825.89*	*$1,484.85*
		Material Cost†................			*5,610.10*	*5,610.10*
		Total Order Cost.............			*$6,435.99*	*$7,094.95*
		Cost per Thousand sq in........			*$0.107*	*$0.118*
		Booked SP per Thousand sq in...			*$0.152*	

* Width change only.
† Original artwork, customer charged separately for cylinders.

order in Exhibit 17-4 is dominated by materials cost, the element of conversion cost being relatively low. While the annual average of materials cost in sales is about 65 per cent, this proportion is not necessarily seen in all orders as each product differs in the ratio of conversion costs to materials. Nevertheless, a substantial PV is generated in spite of the fact that very little conversion is involved. This fact is also supported by the unusually large CPH for this type of work. Normally, this type of work has a low PV and a consequently low CPH. Under this circumstance, management would look to other work which would return more contribution for each hour of an expensive facility. To see how its booked price compares to a price which would give it its desired return on the specific elements of capital employed in this order, management develops a target price from the following profit plan based on the machine-hour rate of the previous chapter:

Total capital employed................ $1,600,000
Desired earnings (Pretax)............. 10%
Annual earnings required............. $ 160,000

Annual profit plan

Planned sales....................... $3,200,000
oop costs
    Direct materials........ $2,080,000
    Conversion............   499,285
    Direct order charges.....   85,215
                                     2,664,500
    Contribution................... $ 535,500 (composite annual PV = .167)
Less: fixed expenses................   375,500
    Planned target profit............ $ 160,000

1. Materials investment turns over four times per year, hence, markup on materials is 10 per cent/4, or 1.025.

2. Markup on oop conversion costs $= \dfrac{(\$3,200,000 - \$2,132,000)}{\$499,285}$ or 2.14

When materials and oop conversion costs are marked up separately in this order, the target selling price is $17,651, thereby providing the company with a favorable pricing variance of $2,749.

It should be noted that when the preparatory costs are a small portion of the total oop costs, larger quantities do not have a large effect on the per pound total oop costs. For example, if the order quantity were for 100,000 pounds instead of for 20,000 pounds:

    oop conversion costs............. $ 3,006.07
    Materials cost..................   79,000.00
        Total order oop costs.......... $82,006.07
        oop costs per lb................ $0.82

Under these circumstances, the seller must be careful about the price discount allowed for the higher quantities. If he follows some sort of an industry price schedule and the discount normally offered for five times the quantity is 10 per cent, the booked price per pound becomes $1.02 less 10 per cent, or $0.918, and the PV under those price and quantity conditions would be .1067, practically one-half of the previous PV. More important, the CPH would fall to $33.79, and this figure might contribute to an overall lower annual contribution figure if facilities were loaded.

Exhibit 17-5 is a sample estimate for printed and converted plastic bags. The difference in the material and conversion cost proportions be-

tween this order and the previous one is caused by the difference in
the cost of raw materials. The example in the previous exhibit used cellophane and passed through only the flexographic printing press. This
order uses polyethylene and runs through a flexographic press as well
as through a bag machine. The price which Nova has to meet is $7.50
per thousand bags. At that price, it shows a PV of .257, certainly better
than the previous job estimated. However, that doesn't mean that the
price of this order is proportionately better than the price of the previous
one. The facts are that the price of this order is worse for the poly bags
than the lower PV price of the previous order is for the cellophane rolls.
The reason obviously lies in the unfavorable pricing variance which this
order shows. So while the PV of .257 is a higher one, it is still not high
enough to reward the company, considering the much greater investment
made in this order—as indicated by the much larger conversion cost
proportion.

Each job should stand on its own for individual evaluation. Even if
a competitive price level is unknown for the poly bag order, the target
price approach should be used. If the customer is the one who shows
the seller what competitive prices are for this type of order, the seller
always has his total oop costs to protect him from going too low. In
terms of the economical employment of his facilities, he can always measure a customer-proposed price by the CPH approach. The method *not*
to follow is to take the booked PV of another order and target a price
on that figure. If the .192 PV of the previous order was used to target
the poly bag order, the price would be $6.90 per thousand bags. The
worst practice of all would be to take all orders at the target profit
plan PV of .167. This practice would deprive the company of orders
which give a "full" or greater return on capital employed in orders—but
which have a lower PV. It could also overcommit converting facilities
to work having a higher PV, resulting in an annually smaller
contribution.

Exhibit 17-6 is an estimate for an expensive product: gravure-printed,
coated, laminated pouch stock. The estimate is for 60 million square
inches, enough for the purchaser to make 4 million pouches. At the
booked selling price, the company gets a satisfactory contribution and
good employment of its facilities. In this case (as is typical practice
in the industry), the customer is charged separately for the etching of
his artwork on the gravure cylinders only if it is original artwork. However, when there is "standing" artwork at another converter for the customer dealt with previously, any new converter is expected to absorb the
cost of this cylinder re-etching work in return for getting the account.
The cost of re-etching is $375 per cylinder; for eight colors, the total
re-etching cost would be $3,000.

Let's now assume that this order, which is priced at the rate of $0.152 per thousand square inches, is not an original artwork job and that the seller therefore has to absorb the $3,000 re-etching cost. Obviously, this fact is going to have an impact on Nova. The total contribution developing from the job without the cost of the re-etching was 60 million times $0.152 less the oop costs of $6,435.99, or $2,684.01. Having to pay for the $3,000 re-etching cost would price the job below oop. So the first thing for Nova to find out (if it cannot raise the unit price) is what the minimum order quantity would have to be to pay at least all the oop costs of the order. To find this minimum order quantity point, it would employ the break-even technique. Without the re-etching cost, the unit contribution is $0.152 less $0.107, or $0.045 per thousand square inches. If every 1,000 square inches of order produces a contribution of $0.045, $3,000/$0.045 would be the quantity which will produce enough contribution to pay for the re-etching. This quantity is 66.7 million square inches. At this price and quantity, the PV and contribution is zero.

On the original basis, when the customer did not require the converter to absorb the re-etching costs, the PV was .296. Now suppose that because of the committing of the most expensive printing facility (gravure), the converter requires a minimum PV of .20 to run the job. The question is what order quantity will be required to provide this PV with the converter still absorbing the $3,000 re-etching costs. To find this quantity, we will use the formula stated in Chapter 11 on page 132.

$$\text{Target unit volume} = \frac{\text{constant order oop costs}}{(1 - \text{PV}) \times \text{unit selling price} - \text{variable order oop costs per unit}}$$

$$= \frac{\$3,206.76}{(1 - .20) \times \$1.52 - \$0.1038}$$

$$= 180.155 \text{ million sq in.}$$

Constant order oop costs

Preparatory	$ 206.76
Re-etching cylinders	3,000.00
Total	$3,206.76

Variable order oop costs

Run, 60 million	$ 619.13
Material, 60 million	5,610.10
Total, 60 million	$6,229.23
Per thousand sq in	$0.1038

When a new machine-hour rate system has been completed and is being used for estimating and pricing, management can employ it at the same time for several other very worthwhile pricing analyses. Among these are testing previous work to see what the contribution would have shown had the machine-hour rate system been in effect, measuring the contribution of work the seller lost because of price, evaluating present sources of profit, etc.

Back-testing Previous Work

Often a company, especially one like the Nova Corp., does a lot of business in repeat orders. If Nova did not previously have a sound-cost-estimating and pricing system, it is possible that the company unknowingly sold below oop cost, and it would want to know this fact at the time an order was repeated. When a handful of customers constitute a large portion of a firm's total output, it is sometimes usual to make special concessions to them. In back-testing, a seller can determine the amount of annual contribution which is provided by these kinds of customers rather than relying on the total revenue figure for evaluating their worth. Thus management has a more objective basis for making any concessions.

Exhibit 18-1 shows a machine-hour rate test form which is used for this purpose in an envelope company. In order to test previous work, it is necessary to locate the original estimate sheets. Then the estimated materials cost, production centers, and the standard hours are brought forward onto this test form. The new machine-hour rates are applied and the new conversion costs developed and totaled. When the total oop costs are subtracted from the selling price at which the order was sold, management can measure the contribution (if any) that was gen-

237

Exhibit 18-1. MHR Test form*

Customer_____ Envelope Type_____ Quality_____
Size_____ Style_____ Paper_____
No. of Colors_____ Salesman_____
Delivery_____ Features_____

Cost Estimate

Production Center*	Hours Required for Order Quantity†	MHR		Conversion Costs	
		oop	"Full"	oop	"Full"
Prep:					
Run:					

Total material cost† × markup =
× markup =
Total oop conversion cost × markup =
Total material cost† × markup =

Total Conversion Costs.........................		
Total Material Costs†	Inside Costs..........		
	Outside Purchases.....		
Total Other Costs	Freight Out...........		
	Commission, etc.......		
Total Costs	Total................		
	Per Thousand........		
Booked, Quoted, or List Price per Thousand.....		
Contribution	Total................		
	Per Thousand........		
PV.....................................		
Target SP	Total................		
	Per Thousand........		
Total Revenue Variance...................		
CPH................		

* To be used on booked and lost jobs and for general testing of list prices.
† Estimated separately or brought forward from existing estimates.

erated. Often, this study leads to a selective booking of future work from both new and existing customers.

Data from such test forms should be sorted by important customers and summarized. This analysis will show the average PV of those customers and is most valuable in making future decisions on pricing. For example, if it is decided that a customer has a characteristic PV, perhaps future pricing should use this PV as a target guide. When a seller cannot escape booking one particular order below oop for one of these customers, a knowledge of overall contribution is helpful in deciding whether to take that order or not. Besides an evaluation of PV, the analysis can be broadened to include facility-hours, CPH, target selling price, and price variance, as discussed in the previous section.

Evaluating Lost Work

When traditional cost-estimating and pricing methods were in effect, management turned down, as well as accepted, work according to arbitrary formulas. The latter activity often led to taking work priced below oop costs. If the price of an order did not look good by traditional cost-estimating yard sticks, it was turned down because management had no idea of the contribution it could have provided. Thus, in the mixture of work lost because of price, there is usually a sizeable number of large contributors. A task for management is to pull out the estimates representing this lost work and have them re-estimated using the machine-hour rate test forms. No doubt there will be some which management is happy it lost because of the negative, zero, or minimum contribution. Others, however, management will regret having turned down—not only, in terms of order contribution but also on the basis of the little facility time required to capture such contribution.

The practical approach to evaluating lost work is to pick out recently lost but important quotations, reestimate them on the machine-hour rate test forms, and, based on the contribution disclosed, try to reawaken interest in the customer (if he has not placed it elsewhere in the interim).

Once the system is completely installed, management should maintain a record which the author calls a "Quotation Mortality Log." This record is a log showing which jobs that have been estimated and quoted do not come to fruition. Very often such a record acts as a control tool for management in appraising the pricing function, especially as it relates to balancing contribution, PV, facility-hours, CPH, and target prices. Frequently, management will find instances where a job was unnecessarily overpriced and thus lost, when it could have been booked at a lower price with adequate CPH, etc.

Evaluating Present Sources of Profits

Estimating forms which provide the same basic information as the machine-hour rate test forms should be used as the regular estimating sheets. If estimates representing present commitments are sorted according to product line or to any other of the company's profit segments, profitability determinations in each of these segments can be made. Exhibit 18-2 shows how such an analysis is made by each of Nova's three

EXHIBIT 18-2. ANALYSIS OF PRODUCT-LINE PROFITABILITY

Profit structure	Total	Product lines		
		(A) Gravure printed extruder-laminator stock	(B) Flexo printed rolls and bags	(C) Plain bags
Sales...................	$4,000,000	$1,500,000	$1,500,000	$1,000,000
oop costs................	3,000,000	1,000,000	1,100,000	900,000
Contribution...........	$1,000,000	$ 500,000	$ 400,000	$ 100,000
PV......................	.25	.333	.267	.10
Fixed expenses...........	700,000	350,000	275,000	75,000
Pretax profit...........	$ 300,000	$ 150,000	$ 125,000	$ 25,000
% of sales...............	7.5	10	8.3	2.5
Total capital employed....	$2,000,000	$ 900,000	$ 600,000	$ 500,000
Return on TCE, %........	15	16.7	21	5

major product lines. Exhibit 18-3 shows how this analysis is carried down to the products which constitute a single product line.

An even more dramatic analysis is shown in the data of a large commercial printing firm. This firm produces a wide variety of product lines—from "toothpicks to Cadillacs." Prior to the installation of a proper profit-planning and pricing system, the company measured the performance in each line on the basis of arbitrary gross profit with no measurement of contribution. One of its major lines was the printing of decorative calendars. Because of the economies effected in printing, the line was thought to be very profitable before the separation of fixed and variable expenses—expecially those variable costs specifically identified with the sale of calendars. Because of this lack of separation, the company had little idea of the amount of specific variable capital that was required to support the calendar line.

Calendars were printed in very large quantities and placed in stock. Orders were received in small quantities from real estate offices, barber shops, insurance brokers, and other people who handed them to their customers as giveaways. Each time one of these orders was received, the calendars were withdrawn from stock by the company and imprinted with the name of the customer. Before the separation and application of the costs of the specific people involved in these tedious transactions, the PV of the calendars was .52, a most respectable contribution rate. However, when the twenty-two people in the sales service and imprint-

EXHIBIT 18-3. ANALYSIS OF PRODUCT PROFITABILITY

Flexo printed rolls and bags	Total	Products in product line B		
		Bags	Cello rolls	Poly rolls
Sales..........................	$1,500,000	$600,000	$400,000	$500,000
oop costs......................	1,100,000	425,000	325,000	350,000
Contribution..................	$ 400,000	$175,000	$ 75,000	$150,000
PV...........................	.267	.29	.187	.30
Fixed expenses.................	275,000			
Pretax profit.................	$ 125,000			
Flexo press machine-hours........	3,950	1,750	1,000	1,200
Contribution per machine-hour....	$101.27	$100	$75	$125

ing departments were recognized and treated as a specific cost and a direct charge to the calendar line, the PV dwindled to .06. Add to that the fact that since the calendars remained in stock for long periods, the cost of its variable capital averaged $0.62 per dollar of sales, whereas most of the other product lines required an average of $0.23. Imagine the company's chagrin when it learned that its major item was barely contributing and in addition required an inordinately large amount of variable capital support. Exhibit 18-4 shows the product-line analysis of the company.

The overall results are rather appalling—a 1.3 per cent return on total capital employed. To improve the performance of the company, the identifiability test was applied, namely, if the calendar line, the line on which the company had built its image and original reputation, is eliminated, would the specific, traceable costs also disappear? The answer was yes; the line was discontinued.

Exhibit 18-4. Product-line Analysis of Commercial Printer

Item	Total	Commercial	Catalogs, brochures, and books	Checks and money orders	Calendars	Posters and maps	Can, wine, and liquor labels	Displays	Christmas cards	Stationery	Direct mail and premiums
Revenue	$3,088,104	$1,012,322	$228,316	$184,218	$978,732	$147,645	$371,198	$62,412	$31,714	$42,941	$28,606
Contribution	$ 985,807	$ 228,785	$ 34,476	$ 60,424	$508,941	$ 27,019	$104,678	$ 8,363	$ 5,423	$ 3,092	$ 4,606
PV	.319	.226	.151	.328	.520	.183	.282	.134	.171	.072	.161
Less: specific transaction costs	192,410	24,632	8,410	4,218	128,780	16,318	8,410	1,142			
Less: commission and royalties	346,500	30,370	11,416		291,134		11,136	1,872			572
Less: inventory-carrying interest costs	47,873	8,231	1,857	228	30,341	322	4,876	128	791	119	980
Net contribution	$ 399,024	$ 165,552	$ 12,793	$ 55,978	$ 58,686	$ 9,379	$ 80,256	$ 5,221	$ 4,632	$ 2,973	$ 3,054
Adjusted PV	.129	.163	.056	.304	.060	.067	.216	.084	.146	.069	.107
Less: common period fixed costs	375,500										
Pretax profit	$ 23,524										
Variable capital employed	$1,097,897	$ 274,380	$ 46,420	$ 11,415	$606,814	$ 16,112	$108,360	$ 6,420	$15,818	$ 2,378	$ 9,780
Variable capital of sales, %	35.5	27.2	20.3	6.2	62.0	10.9	29.2	10.3	49.9	5.5	34.2
Fixed capital	654,000										
TCE	$1,751,897										
Return on TCE (pretax), %	1.3										

242

EXHIBIT 18-5. CONTRIBUTION BY TERRITORY (IBM)

CONTRIBUTION BY TERRITORY

44891

SEPTEMBER 19____

DISTRICT CODE	TARGET PV	ACTUAL PV	CONTN PER HR	BOOKED SP	TARGET REVENUE	CONTR	TARGET CONTR
1	185	212	086	4886	4721	1040	875
2	152	230	096	8797	7994	2025	1222
3	162	200	040	9369	8946	1880	1457
5	131	124	034	26129	26332	3249	3452
6	095	125	070	50150	48519	6278	4647
7	187	206	035	11293	11033	2330	2070
8	123	151	039	43641	42223	6616	5198
10	189	240	051	51738	48493	12440	9195
17	228	076	022	6679	7990	512	1823
20	135	263	121	141092	120229	37199	16336
21	119	154	098	9563	9193	1473	1103
22	097	121	046	8545	8324	1035	814
23	122	208	091	26741	24423	5575	2957
40	216	244	041	2896	2795	707	606
	139	205	069	401519	370915	82359	51755

SEPTEMBER TO DATE 19____

DISTRICT CODE	TARGET PV	ACTUAL PV	CONTN PER HR	BOOKED SP	TARGET REVENUE	CONTR	TARGET CONTR
1	202	163	032	20130	21117	3285	4272
2	149	191	074	61806	58770	11829	8793
3	148	196	036	50525	47629	9949	7053
5	139	171	050	83992	80819	14436	11263
6	118	147	072	77797	75230	11474	8907
7	187	183	042	32786	32948	6008	6170
8	178	147	044	84905	88061	12563	15719
10	164	235	058	268644	245901	63302	40559
17	228	130	030	21682	24434	2840	5592
20	128	227	155	390579	346377	88697	44495
21	105	154	148	45799	43292	7071	4564
22	154	179	058	25522	24786	4569	3833
23	141	198	060	57751	53881	11476	7606
40	210	249	044	4835	4595	1208	968
	149	203	067	1226753	1147840	248707	169794

EXHIBIT 18-6. SALESMAN RUN (IBM)

		SALESMAN RUN					THRU 06/02/YEAR	
PRODUCT LINE	BOOKED REVENUE	CONTRIB	PV	LP HOURS	OFFSET HOURS	CFH	TARGET REVENUE	PRICE VARIANCE
14 FRANK GREENE			CURRENT PERIOD					
LP	98,767	24,454	.248	625		39	93,769	4,998
OFFSET	39,252	12,231	.312	12	88	122	37,903	1,349
NO PRTG	248	62	.250				242	6
TOTAL	138,267	36,747	.266	637	88	50	131,914	6,353
			CUMULATIVE					
LP	434,600	112,059	.258	2,834		39	412,219	22,381
OFFSET	97,101	30,254	.312	34	261	102	96,086	1,015
NO PRTG	4,453	1,351	.303				4,002	451
TOTAL	536,154	143,664	.268	2,868	264	45	512,307	23,847
16 HARVEY CROSS			CURRENT PERIOD					
LP	3,340	1,466	.439	15		97	2,577	763
OFFSET	28,868	12,069	.418		52	232	25,195	3,673
NO PRTG			.000					
TOTAL	32,208	13,535	.420	15	52	202	27,772	4,436
			CUMULATIVE					
LP	33,567	9,973	.297	225		44	31,325	2,242
OFFSET	48,974	20,347	.415		152	133	47,138	1,836
NO PRTG			.000					
TOTAL	82,541	30,320	.367	225	152	80	78,463	4,078

44892

Exhibit 18-7. End Use Listing (IBM)

END USE LISTING   THRU 06/02/YEAR

PRODUCT LINE	BOOKED REVENUE	CONTRIB	PV	LP HOURS	OFFSET HOURS	CPH	TARGET REVENUE	PRICE VARIANCE
132 SPORTING GOODS & TOYS								
			CURRENT PERIOD					
LP	4,962	1,077	.217	27		39	4,838	124
OFFSET			.000					
NO PRTG			.000					
TOTAL	4,962	1,077	.217	27		39	4,838	124
			CUMULATIVE					
LP	112,766	32,166	.285	872		36	104,827	7,939
OFFSET	40,479	11,682	.289	24	52	153	39,005	1,474
NO PRTG	1,365	463	.339				1,208	157
TOTAL	154,610	44,311	.287	896	52	46	145,040	9,570
187 HARDWARE & AUTO SUPPLIES								
			CURRENT PERIOD					
LP	1,491	396	.266	8		49	1,380	111
OFFSET			.000					
NO PRTG			.000					
TOTAL	1,491	396	.266	8		49	1,380	111
			CUMULATIVE					
LP	195,852	43,575	.222	904		48	194,908	944
OFFSET	9,950	2,985	.300		22	135	10,032	- 82
NO PRTG	6,579	1,277	.194				6,320	259
TOTAL	212,381	47,837	.225	904	22	51	211,260	1,121

44883

Exhibit 18-8. Customer Run (IBM)

CUSTOMER RUN   THRU 06/02/YEAR

PRODUCT LINE	BOOKED REVENUE	CONTRIB	PV	LP HOURS	OFFSET HOURS	CPH	TARGET REVENUE	PRICE VARIANCE
0871 AMERICAN CHEM								
			CURRENT PERIOD					
OFFSET	17,071	7,340	.430		28	262	14,353	2,718
			CUMULATIVE					
LP	37,428	9,539	.255	179		53	36,544	884
OFFSET	40,900	16,895	.413		113	112	31,196	9,704
TOTAL	78,328	26,434	.337	216	113	80	67,740	10,588
3240 INDUSTRIAL SUP								
			CURRENT PERIOD					
LP	2,592	544	.210	11		49	2,592	
			CUMULATIVE					
LP	112,478	32,627	.290	910		35	104,512	7,966
OFFSET	40,479	11,682	.289		52	153	39,005	1,474
NO PRTG	1,365	463	.339				1,208	157
TOTAL	154,322	44,772	.290	934	52	45	144,725	9,597
8721 SKELLY PROD								
			CUMULATIVE					
OFFSET	132,061	38,573	.292		4:0	89	143,189	-11,128

Data Processing of Profitability Segments

Profitability determinations in various segments of the company's profit structure are not done for academic interest. Such evaluations made with the methods suggested in this book will tell management more about its company than it ever knew before. To get the most out of its new-found knowledge, management must be equipped to act on these data quickly in order to capture the profit potential revealed by each of the profit segments. While these analyses can be prepared manually, the timing for management becomes slowed down. Of course, there is no substitute for doing it by hand initially, for this technique often debugs much of the format to be used in the future. However, once the formats have been refined, management should seriously consider processing these data automatically, either by using an outside service bureau or by using its own captive electronic data processing facilities.

It may be helpful to the reader to see just how these reports are issued. Exhibit 18-5 is an actual IBM run of territorial profitability for the commercial printer. The following three exhibits are partial weekly IBM runs of a folding-carton manufacturer. Exhibit 18-6 shows the contribution run by salesman, Exhibit 18-7 shows the contribution run by end market, and Exhibit 18-8 shows the contribution run by customer.

Determining the Quality of Pricing

Quality of the pricing function can be evaluated simply by examining period to period the amount of revenue or pricing variance generated. This information is shown for the Nova Corp. in the following tabulation:

Period ended	Booked revenue	PV	Booked contri-bution	Pricing variance	Variance, %
December 31, first year......	$3,337,291	.277	$924,430	$95,341	2.8
December 31, second year...	$3,487,112	.281	$979,878	$45,332	1.3
Net *decrease* in pricing effectiveness.............................					(1.5)

CHAPTER 19 *The Target Pricing Plan*

In previous chapters and sections, we have presented target pricing plans which are designed to mark up materials and conversion costs separately and differently in order to develop a target price which, if booked, is aimed to provide the company with its desired return on the various elements of capital invested in a specific order or product. The approach that was used yielded a flat, uniform, or level markup on all oop conversion costs, regardless of the specific nature of the converting facilities on which the oop costs were incurred.

Limitations of the Level Markup

If an order had $1,000 worth of oop conversion costs and the markup factor was 1.9, the selling price of that order conversion cost was targeted at $1,900. No discrimination was made for the mix of the specific investments in that $1,000 oop conversion cost. Conceivably, that cost could be the result of an order made mostly by hand against an order which required expensive facilities. Yet, under the *level markup* approach, each dollar of oop conversion cost would carry the same markup and same selling price per oop conversion-cost dollar.

When products are converted on joint but rather homogeneous facilities (from the standpoint of facility investment), the level markup approach is an adequate guide to target prices. However, when orders are processed on a variety of alternate facilities whose investment costs vary widely, obviously the level markup acts as an averaging of the target price.

The Differential Markup on Facilities

To develop markup factors which account for the varying investment values of each facility, a separate markup must be developed for each facility. When these different markups are applied respectively to each facility, the second or refined part of the machine-hour rate structure is born. In this process, the "full" machine-hour rate is discarded, and in its place is the pre-extended selling price of the oop machine-hour rate. In effect, the oop machine-hour rate for each facility is extended by its respective markup factor. Thus, to estimate any order, the standard hours are extended by both parts of the machine-hour rate. The first extension and totaling provide the order oop conversion costs; the second

EXHIBIT 19-1. DEVELOPING DIFFERENTIAL MARKUPS ON FACILITIES

Production Center	Present Market Value*	Asset Value of Space†	Total Asset Value	Annual oop Conversion Cost‡	Target§ Markup Margin	Markup on oop Conversion Cost
Extruder-laminator....	$ *350,000*	$ *6,000*	$ *356,000*	$ *85,565*	*$140,355*	*1.6403*
Gravure presses	*650,000*	*20,000*	*670,000*	*178,908*	*264,152*	*1.4765*
Mounter-proofer......	*3,000*	*3,500*	*6,500*	*6,536*	*2,563*	*.3921*
Molder............	*10,000*	*2,000*	*12,000*	*8,035*	*4,731*	*.5888*
6-color 42-in. Flexo....	*150,000*	*9,000*	*159,000*	*42,291*	*62,687*	*1.4823*
5-color 30-in. Flexo....	*60,000*	*6,000*	*66,000*	*35,048*	*26,021*	*.7424*
Large slitter-rewinder..	*80,000*	*4,000*	*84,000*	*49,073*	*33,118*	*.6748*
Small slitter-rewinder..	*12,000*	*1,500*	*13,500*	*10,887*	*5,322*	*.4889*
Bag machines.........	*60,000*	*4,000*	*64,000*	*62,149*	*25,232*	*.4060*
Sheeter..............	*10,000*	*1,500*	*11,500*	*10,793*	*4,534*	*.4201*
Total............	*$1,385,000*	*$57,500*	*$1,442,500*	*$499,285*	*$568,715¶*	

* From CFCS.
† From CFCS × $10/ft.
‡ From AB, CCT, DCB.
§ Total markup margin on oop conversion costs = $1,068,000 − $499,285. See Chap. 17.
¶ Distributed on the basis of $568,715/$1,442,500, or 0.394256 per dollar of asset value.

extension and totaling provide the target selling price of that conversion cost.

Exhibit 19-1 shows how differential markups are developed for each facility. In this technique, the asset value of each production is obtained by adding the present market value of the facilities to the asset value of the space it occupies. In this example, $10 is used as the asset value per square foot and is extended by the net working space occupied by the facilities. Both these data are found on the CFCS. Then the annual oop conversion costs for each production center are developed. This figure is the total of the oop overhead cost found on the AB, the annual amount from the DCB, and the total from the CCT.

Next, we must find the total markup margin on all annual oop conversion costs. In Chapter 17, we developed an example in which the *level* markup on oop conversion costs is 2.14. This figure is derived from the fraction

$$\frac{\$3,200,000 - \$2,132,000}{\$499,285} = 2.14$$

As we stated earlier, the figure $2,132,000 represents the selling price of annual materials cost, and the difference between the two figures in the numerator, $1,068,000, is equivalent to the selling price of everything else in annual sales except materials. That means that the oop conversion costs of $499,285 are being marked up or raised to $1,068,000. Thus, the markup margin is the amount by which these oop costs are raised, or $1,068,000 — $499,285 = $568,715.

EXHIBIT 19-2. DEVELOPING THE SELLING PRICE OF OOP MACHINE-HOUR RATE

Production center	Markup on oop conversion cost	Markup factor	Two-part MHR	
			oop MHR	SP of oop MHR
Extruder-laminator........	1.6403	2.6403	$16.77	$44.28
Gravure presses...........	1.4765	2.4765	26.30	65.13
Mounter-proofer..........	.3921	1.3921	3.84	5.35
Molder.................	.5888	1.5888	4.72	7.50
6-color 42-in. Flexo........	1.4823	2.4823	12.44	30.88
5-color 30-in. Flexo........	.7424	1.7424	10.31	17.96
Large slitter-rewinder......	.6748	1.6748	7.21	12.08
Small slitter-rewinder......	.4889	1.4889	6.40	9.53
Bag machines.............	.4060	1.4060	8.12	11.42
Sheeter.................	.4201	1.4201	6.35	9.02

Once we have found this markup margin, the next task is to distribute it to each production center on the basis of the individual total asset values. To do this task simply, we develop an allocation ratio between total markup margin and total asset values: $568,715/$1,442,500, or 0.394256. In effect, this figure means that a little more than 39 cents of the markup margin is assigned to each dollar of a production center's total asset value. Thus, for the extruder-laminator, the target markup margin on its conversion costs is its total asset value of $356,000 X 0.394256, or $140,355.

To find the specific markup on each production center or facility, we divide the annual oop conversion costs for that facility into their respective target markup margins. Thus, for the extruder laminator, the markup on oop conversion cost is $140,355/$85,565, or 1.6403.

Exhibit 19-2 shows how the refined two-part machine-hour rate is developed. As we said earlier, when the "full" part of the original two-part machine-hour rate is dropped, it is replaced by the selling price of the oop machine-hour rate. First the markups on oop conversion costs are listed; by adding 1.0 to those markups, the markup factor is developed. This factor, when multiplied by the oop machine-hour rate, gives the selling price of the oop machine-hour rate. These figures are shown in the last column of the exhibit. When both parts of this refined two-part machine-hour rate are applied to each production center on an estimate and extended by the standard hours for the order, the result is the total oop conversion costs as well as the selling price of the total oop conversion costs of the order. Adding to this latter figure the selling price of materials and the noninvestment costs gives the target selling price of the order.

Order Target Pricing with the Differentials Markups

Exhibit 19-3 shows a sample estimate on which the refined two part machine-hour rate system is applied. Note that this target price is lower than what the level markup price would produce. Using the 2.14 level markup on all oop conversion costs (in effect, on all production centers), the price would be $0.878 per pound instead of $0.865 per pound. The reason for this lowering of target is principally the lower markup on

EXHIBIT 19-3. SAMPLE ESTIMATE: PRINTED CELLO ROLLS
Quantity 40,000 lb

Conversion Cost and Selling Price

Production Center	Production Standard	Standard Hours	MHR		oop Conversion Cost	SP of oop Conversion Cost
			oop	SP		
Prep:						
Mold plates..........	7	7	$ 4.72	$ 7.50	$ 33.04	$ 52.50
Mounter-proofer........	0.25 per plate	4	3.84	5.35	15.36	21.40
MR–30-in. Flexo.......	5	5	10.31	17.96	51.55	89.80
Run:						
30-in. Flexo..........	350 fpm	114	10.31	17.96	1,175.34	2,047.44
		Conversion Cost and SP.......			$ 1,275.29	$ 2,211.14
		Materials Cost and SP........			31,600.00	32,390.00*
		Total Cost and Target SP...			$32,875.29	$34,601.14
		Cost and SP per lb..........			$0.8219	$0.865

NOTE: Target SP using level markup of 2.14 on oop conversion costs = $35,119.12, or $0.878/lb.
   * Based on markup factor of 1.025.

the 30-in. Flexo press. This specific facility has a markup on its oop conversion costs of 1.7424, reflecting its lower asset value. Had the 42-in. Flexo been the facility selected, the target price would have been higher than what the level markup would have produced because its specific markup on oop conversion costs is 2.4823, reflecting its much higher asset value on which the desired return is to be earned.

Exhibit 19-4 shows another estimate on which the refined two-part machine-hour rate system is applied. However, unlike the former case,

EXHIBIT 19-4. SAMPLE ESTIMATE: POUCH STOCK
Quantity 30 million sq in.

Conversion Cost and Selling Price

Production Center	Production Standard	Standard Hours	MHR		oop Conversion Cost	SP of oop Conversion Cost
			oop	SP		
Makeready:						
Extruder-laminator.........	*3**	*3*	$16.77	$44.28	$ 50.31	$ 132.84
8-color gravure press........	*6*	*6*	26.30	65.13	157.80	390.78
Run:						
Extruder-laminator.........	*250 fpm*	*7*	16.77	44.28	117.39	309.96
8-color gravure press........	*500 fpm*	*3.5*	26.30	65.13	92.05	227.96
Slitter-rewinder............	*150 fpm*	*11.65*	7.21	12.08	84.00	140.73
Conversion Cost and SP..........					$ 501.55	$1,202.27
Materials Cost and SP					2,805.05	2,875.18†
Total Cost and Target SP.......					$3,306.60	$4,077.45
Cost and SP per Thousand sq in...					$0.11022	$0.13591

NOTE: Target SP using level markup of 2.14 on oop conversion costs = $3,948.50, or $.13162/thousand sq in.
   * Width change only.
   † Based on markup factor of 1.025.

the new target price is higher than what would have been produced by the level markup of 2.14 on all oop conversion costs. Even though the slitter-rewinder has a markup on its oop conversion costs of less than 2.14, it is the use of the extruder-laminator and the gravure press which more than offsets the costs with their respective markups of 2.6403 and 2.4765. The target price produced with the differential markup factors then automatically reflects the *investment mix* in each specific order.

Testing Present Business and Rejuvenating Lost Business

If it is appropriate for the company to switch over to the differential markup approach, tests should be made to show to what extent the old

EXHIBIT 19-5. TEST OF NEW TARGET PRICES BASED ON DIFFERENTIAL
MARKUPS BY FACILITY

Estimate No.	Quoted SP	Old Target SP Level Markup	New Target SP Differential Markup	Price Variance	
				Old vs. New Target SP	Quoted vs. New SP
1201	$19,317	$19,308	$19,558	$ 250	$ 241
1218	7,482	7,482	7,738	256	256
1055	17,325	17,325	16,866	(459)	(459)
1209	21,850	15,841	16,321	480	(5,529)
1193	38,000	37,866	38,072	206	72
1203	6,180	6,933	5,891	(1,042)	(289)
0876	31,450	34,281	40,297	6,016	8,847
0977	8,675	8,699	8,496	(203)	179

target prices vary from the new. This action might prompt the restoration of lost business and a better reevaluation of existing commitments. Exhibit 19-5 shows how this analysis should be made for a period which includes an intermix of all orders. In some cases, it will pay the company to sort these data by customers and possibly by any other profit segment which seems appropriate.

Section 6

USING BASIC PRICE DATA
FOR OTHER OPERATING DECISIONS

CHAPTER 20

Managerial Decision Making

The out-of-pocket cost of a product or order is one of the most important and tangible pieces of operating information that is available to management. As a single objective fact about a product or order, the oop cost can be used to measure the contribution which any given price will provide. From this contribution measurement, the contribution per facility-hour can be developed, the most profitable quantity range can be determined, a profit plan can be stated from which separate markup factors on the major elements of oop cost can be developed, and, by no means last, the seller can have a firm knowledge of his pricing floor.

In addition to its value in making these pricing decisions, the oop cost, whether by product, order, department, facility, or period, can be used to make many other operating decisions which managements frequently encounter during their daily routine. The purpose of this chapter is to discuss and demonstrate a few areas for the application of these basic pricing data.

Before we present these areas, it is important to realize that it is not always necessary to have a known selling price in order to make contribution measurements. While sales revenue less oop costs equals contribution, it is also true, irrespective of whether or not a price is involved, that a change in oop implies a change in contribution. That is, if in a given activity area of a company an oop cost increases over a previous level, the contribution decreases, even though no price may be directly involved. This concept will become more apparent as we delve into some of the examples which follow.

Selecting Most Economical Production Facility

The typical multiproduct company makes a variety of different items, some of which are completely different in function and application and some of which have the same function and application but vary in size, capacity, etc. Besides variety of product, there is also great variety in the kinds of equipment used for producing the product. Some equipment is used specifically for one kind of product; other machinery is used as joint facilities to produce many different products.

In the case of a given product, let's say a steel ring requiring many holes to be drilled, either a single-spindle drill may be used, or a more expensive multidrill may be set up to accomplish all the drilling in one pass. The single-spindle drill is faster (and less expensive to set up), but the drilling of the steel ring will take much longer than if it were drilled with the multidrill. But setting up the multidrill takes much longer and is much more expensive. So the question must arise, Which method shall be used to drill x quantity of steel rings? The question is better phrased, Which method will produce the lowest oop cost for x quantity?

Assuming bottlenecks do not exist, both alternate methods are available at the same time, quality factors are the same for both methods, and no other strategic factors are to be considered; the sole economic criterion for setting manufacturing policy is to use that method which will produce the lower oop cost for a specific quantity.

Questions like these probably arise every day in multiproduct, multifacility companies. Unfortunately, they are usually answered by employing rule-of-thumb formulas, "full" costs, and any pet prejudice held by the local foremen or supervisors. Usually, a policy formulated under these conditions (if, in fact, one exists) is an admixture of emotion, pride, prejudice, and arbitrarily exercised autonomy.

An industry in which this question constantly arises is the printing industry. Here we have a meshing of multicolor jobs with single and multicolor presses with a wide range of makeready times and running speeds. For example, a four-color job may be run one pass through a four-color press or two passes through a two-color press. A four-color press may cost more to make ready, but it may run more impressions per hour. The two-color press may make ready faster, but two runthroughs are needed, for which the running speed could be slower. Obviously, if a very large quantity is to be printed, the higher makeready cost of the four-color press dwindles in importance compared with the lower cost of running per thousand. In effect, the higher makeready cost is spread very thinly over a large number of impressions. However, placing this large quantity on the two-color press boosts the run cost to the point where the lower makeready cost has very little effect.

The reverse is also true. If a small quantity is run on the four-color press, the higher makeready cost becomes significant because there is not enough quantity to produce enough savings to make up for the higher makeready cost. But when the small quantity is placed on the two-color press, the savings in makeready cost may offset the higher run cost for the smaller quantity.

The point is that a quantity can be found at which placing the job on either press will be the same. This point is called the quantity crossover point. For order quantities in excess of this crossover quantity, the method which has the higher makeready cost (or first cost) and the lower running cost should be used. Orders less than the crossover quantity should be run on facilities on which the first cost is less and the run cost higher.

As crossover points are established for a host of production alternatives, management can issue an objective policy for equating methods with quantities and thus reduce oop costs and increase contribution. Unlike the contribution produced from pricing, this type of contribution is internally generated irrespective of the sales effort.

As an example of how this technique works, we shall apply it to a commercial printing firm. Here are the facts concerning two of its presses:

Type of press	Speed in./hr	Makeready time, in hr	oop MHR for makeready	oop MHR for run
Two-color........	1,800	4	$23	$23
Four-color........	3,600	11	$51	$58

The company now receives a four-color job which can be run once through the four-color press or twice through the two-color press. The problem is to find the quantity at which the costs of printing the job on both presses will be the same. Then, depending on the specific quantity of the order, the least costly method can be selected. To solve this problem, we call in our old friend break-even:

$$\text{Break-even quantity} = \frac{\text{fixed expenses}}{\text{unit contribution}} \qquad (1)$$

In this case, the fixed expenses are those which are fixed or constant for the job to be run, namely, the first cost or makeready cost. For printing the job on the two-color press, this cost would be twice times 4 hours at $23 per hour, or $184. (Remember that the two-color press has to be made ready two times, one for each pass). The makeready cost on the four-color press would be 11 hours at $51 per hour, or $561. If the job is placed on the four-color press, the company will incur $377 ($561 — $184) more of makeready cost. This additional cost can be justified only by the lower running cost of the four-color press. The running cost per thousand on the two-color press would be twice times $23/1.8 per thousand (M), since the job must run through twice, or $25.56. The running cost on the four-color press would be $58/3.6 per thousand, or $16.10. Thus, even though the makeready cost on the four-color press is $377 higher, the running cost per thousand on that press is $9.46 ($25.56 — $16.10) less. The problem resolves into how many thousand impressions, each of which produces an additional $9.46 of contribution, are required to pay for the additional $377 of makeready cost. Applying the break-even formula, we obtain

$$\text{Break-even quantity (crossover point)} = \frac{\$377}{\$9.46 \text{ per M}}$$
$$= 39,850 \text{ impressions}$$

The formula to use in solving problems involving costs of alternative methods is

$$\text{Crossover quantity} = \frac{\text{change in first costs}}{\text{change in contribution per unit}} \qquad (10)$$

and substituting the above data:

$$= \frac{(\$561 - \$184)}{(\$25.56 - \$16.10)}$$
$$= 39,850 \text{ impressions}$$

Again, the reader is reminded that a difference in oop costs constitutes a change in contribution. Exhibit 20-1 shows how the quantity crossover point is found by means of a break-even chart. Often a visual presentation is easier to understand.

The same type of problem is experienced regularly in a company such as the Nova Corporation mentioned in the previous section. The company has a job which calls for printing cellophane film in rolls and then shipping without converting into bags. The width of the rolls to be printed is 13.5 inches, the customer's web width. The company may run the job through its slower 30-in. flexographic press "two-up" (i.e., two printed images across the web), slit the printed roll at the end of that web, and ship without rewinding. Or it may print the rolls on its faster 42-in. press, "three-up." If it uses this latter method, it will have to re-

EXHIBIT 20-1. FINDING THE LOWEST COST FACILITY
TO RUN ORDER QUANTITY

Data for alternate facilities					
Press	Speed in impressions/hr	Makeready time, hr	oop MHR "run"	oop MHR "makeready"	No. of passes
Two–color	1,800	4	$23	$23	2
Four–color	3,600	11	$58	$51	1

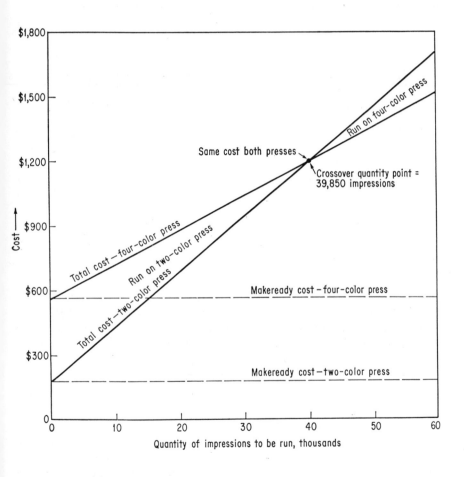

wind the rolls and then send them through its slitter-rewinder. The question, is, What quantity justifies which method? Here are the facts:

Item	Method 1/Method 2		
	30-in. Flexo	42-in. Flexo	Slitter-rewinder
Speed, in ft/min..........	300	700	300
oop MHR: Makeready.....	$10.20	$12.34	$6.34
oop MHR: Run...........	$10.20	$12.34	$6.34
Makeready time, in hr.....	2	5	.25
Output per hour, in lb.....	324	1,057	454
Using these data to compute costs, we have:			
Makeready cost..........	$20.40	$61.70	$1.58
Hr/M lb................	3.08	0.946	2.2
Run cost/M lb...........	$31.50	$11.70	$13.90

Applying Eq. (10) gives us

$$\text{Cross-over quantity} = \frac{(\$61.70 + \$1.58) - \$20.40}{\$31.50 - (\$11.70 + \$13.90)} \text{ per M lb}$$
$$= 7{,}268 \text{ lb}$$

Thus, technically, an order exceeding 7,268 pounds should be run on Method 2, and if less, on Method 1. Again, this concept assumes equal quality from either method, the availability of all three facilities, etc. Usually a crossover quantity is more practical to specify as a range. Thus, one would allow individual supervisory latitude between, say, 7,000 and 7,500 pounds.

Make or Buy?

Practically every manufacturing business operates as a result of a previous make-buy decision. The fact that a piece of equipment is operating means that the decision was to make rather than to buy work produced from that machine. These decisions are not made consciously or frequently but rather continue as "make" once the piece of equipment has been acquired. However, competitive pressures, time commitments to customers, quality requirements, production methods, available working capital, and cost of capital have been changing this picture.

Why make?: One of the major reasons for making rather than for buying is that the required quality cannot be purchased from the outside.

If new products are involved, this reason may be a valid one. Otherwise, the chances are good that outside suppliers will be able to deliver the desired quality. However, if the company attempts to attain a quality level that others cannot obtain, a large possibility of failure exists. Another reason for making is the assurance of controlling the flow of quantity of product and the time when it is needed. From the cost viewpoint, the most obvious reason for making rather than for buying is that the company itself can make the product for less. Of course, there are many other noncost reasons for making, such as the desire to preserve a trade secret. These reasons are strategic and beyond the area of cost analysis.

Why buy?: The reasons for buying are generally the reverse of the reasons for making. The company finds it impossible to make the desired quality, use of vendors' facilities and more specialized skills would be too costly for the purchaser to acquire, the purchaser benefits from the research activity of a skilled supplier, thus allowing the purchaser to keep flexible and up with the times. If the purchaser buys from several suppliers, he has better assurance against delays than if he makes everything himself. Other reasons for buying are to meet emergencies when the purchaser lacks capacity and/or is unable to have work done on overtime or additional shifts, the purchaser has the capacity but wishes to employ it for other more profitable work, the purchaser wishes to reduce the amount of variable capital employed. Cost considerations are, obviously, a desire to buy in order to avoid paying overtime premiums as well as a desire for a lower cost of buying.

Cost evaluations: The cost of making calculated on a unit cost basis is misleading because of the intermixture of fixed costs and volume. When the make-buy decision involves a short term, and plant capacity is not altered, the incremental method is the one to use. Generally, costs which are not changed by the decision are not considered. The reason is that in casting a budget for a period alternately for the make as well as for the buy decision, the costs which remain unchanged would appear in equal amounts in both budgets. These unchanging costs are generally fixed costs. For example, in a company having a seasonal product, the company might decide to make in the slow periods certain items which are normally purchased in busy periods. Under these conditions, fixed costs remain unchanged in either period because of the period nature of the fixed expense. Using the CPH approach, the company would only make in busy period those items which provide the greatest CPH.

A major factor in determining the make-buy decision is the change in the amounts of variable capital being carried and its effect on the working capital picture of the company. Work that is made in the plant requires a higher level of current capital because of additional payroll, raw materials, work in process, etc. Often a company will have raw materials shipped and billed to a supplier to avoid loading up the current investment levels. While this fact may or may not be considered by the supplier in arriving at a price for the purchaser, the incremental amount tends to be below the cost of carrying this additional inventory in the company's plant.

Basis of decisions: The following example is presented to illustrate the mechanics of making a short-term decision to farm out or not. The Nova Corporation is considering what to do about a regular piece of business

EXHIBIT 20-2. MAKE OR BUY?

| Cost elements | 20,000 lb per month | | | |
| | Make | | Buy | |
	Per lb	Total	Per lb	Total
Direct material cost..................	$0.350	$ 7,000		
Conversion cost: oop................	0.325	6,500		
Conversion cost: fixed..............	0.250	5,000		
Total oop.........................	......	$ 13,500	$0.80	$ 16,000
"Full" costs.....................	......	$ 18,500		
Average capital employed:				
Cash and accounts receivable........	$ 88,000		$ 99,000	
Inventory.......................	463,000		302,000	
Total variable capital.............	$551,000		$401,000	

$$\text{Return on average capital employed} = \frac{\text{increase in annual contribution}}{\text{increase in variable capital}}$$
$$= \frac{(\$16,000 - \$13,500) \times 12}{\$150,000}$$
$$= 20\%$$

which involves 20,000 pounds per month of flexographically printed plastic film. The company can buy this printed film at 80 cents per pound, or it can make it in its plant for 92.5 cents per pound, "full" cost. In addition, if the company makes the film itself, the average variable capital employed rises by $150,000 per year. Exhibit 20-2 shows the details of the comparisons.

The first thing to notice is that the $0.25 per pound and $5,000 per month figures are unitized fixed costs and are not tangibly related to this decision because the company has the press anyway but perhaps wishes to use it on more profitable work. The determining costs are the oop costs of $13,500, which are incurred directly with the make and are not incurred without the make. The use of the "full" costs would mislead the company into believing that if it farmed this work out, it would be saving 12.5 cents per pound. The allocated fixed portion of the "full" costs, readers will remember, is developed from an expected forecasted level of activity. If, in this example, activity was understated, the "full" costs are inflated to the point where they might deprive the company of a sizeable amount of contribution. Buying for 80 cents per pound may seem attractive if "full" costs are considered, but "full" costs are not cash outlay costs. Since the company already owns a press, the period fixed costs are unchanged and inescapable unless the machine is sold. Therefore, both situations should be analyzed by comparing cash in versus cash out versus the change in current capital.

Cash in and out versus capital change: If this company's oop costs are 67.5 cents for making and 80 cents for buying, obviously it makes a tangible cash saving of 12.5 cents per pound by making. The question to be answered is how much will current capital rise to support this internal production effort and what return on this additional capital will be provided by the cash savings (increase in contribution).

The annual increase in contribution is the monthly cash saving of ($16,000 — $13,500) × 12, or $30,000. To generate this saving, an additional $150,000 in current capital must be invested annually. The annual return on this incremental investment is therefore $30,000/$150,000, or 20 per cent. The formula for making this kind of decision to arrive at the rate of return is

$$\frac{\text{incremental contribution}}{\text{incremental investment}}$$

Summarizing:

1. Fixed costs should not be considered, since these can only be unitized or allocated costs. The facility now exists in the company and does not involve getting new equipment to support the make or disposing of equipment if the company decides to buy.

2. Make-buy decisions, when the facility exists in the manufacturer's plant, should be made only on an oop basis by comparing the comparative cash inflows and outflows.

3. Any tangible cash savings must be compared to the amount of additional current capital that is required to generate such savings. This provides the ultimate appraisal of the return on variable capital.

Justifying Capital Expenditures for Equipment

This topic might be amended to read "Investing to Make versus Continuing to Buy." Basically we have the same factors of make-buy, except that before the decision is made the company does not own the equipment which is intended for the make. In the former make-buy, the equipment already exists in the company's plant. Therefore, in a make-buy decision involving a new capital expenditure, both oop costs as well as *period* fixed costs must be considered. The basic concept to be used involves the oop costs as the only *unit* cost factor; the fixed costs of owning the proposed new equipment are to be treated as an annual period cost. Since the purpose of this chapter is to show how the basic pricing costs are used for making these decisions, only the economic approach is discussed. Strategic factors involving long-range planning, changes in markets, and customer buying habits are beyond the scope of these discussions.

Now let's take an example in which the Nova Corp. is considering the acquisition of a free-blown extruder to extrude its own plastic sheeting instead of continuing to buy sheeting from vendors. Here are the facts:

Type of cost	Make	Buy
Total oop cost per pound...............................	$0.29	$0.33
Capital cost of extruder..................................	$100,000	
Specific annual fixed costs associated with acquisition........	$11,200	

The annual fixed ownership costs consist of depreciation (in this example, using a ten-year straight-line term), finance charges, and the specific annual cost of space to be occupied by the extruder. No other fixed charges are included. Even though the space costs may be thought of as a charge which remains unchanged with or without the extruder, we include it on the basis that occupancy by the extruder could displace another facility which might be purchased in the future. Before continuing, it might be interesting to note that the classic approach to justifying equipment acquisition is to charge the proposed operation with "full" costs in making the comparison. Obviously, such fixed costs as administrative, executive, clerical, etc. remain unchanged with or without the extruder. Including these could prompt management into making the acquisition when in fact it should not, and vice versa.

Basis of decision: Here, again, we use the break-even technique to get our answer. From the above figures it is clear that for each pound made in the plant, a 4-cent contribution will be obtained $0.33 — $0.29). All that remains in this first step is to see how many pounds annually are required (each pound of which provides a 4-cent contribution) to pay completely for the specific annual fixed costs directly associated with the extruder. To determine this figure:

$$\text{Break-even quantity} = \frac{\text{fixed expenses}}{\text{unit contribution}}$$
$$= \frac{\$11,200}{\$0.04 \text{ per lb}}$$
$$= 280,000 \text{ lb}$$

Before there can be any profit in the year from the internal use of the extruder, at least 280,000 pounds of plastic film have to be used. If 300,000 pounds are expected to be used, the first 280,000 go to pay fixed expenses, and the remainder 20,000 is the amount on which net contribution is earnable. This remainder amounts to a profit of 20,000 × $0.04, or $800. While the $800 is a clear incremental profit in terms of profit and loss, is $800 an adequate return on the investment in the extruder? This question brings us to the second part of the problem.

What return on investment?: Obviously, not only must the annual consumption of film be great enough to yield a profit on the operation of the extruder, it must also be large enough to provide an adequate return on the specific investment in the extruder. The investment is not only the acquisition cost of $100,000 but also the supporting variable or current capital required, as follows:

```
Incremental fixed capital................  $100,000
Incremental variable capital............    180,000
Increase in total capital employed........  $280,000
```

Nova management projects its annual expected consumption at 800,000 pounds. Now, considering the contribution per pound, the annual fixed expenses, and the increase in total capital employed, the company wishes to know what return on capital it will get at the 800,000 annual poundage figure. To find the answer to this problem, it must be recognized that net contribution will be generated only above the break-even quantity of 280,000 pounds per year. Therefore, the net annual contribution (and incremental profit) will be (800,000 − 280,000) × $0.04, or $20,800. Then the formula stated in the previous decision is used:

$$\text{Rate of return} = \frac{\text{incremental contribution}}{\text{incremental investment}}$$
$$= \frac{\$20,800}{\$280,000}$$
$$= 7.4\% \text{ (pretax)}$$

Targeting unit contribution: While it is not our purpose to argue what percentage constitutes a satisfactory rate of return on invested capital,

for this is a highly individualized question, we do wish to suggest approaches for finding investment answers based on the changing desires
For example, Nova decides to make this acquisition if it can earn a
least a 20 per cent return (pretax) on the proposed investment in the
extruder. The management feels it cannot honestly project an annua
volume of more than 800,000 pounds. Therefore, it wishes to know how
much higher the contribution must be in order to give it its desired
return at the same projected volume. To find the answer to this question
we take the basic return on capital formula and expand it:

$$\text{Rate of return} = \frac{\text{incremental contribution}}{\text{incremental investment}}$$

$$= \frac{(\text{new unit contribution} \times \text{consumption}) - \text{fixed expenses}}{\text{total capital employed for investment}}$$

Since we know all the values in this formula except the new spread
between oop costs to make and oop costs to buy (the new unit contribution), we can readjust terms so that we can solve for the unknown value
thus:

$$\text{New unit contribution} = \frac{(\text{TCE} \times \text{rate of return}) + \text{fixed expenses}}{\text{annual consumption}}$$

$$= \frac{(\$280,000 \times .20) + \$11,200}{800,000}$$

$$= \$0.084 \text{ per lb}$$

If management can increase the spread between inside and outside oop
costs to 8.4 cents instead of 4 cents, the 800,000 pounds of annual consumption will provide a 20 per cent pretax return on the additional total
capital employed. While this procedure shows how to arrive at the
correct answer, the implementation of this answer may well be impossible
to achieve. Admittedly, the increase in spread will not be the result
(usually) of artificially showing a higher outside buy cost, but it will
rather be accomplished (if at all) by a reduction in internal oop costs.
Management must be prepared to defend how it can bring the oop
make costs down another 4.4 cents; otherwise the decision to acquire
will be a case of wishful thinking.

Targeting annual consumption: Now Nova begins to program some
internal reductions in oop costs and examine its markets to determine
if it can intensify its penetration to provide additional annual consumption. At the same time, it decides to be satisfied with a 15 per cent
return on the investment in the extruder. The company believes it can
reduce internal oop costs by 1.5 cents, thereby increasing the unit contribution to 5.5 cents. Now the question is what annual consumption

must Nova have to provide a 15 per cent return on the incremental TCE, with the aforementioned increase in unit contribution. This question is more involved because the variable capital portion of the TCE changes with volume; we don't know either the annual consumption required or the amount of the TCE required to support that unknown amount.

But we do know the following: if we let x equal the unknown annual consumption:

Fixed capital.. $100,000
Variable capital for 800,000 pounds was $180,000. Therefore, variable capital per pound equals $0.225 and the annual variable capital... $0.225x
Total capital employed................................. $0.225x + $100,000

Again returning to the basic formula and expanding

$$\text{Rate of return} = \frac{\text{incremental contribution}}{\text{incremental investment}}$$

$$0.15 = \frac{\$0.055x - \$11,200}{\$0.225x + \$100,000}$$

$$\text{Required volume} = 1,232,941 \text{ lb annually}$$

Perhaps a simpler formula could be used to recognize that

$$\text{Required contribution} = \text{return on TCE} + \text{fixed expenses}$$
$$\$0.055x = 0.15(\$100,000 + \$0.225x) + \$11,200$$
$$x = 1,232,941 \text{ lb annually}$$

For those who do not want to bother with transposing terms in the equation, the formula may be restated as

$$x = \frac{\text{annual fixed expenses} + (\text{fixed capital} \times \text{desired return})}{\text{contribution per lb} - (\text{variable capital per lb} \times \text{desired return})}$$

substituting the known values directly in this equation gives:

$$x = \frac{\$11,200 + (\$100,000 \times .15)}{\$0.055 - (\$0.225 \times .15)}$$
$$x = 1,232,941 \text{ lb annually}$$

Sales Incentive Compensation Plans

The traditional sales incentive compensation plan takes the form of paying as commission, a percentage of the sales revenue booked by the salesman. Some plans combine this figure with a flat drawing; others pay solely a commission on sales. Some plans differentiate the percentage commission on the basis of the product line sold, or the profits ostensibly generated by various products, etc.

This incentive for generating revenue is misplaced and can actually be harmful in restricting profits when the wrong kind of revenue occupies all the capacity of a company. When a flat commission is paid on sales revenue, the company is implying that all sales revenue dollars have the same value to the company. As we have demonstrated throughout this book, each revenue dollar does not contain the same amount of oop cost and therefore doesn't provide the same contribution as all other sales dollars.

A company's profit performance in an operating period is measured by the total amount of contribution generated minus the period fixed expenses. Thus, once the company has fixed its period expenses, it is in the business of generating contribution dollars, irrespective of the sales dollars booked. If this is the case, the incentive emphasis should be placed where it will generate the greatest amount of contribution dollars. In client companies where commission is paid on contribution, there has been a complete turnabout in profits. More annual profits were made on less sales without threatening the maximum capacity limits of the companies and without exceeding the working capital ability of the firm. Most important, *companies* were able to direct their own product mix.

In companies which use different commission rates to reflect different gross profits of different products, the result can be as negative as a flat commission on all revenue dollars; in some cases the result can be much worse. Since the unit gross profit of a product, order, or product line is based on an arbitrarily unitized fixed expense, the measurement of contribution is obscured, and the company could wind up paying more commission on less profitable work—work which provides a lower level of contribution—and vice versa.

If a company makes two products which show the following data

Item	Product A	Product B
Selling price.......	$10.00	$10.00
oop cost..........	6.00	9.00
Contribution......	$ 4.00	$ 1.00

and a 5 per cent flat commission rate is being used as sales incentive compensation, the booking of both orders would pay the salesman 50 cents each. Obviously, though, Product A is making four times the con-

tribution of Product B, and yet the sales reward is the same. In a more
dramatic case, suppose we have the following two orders

Item	Order C	Order D
Selling price.......	$4,000	$10,000
oop cost..........	2,000	9,500
Contribution......	$2,000	$ 500

in which the flat 5 per cent commission rate is paid. The commission
paid on Order C would be $200, and $500 would be paid on Order
D. In this case, the company is paying 2½-times the reward for an order
which makes one-fourth of the contribution. Doesn't make sense, does
it? Not only does the Order D make one-fourth the contribution, it involves the company in four and three-fourths times the amount of working capital. Order D may also require more storage space, if a large
portion of the oop cost is for raw materials, and may also commit the
company's facilities out of proportion to the contribution generated (low
CPH). In effect, paying a commission on revenue dollars steers the salesman in the wrong direction—to wherever he can book the most sales
dollars for least amount of selling time. This type of equation is a definite
limiting factor in the profit-making ability of the firm and deprives the
company of designing its own product mix. Under these circumstances,
the product mix becomes a function of the salesmen's needs for income
instead of the company's need for contribution.

Basic approach: Obviously, then, the most equitable sales incentive
plan for the company is the paying of a commission rate on contribution
dollars. No differential commission rates need be employed, because, unlike revenue dollars which have infinite differences in value (contribution), the contribution dollar is always the same shade of green. Each
contribution dollar has exactly the same value because it cancels an equal
dollar of fixed expenses on the road to annual profit. Once such a plan
is installed and is working and clearly understood by the salesmen, the
company benefits immeasurably.

The problems with such a plan are in its initial phases, during the
switchover from commission on sales to commission on contribution dollars. Salesmen become insecure and worried that they will wind up with
less income by the end of the year. While this might be true if the
switchover is done without an orientation period, the practical approach
is to switch over to the commission on contribution but then pay a
subsidy to the men for a limited time, based on the difference between
what they earned on the new plan and what they would have earned

on the old plan. However, the orientation period must be used to educate and counsel each salesman and to steer them into the paths of higher contribution per revenue dollar. Then, as each salesman aims for work of higher contribution, as has been experienced, the subsidy disappears, and the men begin to produce in excess of their former levels under the old plan. The percentage selected must aim to accomplish this result with lower net selling cost. The switchover is not easy because we are dealing with people who don't fit the nice arithmetic patterns of profit and who for centuries have thought of sales performance in terms of sales revenue dollars.

To get such a plan started, it is first necessary to tabulate the immediate past performances of each salesman. Taking the last twelve

Exhibit 20-3. Test of Sales Commission Applied to Contribution

Salesman	Bookings Last Twelve Months	Booked Contribution	Alternate % of Contribution		
			15	20	25
D. Greene..........	$184,190	$27,194	$ 4,079	$ 5,439	$ 7,799
H. Horvath..........	150,156	28,120	4,218	5,624	7,030
G. Sweeney..........	229,372	31,526	4,729	6,305	7,882
J. McCann.........	128,782	26,106	3,916	5,211	6,517
M. Foster..........	299,764	50,792	7,619	10,158	12,698
L. Lyons...........	149,362	20,428	3,064	4,086	5,107
F. Monas..........	137,364	22,474	3,371	4,495	5,619
T. Gorman.........	325,240	93,114	13,967	18,623	23,279

months' data, we list the salesman's sales and earned commissions. Then (having developed the applicable estimated oop cost of those sales), the respective contributions are listed. Since the amount of contribution in the sales dollar is less than the sales dollar itself, a commission percentage larger than the commission on sales revenue must be selected. Often, this figure has to be experimented with in order to get a sufficient stimulus for the salesman in keeping with a reasonable sales cost to the company. Exhibit 20-3 shows such a tabulation and the test results of applying various commission percentages on contribution dollars.

It should be kept in mind that these experimental incomes based on contribution are the result of what happened in the past when men pushed only for sales revenue, irrespective of the contribution levels. The new commission plan should not attempt to equate with present or immediately past earnings. It is, of course, the individual salesman's placing of emphasis on higher contribution work that will result in higher than present commission earnings. However, we do get a number of clues from even this first step in designing the commission-on-contribution plan. When a man's record shows a large gap between present income and any of the alternate plans on contribution, the average PV of what the man booked was low. An analysis of each salesman's list of accounts will bring to light those orders which bring in lots of revenue but little contribution. The sales manager can point out the effect on income of substituting higher PV work as part of his counseling during the orientation period.

Incentive for target revenue: The above is not the entire scope of a suggested sales incentive compensation plan. The three alternate percentages shown place full emphasis on the gross contribution booked without any other factor entering into the determination of a fair relationship between the benefit to the company and the reward to the salesman. What the basic incentive does not include is a consideration for target revenues represented by the booked sales and the extent to which salesmen booked above or below these targets. Surely, if a salesman booked an amount of contribution above the targeted contribution, it is worth more to the company and constitutes a greater man-effort than that same amount of contribution booked below target. It is suggested, then, that this factor be included in the design of the plan.

If the sales incentive plan was to end at simply the flat commission on contribution, it would be inequitable because, as we have seen, a low PV (small contribution) could produce the target return on capital (high turnover of material, low turnover of oop conversion cost). On the other hand, a high PV (large contribution) could produce less than the target return because a price doesn't compensate sufficiently for a high turnover of oop conversion cost. Therefore, an acceptable plan is one which establishes a flat commission percentage on contribution and then adds another factor for motivating salesmen to get up to and over target contribution (target revenue). A typical plan is 13 per cent on gross booked contribution in an order plus or minus 4 per cent on revenue variance between booked and target revenue. It is applied as plus 4 per cent on top of the gross contribution in excess of target and minus 4 per cent from the gross contribution on that portion of contribution which is below target. The base contribution percentage, as well as the plus or minus percentage, is an empirical selection to suit the company's needs as dictated by its specific operating characteristics. The variance percentage need not be in the same plus or minus amount. For example, a plan might be 16 per cent on base contribution plus 7 per cent minus 3 per cent from target revenue.

The following is a simple case of the way such a plan might operate when two orders for the same revenue are booked:

Order A

Booked revenue...............................	$10,000
Target revenue................................	9,000
Booked contribution...........................	3,000
Base commission on contribution = 16%.........	$ 480
Plus: 7% on variance of $1,000.................	70
Salesman's income...........................	$ 550

Order B

Booked revenue...............................	$10,000
Target revenue................................	11,000
Booked contribution...........................	3,000
Base commission on contribution = 16%.........	$ 480
Minus: 3% on variance of $1,000................	(30)
Salesman's income...........................	$ 450

Again, experiments should be performed by varying both the gross contribution commission as well as the added commissions for revenue variances until a balance is achieved which matches salesmen's rewards with their efforts and value received by the company. In some companies in which product lines have vastly differing investment levels, different groups of percentages can be used.

Exhibit 20-4 shows how the dual percentage plan is applied to the data of the salesmen appearing in Exhibit 20-3. In a typically low-PV business (see Chapter 14), if the emphasis is wanted on gross contribution, a plan like the 20 per cent ± 10 per cent may be used. When high investments characterize the company structure, emphasis should be placed on attaining target revenue and a plan such as the 10 per cent + 20 per cent − 5 per cent may be used.

Other factors: The contribution approach to sales incentive compensation is effective but should include other factors which the company may wish to emphasize, such as new accounts, new product penetration, new market penetration, level of travel, and entertainment expenses. Otherwise, these factors may be included in the overall compensation plan for sales managers. Paying the traditional override to sales managers on the basis of the total sales revenue bookings of their departments is just as ineffective as the payment of commission on revenue to individual salesmen. Tying the sales manager into sales department booked contribution gives him a positive objective stimulus to improve the profit position of his company.

The commission-on-contribution concept should always be applied to booked or estimated contribution and *not to actual* contribution. Salesmen are responsible for getting a price based on the estimated oop costs. Tying them into actual contribution alternately penalizes and rewards

EXHIBIT 20-4. SALES COMMISSION ON CONTRIBUTION ± REVENUE VARIANCE

Salesman	Target Revenue	Revenue Variance	Alternate Plans: % on Contribution ± Variance %	
			20% and (±10%)	10% and (+20% − 5%)
D. Greene........	$172,618	$11,572	$ 6,596	$5,034
H. Horvath.......	164,370	(14,214)	4,203	2,101
G. Sweeney.......	208,741	20,631	7,368	7,279
J. McCann.......	142,558	(13,776)	3,833	1,922
M. Foster........	292,264	7,500	10,908	6,579
L. Lyons.........	121,781	27,581	6,844	7,559
F. Monas.........	124,890	12,474	5,742	4,742
T. Gorman.......	361,442	(36,202)	15,003	7,501

	Incentive Income as % of Booked Sales	
D. Greene..............................	3.58	2.73
H. Horvath..............................	2.79	1.34
G. Sweeney..............................	3.21	3.19
J. McCann..............................	2.98	1.49
M. Foster..............................	3.64	2.20
L. Lyons..............................	4.58	5.06
F. Monas..............................	4.18	3.45
T. Gorman..............................	4.62	2.31
Department..............................	3.77	2.66

them for production performances which are beyond their control or responsibility.

Production Incentive Plans

Measuring the difference between estimated standard oop production cost and actual is, in effect, a measurement of the change in contribution. If actual performance or productivity is better than estimated, the actual contribution that develops is above the estimated contribution expected at the pricing point. Thus, the contribution to the "pool" is made from the production as well as from the pricing sources. If the actual performance is worse than estimated, the estimated contribution at the pricing point is diluted to the extent of the unfavorable performance variance and the deposit to the pool is lowered.

This measurement of the change in contribution can be the basis for paying financial wage incentives to production workers, foremen, supervisors, and plant managers. The measurement point can be the individual worker's productivity, the output of machines, the performances of departments and entire plants. Such a plan is equitable both to the company as well as to individuals if the standard hours are scientifically established and applied to both the pricing of the estimate as well as to the measurement of productivity. Estimating the costs at standard effort, i.e., at a pace which workers can normally attain in earning their base hourly pay rates, protects the company in pricing and also provides a bench mark which workers can exceed by applying extra effort. However, if the extra-pay-for-extra-effort concept is applied directly to the

EXHIBIT 20-5. VARIANCE IN PRODUCTION CONTRIBUTION BY CENTER

Production Center *104*   Oop MHR *$32*   Week Ended *Aug. 24*

Date	Job No.	Actual		Estimated		Variance	Change in Contribution
		Elapsed Time	Quantity Produced	Standard per Hour	Earned Hours		
8/20	4214	3	2,500	1,000	2.5	(0.5)	$ (16.00)
20	4312	5	6,600	1,200	5.5	0.5	16.00
21	4111	2	2,000	800	2.5	0.5	16.00
21	4716	6	6,600	1,000	6.6	0.6	19.20
22	4219	8	6,300	900	7.0	(1.0)	(32.00)
23	4610	4	3,750	750	5.0	1.0	32.00
23	4311	4	3,000	750	4.0		
24	4710	3	3,200	800	4.0	1.0	32.00
24	4414	3	3,150	900	3.5	0.5	16.00
24	4215	2	2,600	1,000	2.6	0.6	19.20
Worker performance........		40	.....	.....	43.2	3.2	$102.40

tangible savings accomplished by such efforts, management has an objective and defensible basis for paying wage incentive premiums. Needless to state, this plan must operate within the framework of quality control to ensure that productivity gains are not made at the sacrifice of end quality.

Worker incentives: Data for the payment of wage incentive premiums to workers come from a period production-center variance report. Such a report is compiled by period, i.e., weekly, monthly, etc., and reports the actual work which has passed through the center, irrespective of the start or completion of jobs. Such work is evaluated by the standards used in price estimating and then compared with the standard hours estimated to determine the direction and extent of any variance. Exhibit 20-5 shows such a variance report for one production center, manned by one worker. The actual results of conversion show that a contribution of $102.40 above the estimated contribution (at the pricing point) has been earned by the extra effort of that particular worker. When these variances are zero, the contribution estimated in pricing reflects the actual profit trend for that period.

This type of production-center period variance report is simple to compile from the daily production tickets and can be automated with EDP to accelerate the evaluation and speed of taking necessary remedial action. The elapsed time and actual production are extracted from daily tickets, and the standards are posted from the order estimate sheets. Then the actual production is converted into standard hours by dividing standard hourly production into actual production. If a productivity measurement is desired, elapsed hours are divided into earned hours. In this illustration, the productivity is 108 per cent.

The extra effort put forth by this worker generated an additional $102.40, which was made available solely because of his extra efforts. Management policy will determine what portion of this premium is distributable to the worker.

We would be remiss if we did not point out that there are other variance measurements to be performed in the profit-planning function. One of the most important is the comparison of actual with estimated material cost. This measurement, though, is related to the specific order without reference to the period and can be determined only after a job has been closed out. This variance is valuable in determining the equity of a price and forms the basis for possible price revisions on repeat orders. In any type of variance report on which management will pay incentive premiums or for which it will hold people responsible, it is important to realize that only those elements of cost within the control of the worker should be the subject of such variance measurements. Including the element of allocated or unitized fixed expense is the traditional measurement of activity variance and belongs properly within the responsibility of the sales department, if, in fact, any activity forecast can ever be that accurate.

Supervisory incentives: Proper foreman and supervisor incentives have many factors, including quality, indirect labor support, absenteeism, labor turnover, accident rate, etc. However, the base against which the other factors are applied is the departmental variance on oop conversion costs. This concept is essentially the same as for the individual worker and is shown in Exhibit 20-6. In this case, the department increased period contribution by $450.21 as a result of the combined efforts of the foreman's department workers. Productivity can be evaluated in two ways: in terms of effort and in terms of cost. Productivity of effort uses actual to earned *hours,* $298/288$, or 103.5 per cent. To get productivity in terms of cost, it would be necessary to extend elapsed and earned hours by their respective oop machine-hour rate and then make the com-

EXHIBIT 20-6. VARIANCE IN PRODUCTION CONTRIBUTION BY DEPARTMENT

Department   *C*   Week Ended   *Aug. 24*

Production Center	Elapsed Hours	Earned Hours	Variance	oop MHR	Change in Contribution
101	40	38.1	(1.9)	$41.70	$ (79.23)
102	56	62.8	6.8	57.20	388.96
103	48	51.0	3.0	24.60	73.80
104	40	43.2	3.2	32.00	102.40
105	32	29.7	(2.3)	32.80	(75.44)
106	48	46.0	(2.0)	28.30	(56.60)
107	24	27.2	3.2	30.10	96.32
Department performance..	288	298	10	......	$450.21

parison. This latter figure is not too useful for measuring effort. However, the difference between the two will be equal to the change in the contribution figure.

Plant management incentives: The approach to this measurement follows the same concept of the former two as shown in Exhibit 20-7. The

EXHIBIT 20-7. PLANT-WIDE VARIANCE IN PRODUCTION CONTRIBUTION

Week Ended   *Aug. 24*

Department	Elapsed Hours	Earned Hours	Performance, %	Change in Contribution
A	840	912	108.6	$3,412.18
B	518	560	108.1	1,380.11
C	288	298	103.5	450.21
D	412	419	101.7	318.48
E	180	162	90.0	(618.98)
Plant-wide performance......	2,238	2,351	105	$4,942.00

overall plant-wide productivity of 105 per cent has resulted in an increase in period contribution of $4,942. As in the former two cases, this contribution increase can be used as the basis for paying a direct financial incentive to the plant manager.

Index